Picturing
the World

*ALA Editions purchases fund advocacy, awareness,
and accreditation programs for library professionals worldwide.*

Picturing the World

Informational Picture Books for Children

Kathleen T. Isaacs

AMERICAN LIBRARY ASSOCIATION
CHICAGO   2013

KATHLEEN T. ISAACS spent many years as a teacher, with intermittent stints as a school and public librarian. She has taught in schools and universities in Baltimore, Washington, Hong Kong, and Xi'an, China, and has traveled extensively in many parts of the world. She has chaired selection committees for ALSC's Sibert Award, ALSC's Notable Children's Books, and USBBY's Outstanding International Book Committees, and twice served as a member of ALSC's Newbery Award committee. Most recently, she has been teaching children's literature in the education program at Towson University in Maryland. She regularly contributes articles and reviews to professional publications.

© 2013 by the American Library Association. Any claim of copyright is subject to applicable limitations and exceptions, such as rights of fair use and library copying pursuant to Sections 107 and 108 of the U.S. Copyright Act. No copyright is claimed for content in the public domain, such as works of the U.S. government.

Printed in the United States of America

17 16 15 14 13   5 4 3 2 1

Extensive effort has gone into ensuring the reliability of the information in this book; however, the publisher makes no warranty, express or implied, with respect to the material contained herein.

ISBNs: 978-0-8389-1126-6 (paper); 978-0-8389-9488-7 (PDF); 978-0-8389-9618-8 (ePub); 978-0-8389-9619-5 (Kindle). For more information on digital formats, visit the ALA Store at alastore.ala.org and select eEditions.

Library of Congress Cataloging-in-Publication Data
Isaacs, Kathleen T.
  Picturing the world : informational picture books for children / Kathleen T. Isaacs.
    pages   cm
  Includes bibliographical references and indexes.
  ISBN 978-0-8389-1126-6 (pbk. : alk. paper) 1. Picture books for children—United States—Bibliography. 2. Picture books for children—Educational aspects. I. Title.
  Z1033.P52I83 2013
  011.62—dc23

                                                                              2012010059

Cover design by Kirstin Krutsch. Cover illustration © Shutterstock, Inc.
Text design by Karen Sheets de Gracia in Adobe Caslon Pro, Minya Nouvelle, and Avenir.

∞ This paper meets the requirements of ANSI/NISO Z39.48-1992 (Permanence of Paper).

To my children and my children's children,
whose reading fueled a career.

Contents

Author's Note *ix*

1   What Are Informational Picture Books? *1*
What Is an Informational Book? *3*
What Is a Picture Book? *7*

2   Choosing Good Informational Picture Books *13*
Subject and Child Appeal *13*
How the Story Is Told *14*
How the Story Is Pictured *16*
Accuracy, Sources, and Additional Tools *18*
Awards and Best-of-the-Year Lists *18*
The Books in This List *20*

3   Ourselves and Our World at Home and School *23*
Families *23*
School *25*
Pets *27*
Our Bodies *29*
Our Health *32*

4   The Natural World around Us *37*
Looking at Nature *38*
Environments and Ecosystems *41*
Plants *46*
Animals *48*
Fish *54*
Amphibians and Reptiles *56*
Birds *59*
Mammals Other Than Humans *62*
Insects and Spiders *68*
Other Invertebrates *72*

Extinct Animals *73*
How the Earth Works *77*
Stars and the Universe *79*
Mathematics *80*

5   The World We Make *85*
Food and Farming *85*
Construction, Equipment, and Things That Go *90*
Inventors and Inventions *93*
Flight and Space Travel *97*

6   The Things We Do *101*
Writers *101*
Art and Artists *103*
Music and Musicians *109*
Theater and Performers: Actors, Dancers, and Entertainers *112*
Sports and Athletes *116*

7   The World of Faith and Festivals *125*

8   Our World in History *135*
Places through Time *135*
Events *140*
People *144*

9   Our World Today *155*
Around the World *155*
People *163*

*Appendix: A List of Awards and Best-of-the-Year Book Lists Mentioned in the
    Annotations 169*
Title Index 175
Author and Illustrator Index 181
Subject Index 187

Author's Note

WHEN MY CHILDREN WERE very young, my mother-in-law decided to continue a grandparent present tradition dating back to my husband's childhood, a personal book-of-the-month club. Every year at Christmas, she gave me a large check; for the rest of the year, I purchased a book for each child every month. The children dutifully wrote thank-you notes for each book. (This made it a twofer present, encouraging both reading and writing). I've continued that tradition for my grandchildren. Somewhere along the way, all those years of buying, reading, and giving children's books turned into a career. Working as a librarian and teacher, reading, reviewing, discussing, and evaluating, I've had the opportunity to admire a great deal of wonderful work by writers, illustrators, editors, and designers of children's books. Within this small selection, I hope readers will find books that they will enjoy sharing with children as much as I have enjoyed the many I have shared over a great many years.

Credit for the concept of this book goes to Patricia Cianciolo, who began writing about illustration in children's books in 1970, not long after I started looking at them as an adult. After several successful picture book bibliographies, she wrote *Informational Picture Books for Children* (ALA Editions, 2000), an annotated bibliography of titles published in the 1990s. That publication paved the way for this new selection.

1

What Are Informational Picture Books?

What we too often forget when considering the importance of nonfiction reading is the pleasure, the art, the wonder of it. We do not want to develop students who read nonfiction just for function, or for school success, but students who read nonfiction for enjoyment, to be fascinated, to discover.

—NELL DUKE[1]

WHAT ARE INFORMATIONAL BOOKS? "Great stories that have the added advantage of being true." That's how Dinah Stevenson, longtime children's book editor and publisher, described them as we chatted in her ALA exhibit booth, surrounded by new and intriguing titles (pers. comm.). Nearly all informational books are about concrete subjects, things that can be seen and heard and touched, the lives of real people, places that can be visited, or the stories of real events. That connection with the real world is the heart of the attraction of informational books. "Kids . . . want to know truths," Susan Kuklin, a prolific nonfiction author, wrote about her work.[2] Parents and teachers seeking to encourage young people to become readers will find such books an excellent bridge between their children's lives and personal interests and the larger world waiting for their discovery. For young children, parents and teachers begin with picture books.

FACING PAGE ART FROM

Book Fiesta by Pat Mora

Text copyright © 2009 by Pat Mora; illustrations © 2009 by Rafael Lopez. Used by permission of HarperCollins Children's Books.

From birth—and perhaps even before—children strive to learn about the world around them. Throughout their childhood, books help in this task. Books with pictures are a natural starting point, since visual literacy starts long before a child can decode words on a page. Well before children can read, they can follow the pictures and put together the information they need to ask and answer questions and to grasp a story. For early readers, pictures continue to provide helpful cues to the text. Even for adults, it's said, a picture is worth a thousand words. Today, in a world of ubiquitous screens and images, children expect to learn about their world through pictures. And advances in laser scanning technology and other changes in book production over the last forty years have made it possible to produce reasonably priced books with astonishing images on every page. A wealth of attractive and interesting picture books has been the result. Those that are factual, as well, are informational picture books.

"We are in the Golden Age of Picture Book Biography," author and blogger Marc Tyler Nobleman writes.[3] He argues that informational picture books are really for all ages, splendid introductions to a subject because "concise writing is in high demand," and "everyone likes pictures." On another blog, hosted by a group of nonfiction authors, there was extensive discussion of the importance of picture books in late 2010, reacting to a controversial *New York Times* article about the genre.[4] "The form ... allows readers time and space to contemplate the science ideas as they look back and forth between the visuals and the text," wrote Melissa Stewart. "Besides being so compelling and delicious, the artwork in picture books can often teach kids more about a complex subject than the text," Roz Schanzer added.[5] Responding to the same provocative article, the children's book director for Global Fund for Children (which produces books about children around the world, photo essays designed for young readers and listeners) wrote to an electronic mailing list, "Our nonfiction picture books continue to be in demand."[6] These authors, illustrators, and publishers are referring to books about a wide variety of subjects, but all agreed that the picture book format is both popular and effective.

There is no question that these colorful books are eye-catching. Even my college students, in training to be teachers, confessed that when they chose books to read for the class they looked at the covers and the pictures. In evaluating informational books they wrote comments such as "The pictures grabbed my attention" and "The book had real pictures which made it engaging and brought it to life." There is no lack of books to choose from. According to Bowker—a company that charts publishing trends for libraries, publishers, and booksellers—of over 14,000 informational books published for young children in 2008, half were illustrated. Most of those 7,000 new and backlist titles do not rely on illustration heavily enough to be considered picture books, but a substantial number certainly were (R. Staats, Bowker, unpublished data). It can be hard to know how to choose among them.

In January 2011, the Association of Booksellers for Children and Bowker Pubtrack announced the results of a study that surprised and pleased many in the children's book world. Among its conclusions: consumers still value books and reading over all other media in children's lives; and, parents, teachers, relatives, librarians and booksellers are the most important influences in their reading choices.[7] If we have that responsibility, we need to educate ourselves to be the most positive, knowledgeable influences we can be. This is where selection tools such as this book, review magazines and websites, award lists, and library and bookseller's suggestions come in. We need many pairs of eyes, many readers to assess the available books and find the best and the most appropriate for the young readers we serve.

The 250 books annotated in the chapters that follow represent one person's selection of excellent books published in the last five years that are intended to convey information to child readers through a combination of text and pictures. I've selected books included on a variety of award and best books lists as well as books that may have been overlooked.

My target reader set for this selection includes children from 3 to 10. At age 3, children understand that an image can represent a reality.[8] They can apply what they have learned from a picture to their everyday lives. Not long after that, they come to understand the difference between a made-up event and reality.[9] During elementary school, parents, teachers, and librarians reinforce this distinction by actively teaching the concepts of fiction and nonfiction. Most children come to understand this reasonably quickly, although, as with any other developmental turning point, the exact age varies. But plenty of children are encouraged to keep believing some stories long after others have consigned them to a fantasy world. (A teacher I know recalled one of her worst moments, when she mentioned the tooth fairy to her fourth graders and realized from their shocked expressions that several were still believers.) Elementary school children will ask, "Is that true?" "Did that really happen?" It is helpful to offer books to children that will help them distinguish between real and make-believe. And it's important that their "true" books be genuinely true.

In choosing books for this selection, I was looking for a range of books of demonstrated quality among the larger number that might be categorized as informational picture books. By nature, I am not a person who likes hard-and-fast definitions, and these categories are particularly slippery: What is a picture book? What is an informational book? What do librarians, teachers, publishers, and book reviewers mean when they use this phrase? Most people seem to use the terms comfortably, but when asked about particular books, it turns out that the edges of these concepts are fuzzy. What follows are answers I've come to in compiling this selection and some examples of books that others might categorize differently.

WHAT IS AN INFORMATIONAL BOOK?

I recently spent a week at the beach with a friend's grandchildren. These two boys, ages 5 and 7, had great imaginations. They used fantasy characters and fantasy tropes in their own play, and happily listened to their grandmother's made-up stories. But they also enjoyed looking at and listening to picture books. They didn't care or even seem to notice whether the text was prose or poetry, whether information was embedded in a fictionalized story. They did care about the connection to their real world. They heard poetry from talking sea creatures, a nonfiction book about an undersea explorer, and a nearly wordless picture book about friendship and cooperation starring seals. They liked them all. What appealed about all those books was the connection to their immediate, personal experience.

For the young child—as for adults—in a sense, everything is informational. We come to understand our world as much or more from the facts offered by the stories we read and the movies and shows we see, as we do from the more straightforward reportage. Unless they are told otherwise, children expect that what they read and hear will be true. Even adults need reminders and context clues to distinguish fact from fantasy.

An informational book is written to inform readers. The intent matters. The phrase *informational book* is often used interchangeably with *nonfiction*. The latter is a library term, describing everything not shelved in the Fiction and Picture Book sections in libraries using cataloging systems based on versions of the Dewey decimal system. Mythology and folklore are often given Dewey numbers and shelved in nonfiction collections, but they are not informational. They are usually reworkings of traditional stories; informational in intent only in the way they introduce children to a perhaps unfamiliar story. Poetry, too, has its own section and specific number among the nonfiction books. Poetry is a form, like short stories or comic books or graphic novels. Poetry can be used to convey facts, distill an experience, or describe something wholly imagined. It might or might not be informational.

Adults who deal with children have been grappling with this definition for generations, especially as they tried to identify the best of such books. The oldest award for children's informational books is the Orbis Pictus Award, given by the National Council of Teachers of English to books whose "central purpose [is] the sharing of information."[10] According to the criteria for the Sibert Informational Book Award (given by the Association for Library Service to Children, or ALSC, a division of the American Library Association), an informational book conveys "documentable factual information."[11] But documentation is often missing from a book for young readers. And can it have fictional elements? Does it make any difference if it is told as a narrative as exposition, as a series of facts, as a poem? It does make a difference for these awards, but is the difference meaningful for the reader or for the adult who is guiding the reader?

Exposition has been the customary way to deliver facts to adults, but there is a long tradition of conveying facts to children through story. Notable examples include Holling Clancy Hollings's Great Lakes–traveling *Paddle to the Sea* (1941), David Macaulay's *Cathedral* (1973), and subsequent titles such as *Mosque* (2003), all published by Houghton Mifflin. Many would argue—and some brain research supports the idea—that we all learn better through story because stories engage our emotions.[12] In her 1979 edition of *Children's Literature in the Elementary School*, Charlotte Huck offers several examples of "informational picture books" that are "exceptions to the rule that says information is distorted by a veil of fiction."[13] They present information about a subject but it comes through imagined narrators and situations.

The imaginary Ms. Frizzle has piloted a generation of schoolchildren through science and social science topics. I've included a recent Ms. Frizzle title, *The Magic*

School Bus and the Climate Challenge (by Joanna Cole, Scholastic Press, 2010). Reviews of this and others in the series in *The Horn Book* have appeared in the informational book section. Explaining that placement, Roger Sutton, the magazine's editor, told me: "In the case of the Magic School Bus books . . . the distinction between the fictional/fantasy elements and the information about science is clearly underlined, with the balance tipping in the direction of the latter" (pers. comm.). Elementary school readers can tell what is fantasy and what is fiction, not only through their own sense of what can actually be true but also through explanations in the back matter. And, in these titles, there is more information than story.

The sun is the imagined narrator in Molly Bang's *Living Sunlight* (Blue Sky Press, 2009), but both the intent and the effect are informational, explaining how the sun's light energy becomes the energy for life on earth. In *My Little Round House* (Groundwood Books, 2009), a description of Mongolian nomadic life, Jilu's first-person story begins in his mother's womb. (Helen Mixten adapts the story by Mongolian author/illustrator Bolormaa Baasansuren.) James Rumford's *Silent Music* (Roaring Brook Press, 2008) is a completely imagined story introducing the beautiful Arabic script in a realistic Baghdad setting. The manatee's experience in Jim Arnosky's *Slow Down for Manatees* (G. P. Putnam's Sons, 2009) has been distilled from an actual event. The naturalist has organized it into a narrative whose purpose is not the story arc but the information he is conveying. There is no anthropomorphization. I've included all four of these books. In spite of imagined elements, they are informational picture books. The line I've tried to draw reflects both the author's intent, as far as I can discern it, and my judgment of how the reader will experience the book.

But what if parts of an apparently true story have been changed? Facts matter. Librarians have long consigned the imagined childhood events and made-up conversations of the Childhood of Famous Americans series to the category of historical fiction. It is fiction with a didactic intent. The back cover of current editions calls them "fictionalized biographies." Still, plenty of picture-book biographies are published today with imagined dialogue. "I think that invented dialogue simply cannot exist in nonfiction," writes Vicky Smith, children's editor for *Kirkus* magazine, when asked about the difference between that magazine's categories: picture book, informational picture book, and nonfiction (pers. comm.). For that magazine, as a rule, books with imagined dialogue are either described as picture books or fiction.

Informational picture books are an extension of the nonfiction continuum. But looking at library cataloging, even from the Library of Congress, we see again that there are no hard-and-fast rules. And even *Kirkus* has made exceptions. For the most part I have avoided using biographies and histories with extensive imagined dialogue. Where there are other invented elements, I have tried to point them out. A book that deals with exactly this issue, and which I included in this selection, is *Abe Lincoln Crosses a Creek* (Schwartz & Wade Books, 2008) where author Deborah Hopkinson and illustrator John Hendrix make a point of showing how the imagination of the creators shapes the story.

The phrase *narrative nonfiction* is often used to describe informational books that use techniques of fiction: stories told with a narrative arc, developed settings and characters, rising and falling action, dialogue and interior monologue. These increasingly popular techniques are particularly appropriate for biographies and historical accounts. The dialogue and personal thoughts in these books will come out of the writer's research. A skilled writer such as Barbara Kerley can take quotations from primary sources and fit them into a new narrative, as she did in her biography of President Theodore Roosevelt's daughter, *What to Do about Alice?* (Scholastic Press, 2008). But narrative nonfiction is not the only possibility; informational books for young readers and listeners take other forms as well.

Traditionally, informational books for schoolchildren were written in a straightforward fashion, with topics introduced and highlighted by chapter headings and subheadings, and with clear topical or chronological organization. Many subject books intended for the school and library markets and some informational titles sold in bookstores are still presented that way. Deborah Heiligman's *Celebrate Diwali* (National Geographic, 2006) and other books in that excellent series on religious holidays are good examples.

Changes in book production have led to the rise of the photo essay, in which the pictures are the attraction and deliver much of the information while the text may be limited to a few lines and photo captions. There may be dual narratives, where a simple text for younger readers and listeners accompanies a more complex one. Often the subject is put into context by an afterword, intended for an older reader or adult. Nic Bishop's series for Scholastic, including *Spiders* (2007), *Frogs* (2008), and *Lizards* (2010), is an appealing example.

In her groundbreaking *Radical Change* (H. W. Wilson, 1999), Eliza Dresang referred to some books as "handheld hypertext,"[14] texts that don't require linear reading. These don't provide a narrative. Instead, the child reader constructs the narrative using text and illustration together as well as clues provided by the design. Scholastic's Magic School Bus series is one example. Simon & Schuster's Insiders series goes even further toward the reference book end of the continuum. A local librarian told me that an Insiders volume was her son's favorite bedtime story long before he could read; well loved to the point that the family finally limited him to one double-page spread per evening. As soon as he could sound out words, he was reading these complex books on his own, puzzling out the informational bits whose illustrations had attracted his attention. MetaMetrics' Lexile Framework for Reading, an often-cited measurement of text difficulty, codes some of these books IG, "illustrated guides," a category that covers the range from encyclopedias to books presented topically in single or double-page chunks. In these books "text pieces could be moved around without affecting the overall linear flow of the book."[15]

Finally there are interesting new hybrids. The text of Jason Chin's *Redwoods* (Roaring Brook Press, 2009) reads like an extensive encyclopedia entry. The illustrations show the boy's fantasy journey into the forest and up to the top of a tree, demonstrating what an able nonfiction reader might be doing with material that seems, on its surface, bland.

Everyone likes to learn new things. When children or adults say they prefer fiction, they may well be thinking more about style than about content. Some readers like to amass facts and skip around in their reading; others love a good story but retain all of its background; still others want information organized clearly so they can see what's important. Some prefer photographs, something that looks like the real thing; others like the additional emotional and informational content that a good artist can convey. These differences are more a matter of taste than a matter of definition.

In any preschool or day-care center, informational books are an important part of the library. Such books may have talking toothbrushes and anthropomorphized animals. Invented dialogue and imagined incidents have always been part and parcel of the presentation of information to the very young. At what point should teachers and librarians insist on total accuracy and realism in the books they recommend? And at what point does a subject become too complex to be explained correctly to a child? These are questions without easy answers. The common sense response is "It depends." Rather than eliminate books with fictional elements and possibly misleading simplification, I have included some whose purpose is obviously informational but have pointed out such embellishments in my annotation.

WHAT IS A PICTURE BOOK?

The second part of the phrase *informational picture book* is an equally blurry category. Most adults remember informational books from their childhood as a sea of gray type, dull in presentation even if the subject was interesting. A college junior in my children's literature class wrote in her reading response journal, "If informational books could be like picture books, it would be great." The good news is that today, they are. Changing expectations and tastes, as well as advances in printing and publishing that have reduced the cost and complexity of adding color illustrations, have led to a situation where more often than not, an informational book, even one for readers in grades six through ten, is illustrated on nearly every page. Books in Houghton Mifflin's Scientists in the Field series, such as Pamela Turner's *The Frog Scientist* (2009) or Sy Montgomery's *Tarantula Scientist* (2007), have considerable appeal even for reluctant readers because of the eye-catching photographs that add to the information in the text. National Geographic's award-winning Face to Face series features photographs and personal encounters described by naturalists who have studied all sorts of appealing creatures: butterflies, manatees, penguins, elephants, lions, and many more. A patient listener with a special interest will certainly enjoy seeing these, but they are beyond the usual understanding of picture book.

In a well-edited picture book the illustrations have "collective unity," a phrase ALSC uses in its definitions for its well-known Caldecott Award. A picture book "essentially provides the child with a visual experience." It has a "story-line, theme, or concept developed through the series of pictures of which the book is comprised."[16] The adult trying to categorize books has to look beyond thematic unity to see if these pictures actually extend or simply support the text. Do they tell a story—at least the story of the text, or (very likely) something more? Or do they just illuminate incidents? Sometimes the story may seem lacking, but the illustrations are striking enough to draw readers into the book and keep them there. That seems to be the case with the Insiders books, whose computer graphic imagery gives a striking 3-D effect. These images are intriguing enough to some early readers that they are willing to expend extra effort to decode the text. The text in these books comes in digestible bites while the images add to and extend the reader's understanding.

A picture book, one publicist told me only half in jest, is a book for a picture book audience. Others define it as one that can be read in one sitting. They are imagining the "traditional picture book experience," an adult with a child on the lap or several nestled close by, possibly at bedtime. Or they picture an adult reading to a group, skillfully showing the illustrations while simultaneously speaking the text. Books for reading aloud can have substantially more difficult text, laid out on the page in more complex ways, than books designed for young readers to read themselves. Books for reading to a group need illustrations that show well across a room. In the annotations that follow, I have sometimes pointed out books that I thought would make especially good read-alouds.

Some adults complain that today's children can't or won't sit still to listen for an extended period. But today's children aren't limited to books that can be read in one sitting or to stories that march sequentially to a clearly defined ending. They are comfortable dealing with a variety of stimuli and constructing their own understandings. Those of us who read to very small children try to teach them to begin at the beginning and progress through to the end. But their lives don't feel like that, and their own natural inclinations often lead them to skip some pages, linger on others, go back and forth, and make their own narrative. In a world where, increasingly, other experiences reinforce their ability to attend to a variety of stimuli at the same time, the single linear path of an old-fashioned picture book is just one of many possibilities. And in truth, information is like that. It comes in bits and pieces that we need to put together ourselves. With few exceptions, scientific knowledge is accumulated by a variety of researchers working at different times and places and not even always in the same field. Historians look at masses of different documents to pull together a coherent picture of an event. It is appropriate to include informational books for young people that model something of that experience.

In limiting this selection to books for children from ages 3 to 10, I have excluded books meant for the earliest use: concept books, counting books, and early alphabet books of the sort simply designed to teach letters. At the other end of the scale I have excluded titles whose text could not be understood by an able 9- or 10-year-old. Children will read or listen to anything that truly interests them; they should not be limited by age and grade-level distinctions. But with so many good books to choose from, there needed to be some limits.

To sum up my working definition, an informational picture book is a book both intended and experienced as one that conveys information through a marriage of text and pictures. This information is factual and up to date. It can be documented, and it has been presented appropriately for child readers or listeners ages 3 to 10. This sounds straightforward but it's a definition with blurry edges, not as easy to apply as it sounds. Here are just a few more examples, books using extensive fictional elements or traditional literary forms for informational purposes:

Mark Foster's *Whale Port* (Houghton Mifflin, 2007) imagines a New England coastal settlement, following its growth and change through the years to describe the history of whaling ports. At first, illustrations stretch across a double-page spread, with a paragraph of text on or under the illustration, a typical picture book composition. But then there are pages with more extensive text and smaller, carefully labeled illustrations. Tiny sketches add information that does not appear in the text (varieties of harpoons; the specialized tasks of crew members on a whaling ship; how whalebone was used in a lady's corset). In spite of the extensive, expository text, the relatively difficult vocabulary, and the composite, imagined place and families, this title—reminiscent of David Macauley's work—belongs on this list. The intent is to inform; the experience is informational; the reading level is age appropriate; the pictures extend the text.

Joyce Sidman's *Ubiquitous* (Houghton Mifflin, 2010) is a collection of poetry celebrating life forms that have long flourished on our planet. Each poem is accompanied by a paragraph of factual information, and the whole is meticulously sourced. Similarly, Pat Mora's *Yum! ¡Mmmm! ¡Qué rico!* (Lee & Low Books, 2007) describes food plants native to North and South America in haiku. Again, her information is sourced. In both cases, though the form is literary, the content is factual and the illustrations, on double-page spreads, extend the text.

Jacqueline Jules's *Unite or Die* (Charlesbridge, 2009) uses the framework of a school play to present the Constitutional Convention of 1786–87. A simple narration and speech balloons are brought to life by the cartoons depicting various parts of the play. Text and pictures work together in the synergistic way that characterizes a picture book. This is not a subject for preschool children, but the Constitutional Convention does turn up in elementary curricula, and some children are interested in U.S. history long before they have been exposed to it in school. In relatively few lines, the author gets the important issues across and details of the staging shown in the illustrations help make the concepts clear.

In Carole Boston Weatherford's *Moses: When Harriet Tubman Led Her People to Freedom* (Hyperion Books for Children, 2006), God speaks and Harriet replies. This imagined or recollected dialogue is set off by the use of different fonts and is based on Tubman's own accounts.[17] Almost every professional reviewer and the catalogers at the Library of Congress define this as an informational book. Librarians, reviewers, and bookstore managers categorize books like these on a case-by-case basis, and there is no unanimity. But they all seemed to belong in this selection.

NOTES

1. Nell K. Duke, foreword, in *Reality Checks: Teaching Reading Comprehension with Nonfiction K–5*, by Tony Stead (Portland, ME: Stenhouse Publishers, 2005), ix.
2. Susan Kuklin, "Why I/You/We Continue to Write for Kids," *I.N.K.*, February 11, 2011, http://inkrethink.blogspot.com/2011/02/why-iweyou-continue-to-write-for-kids.html.
3. Marc Tyler Nobleman, "The Golden Age of Picture Book Biography," *Noblemania*, April 26, 2009, http://noblemania.blogspot.com/2009/04/golden-age-of-picture-book-biography.html.

4. Julie Bosman, "Picture Books No Longer a Staple for Children," *New York Times*, October 7, 2010, www.nytimes.com/2010/10/08/us/08picture.html.

5. David Schwartz, "Are Picture Books Dead?" *I.N.K.*, October 25, 2010, http://inkrethink .blogspot.com/2010/10/are-picture-books-dead.html.

6. Cynthia Pon and Maya Ajmera, "In the Picture Book Kitchen (re: A Paucity of Picture Books)," *CCBC-Net*, November 12, 2010, http://soe-b5.ad.education.wisc.edu/ccbc -net/2010-11/16412.html.

7. Kristen McLean, "The Children's Book Consumer in the Digital Age: Takeaways from the ABC/Bowker Pubtrack Survey," *Bookselling This Week*, February 10, 2011, http:// news.bookweb.org/news/children%E2%80%99s-book-consumer-digital-age-takeaways -abcbowker-pubtrack-survey.

8. Judy S. DeLoache and Nancy M. Burns, "Early Understanding of the Representational Function of Pictures," *Cognition* 52, no. 2 (1994): 83–110.

9. Adrienne Samuels and Marjorie Taylor, "Children's Ability to Distinguish Fantasy Events from Real-Life Events," *British Journal of Developmental Psychology* 12, no. 4 (1994): 417–27.

10. "NCTE Orbis Pictus Award for Outstanding Nonfiction for Children," www.ncte.org/ awards/orbispictus, last accessed April 4, 2012.

11. "Terms and Criteria: (Robert F.) Sibert Informational Book Award," www.ala.org/ala/ mgrps/divs/alsc/awardsgrants/bookmedia/sibertmedal/sibertterms/sibertmedaltrms.cfm, last accessed April 4, 2012.

12. Eric Jensen, *Brain-Based Learning: The New Paradigm of Teaching* (Thousand Oaks, CA: Corwin Press, 2008).

13. Charlotte S. Huck, *Children's Literature in the Elementary School*, 3rd ed., updated (New York: Holt, Rinehart and Winston, 1979), 539.

14. Eliza T. Dresang, *Radical Change: Books for Youth in a Digital Age* (New York: H. W. Wilson, 1999), 106.

15. "Lexile Codes: IG: Illustrated Guide," www.lexile.com/about-lexile/lexile-codes/ #IllustratedGlossary, last accessed April 4, 2012.

16. "Terms and Criteria: Randolph Caldecott Medal," www.ala.org/ala/mgrps/divs/alsc/ awardsgrants/bookmedia/caldecottmedal/caldecottterms/caldecottterms.cfm, last accessed April 4, 2012.

17. Carole Boston Weatherford, "Q&A: Moses: When Harriet Tubman Led Her People to Freedom," www.caroleweatherford.com/moses.htm, last accessed October 22, 2011.

2

Choosing Good Informational Picture Books

ADULTS CHOOSE CHILDREN'S BOOKS for a variety of reasons. They may be buying them for their children or for gifts. They may be helping children make their own choices, or making selections for a library or bookstore, or choosing books for a classroom or a story time. Whatever the reason, there are four elements to consider in picking a children's book. One is the subject and its potential appeal for the child. Another is the text. A third is the visual experience of the book—its illustrations, design, and production. The final element is the use of sources and additional tools a book may provide for a child's enjoyment or education.

SUBJECT AND CHILD APPEAL

When choosing a good book for a child the adult should, if possible, be guided by the child's own interests. Often this is easy. One child is fascinated by trucks, another by dinosaurs. A third wants to know everything there is to know about soccer. Some children like to learn about real people, of today or yesterday; they may be looking for heroes or for people like themselves. Others are budding naturalists or astronauts. Sometimes children don't know right away what they're interested in; they need

FACING PAGE ART FROM

Biblioburro: A True Story from Colombia written and illustrated by Jeanette Winter.

to explore. The lists that follow include a wide variety of subjects, both familiar and unusual. They are a place to start.

Any good teacher, parent, or leader will also be thinking about the child's next step. Sometimes, children's minds need stretching. Educators talk about the *zone of proximal development*—that area between the skills a child already has and what he or she still needs to learn, between what can be done on one's own and what requires help. The best learning choices for children lie in that space; they build on what the child knows. But sometimes readers just want something comfortable, something that reinforces what they already know. That's an appropriate choice, too. Whatever the topic, it should be a subject of interest and value to children. Look for books that make a connection to the child reader. There should be some way the child can find himself, his interests, experiences, and understanding of the world in the book.

By necessity, an informational picture book is a small slice of information about a subject. *Which* slice matters. The author's and illustrator's choices should have some purpose. Usually, the creator is using something small and particular to suggest or represent something larger. Informational picture books also open doors. If what they learn engages them, children will want to read more. So, a book about an ecosystem will pick a few appealing species to represent the whole system. A biography may concentrate on a few moments in the subject's life, moments that may be high points in the life story or that may connect with the reader in ways that invite further exploration.

Obviously, the book should be free of bias. But beyond looking at the slant of a particular book, when choosing books for children, we should also consider what other books the child is reading or has available to read. Broad gender, racial and socioeconomic representation can't be expected in a single volume. So, parents, teachers, and librarians will want to make sure that their collections have breadth. Books about slavery are important, but children should also hear about African American success stories. Nowadays it is easy to balance collections of biographies of famous men with well-done biographies of successful (if not so famous) women.

HOW THE STORY IS TOLD

A well-written informational book is written with passion and enthusiasm that leave the reader with a sense of adventure and excitement. It has a clear, logical organization. It is told with clarity and directness, using rich, appropriate language and equally rich, appropriate examples. It is accurate and avoids anthropomorphism.

Sportswriter Fred Bowen's passion for baseball comes through in *No Easy Way* (Dutton Children's Books, 2010), about the great hitter Ted Williams. The story of the Red Sox superstar's hard work and dedication is told conversationally, but Bowen adds deeper meaning and suspense by paying particular attention to the choice Williams faced at the end of the 1941 season: should he sit out the last games and protect his .400 batting average, or keep playing and take the chance of slipping below that mark? Bowen's focus on those pivotal games demonstrates something about the player himself as well as the excitement of the game.

Barbara Kerley shows similar enthusiasm about the subject of her biography, *What to Do about Alice?* (Scholastic Press, 2008). Even the subtitle has a sense of excitement: *How Alice Roosevelt Broke the Rules, Charmed the World, and Drove Her Father Teddy Crazy!* The exuberant telling and humor add to the appeal. Kerley finds examples that illustrate the adventure of being the President's daughter as well as her subject's personality: Alice greets White House guests with a snake and dives into a swimming pool with all her clothes on.

The choice of narrative style will help determine the organization. If the author tells a story, is it chronological? After a page of background describing the ship's construction, Don Brown tells the story of the sinking of the *Titanic* step-by-step in *All Stations! Distress!* (Roaring Brook Press, 2008). The events are easy to follow. Sometimes an author will provide an opening narrative hook before moving to the beginning of the story and proceeding chronologically. Even quite young children can understand flashbacks, and the narrative hook explains why the subject might be important to the young reader. *Listen to the Wind* (Dial Books for Young Readers, 2009) by Greg Mortenson and Susan Roth begins with a statement from the children of Korphe, in Pakistan: "We study in the school that we helped to build." Then the children who narrate the story describe Dr. Greg's first visit and his return with material to build their school. The narrative hook connects young American readers and listeners with this faraway place.

Some books are organized topically, with a different subject on each double-page spread. The table of contents in John Long's *Dinosaurs* (Simon & Schuster Books for Young Readers, 2007) shows that even in this Insiders series text, there is a clear topical organization, first presenting the subject in general and then telling about particular species, grouped into meat eaters and plant eaters. Sometimes the one-topic-per-spread format can dictate the content so rigidly that some subjects seem slighted while others are overdeveloped. The designers of the Insiders series get around that problem by varying the amount of text on a page.

The story should be told with interesting language appropriate to the child's language level. There is nothing wrong with technical words. Unfamiliar new words that aren't defined in context may well be glossed over and ignored. But children are sponges, ready to soak up new vocabulary. It helps if new words are defined as they are used and, perhaps, in a glossary in the back matter. Clarity and directness make a text easier to understand. Look for language that isn't hackneyed, even in books for the youngest child. Lively verbs, fresh turns of phrase, precise language, and appropriate imagery all enhance storytelling, and even exposition of facts. Here is Jean Craighead George describing the return of wolves to Yellowstone National Park:

> Flowers filled the valley. Bees and butterflies that fed on the flowers returned. Warblers sang. Hummingbirds brightened the valley. Like pieces in a kaleidoscope, the broken parts of the wilderness were tumbling into place.
>
> The wolves were back.[1]

And here Carole Boston Weatherford describes what the young John Coltrane heard:

> Before John was a jazz giant,
> he heard big bands on the radio
> and a saxophone's soulful solo,
> blue notes crooning his name.[2]

Stories should be told with rich, appropriate examples. Authors select a particular event or series of events and particular examples to make a general point, create a narrative arc, or develop a larger theme. In evaluating a book, ask: Is the story cohesive? Do the examples work together to tell a story a child will understand? Think about what has been included and what was left out. Do the specific examples or story chosen for the child reader leave an appropriate general impression? I chose not to annotate John Hendrix's memorable *John Brown* (Abrams Books for Young Readers, 2009) because I am uneasy about a text that portrays Brown as an ultimately sympathetic character while the horror of his act is shown only once, in a double-page spread of a dead man at Harper's Ferry. If I were to read this book to young people I would want to discuss the use of violence for positive ends.

A good informational book is accurate. The information should be clear and up to date, with clear distinction between facts and theories, and between historical data and suppositions. Generalizations should be supported by specific details. The subject should not be so oversimplified as to leave an inaccurate impression, and the book should include enough of the significant facts so the subject is accurately represented.

Have chronologies been adjusted or details been made up? Sometimes an author will tell us. If details are supposed or imagined on the basis of other information, some authors use words like *might have*. But others freely imagine feelings and even conversations among their real characters. In the annotations in following chapters I have tried to note instances of imagined dialogue, feelings, or events, and I have included only a few books that make significant use of fictionalized material. An adult reading to or with a child can help children see the difference by asking, "How do you suppose the author knew that?"

If there are fantasy elements in an otherwise informational book, the distinction should be clear. Dinosaurs did not share their world with humans, but humans can be used as part of a measuring scale. Avoiding anthropomorphism seems simple, but it is difficult not to imagine that animals share our feelings and our motivations. Sometimes otherwise excellent titles about the natural world will use language that suggests that animals are thinking in ways that humans think.

HOW THE STORY IS PICTURED

Illustrations should match the subject and tone, convey the story and/or add additional information. In the best picture book biographies, the illustrations will convey far more about the time and place than the text can do. In the best nature books, illustrations can bring the child much closer to the subject than they are likely to get in real life. Artists such as Wendell Minor and Jim Arnosky and photographers such as Nic Bishop are skilled at showing animals in the context of their environment, adding a great deal to the text. Illustrators such as Brian Selznick go to great lengths to research the time and place of their story, making sure that details in the illustrations are as truthful as those in the text.

Just as authors select details that are most appropriate to tell the story to a child audience—and perhaps that give a sense of its larger importance—illustrators need to choose carefully what they are going to show. The pictures may emphasize important points or add details that the words don't convey. They may even tell a whole separate story, but one that is still accurate and relevant.

The choice of medium, the color palette, and the design can support or be at odds with an author's text. Leonard Jenkins's illustrations for Deborah Hopkinson's *Sweet Land of Liberty* (Peachtree, 2007) are dark, full of crayon scribbles and sharply defined edges. They suggest the jumble of mixed feelings surrounding Marian Anderson's concert at the Lincoln Memorial in 1939. Illustrating Karen Fox's *Older Than the Stars* (Charlesbridge, 2010), Nancy Davis uses special text effects at the beginning, evoking the chaos of the beginnings of the universe.

Illustrations should be well crafted. Children's-book illustrations may be photographs, or may be painted, drawn, carved or etched and printed, scratched, pasted, and digitally generated or enhanced. For the annotations in this book I have usually made note of the medium (helpful publishers include that information in the book), but I haven't gone on to specify the many possibilities of paper, canvas, or board from which the artist may choose. Styles vary from realistic to quite abstract. Children between 3 and 10 don't seem to have difficulty with abstractions, as long as the style is consistent. They enjoy cartoons. What they don't like are realistic pictures that aren't realistic—awkwardly portrayed people or animals, and scenes that are hard to make out.

Illustrations that vary in size and placement on the page keep the reader's interest. Illustrations should not lose details as they cross the gutter. Photographs should be large enough to see easily, clearly identified, and well reproduced. Text and illustration should be well integrated. Child readers should not have to leaf through the book to find an explanation for a picture. When the text mentions something unfamiliar, there should be a picture to help the reader understand what it is.

For traditional picture books, the key is the page turn. The pictures and graphic elements, including the font, will guide readers through the book. Many modern informational picture books can be read on two levels, with the information on a page summarized or introduced by words or simple sentences in a larger font. Others have a short picture-book text and several pages at the end that give a more thorough treatment to the subject.

Finally, a picture book for young readers should be sturdy enough to last through repeated readings. Foldouts, pop-ups, tabs, and the like should not tear after just a few sessions. Children reread books they like, often over and over. Invitations to interact with the physical book are very appealing, but they can also become a disappointment if they don't last.

ACCURACY, SOURCES, AND ADDITIONAL TOOLS

A well-written informational book presents facts and chronology that are correct and can be independently verified; the overall impression is proportionate and balanced. Writers of informational books choose the details they include in their text. They may have to simplify ideas, omit events that seem irrelevant to their particular focus or inappropriate for the audience, but the narrative as a whole should not be misleading.

Even for the youngest readers, an author can indicate where he or she got information for the book. For middle graders, sometimes an illustrator's afterword explains his or her research as well. This can range from a list of sources to an explanation of photographic methods authors such as Nic Bishop and Pamela Kirby provide. At the very least, a line thanking an expert for looking at the book is helpful. Sometimes this information can be found on the copyright page, and sometimes in more extensive back matter. As I evaluate books, I appreciate authors who have added information about their research methods and sources to their own or their publisher's website, but this information should be a supplement, not a substitute, for some acknowledgement in the book. Web resources are grand, but many children, especially young children, don't have ready access to the Internet. Along with sources, the back matter should provide suggestions for further reading. Having opened a door to a subject, the author should invite the young reader through it.

For elementary school readers, maps and time lines are important. Every exposure to these graphical representations of space and time helps a child develop his or her own mental map and sense of history. In families and preschools where map reading is encouraged, even preschoolers can find their own place in the world, a starting place for broader connections.

Finally, it is really helpful to have page numbers and an index. The index does not need to be traditional; it can be made of pictures. In *How to Clean a Hippopotamus* (Houghton Mifflin Harcourt, 2010) Steve Jenkins and Robin Page have provided miniature reproductions of each double-page spread along with additional information about animals. These books are teaching young readers *how* to find information in books, with the index as their tool. In books for elementary school readers—who may be reading for school reports or to learn about a particular passion—an index should be required.

AWARDS AND BEST-OF-THE-YEAR LISTS

In choosing books to consider for this selection of informational picture books, I began with a variety of notable book lists. Different awards honor books of a particular genre, or books that deal with a specific subject area, or books whose creators meet specific criteria. Because of the narrower focus of their selections, these awards also tell potential readers something about the book. In my annotations I have tried to include awards that can give readers a better sense of which children may like the book. Publishers' websites often give more complete lists of a particular title's awards.

Book awards and notable book lists are curious things. They depend enormously on the chemistry of a particular committee and members'·interpretations of the criteria for particular awards. Those criteria range widely. Each committee looks at a different selection of books. Some cast a broad net; others are more closely focused. Members of the National Science Teachers Association (NSTA) look for excellence in science writing; those in the National Council of Teachers of English (NCTE) look, in part, for books that deal explicitly with language. Some awards and best books lists only consider the pictures, some only the words; most look at the combination. Some have quite explicit criteria for literary or pictorial excellence; others weigh thematic or informational content or child appeal more heavily. Many awards are limited to books published in this country; others include books published in Canada and elsewhere and distributed here. In looking at award lists for help in choosing good children's books, there are several things to keep in mind. First, it is important to know the specific criteria for a particular award. Some guidelines refer vaguely to "generally acceptable criteria of literary excellence," others define excellence in terms of the writer's craft, still others are more concerned with a book's message. Some award lists have many titles to choose from; others relatively few. Suggested readership age or grade ranges, the nationality or ethnicity of the author or illustrator, even the ability of a publisher to provide multiple examination copies—all these things affect the choices an award committee makes. More information about the awards I've included appears in the appendix.

Looking at individual award criteria also reveals why it is so hard to find an exact definition for an informational picture book—a struggle I described in the first chapter. In identifying the genre of the books they honor, different award committees use different definitions. Especially for the very young, and especially in the social sciences, fiction and poetry are often included in the "informational" category.

Finally, and not too surprisingly, in almost all these reading lists the emphasis is on fiction. Unless the award or book list is specifically targeted at nonfiction, the lion's share of titles will be fiction. Yet many readers read both fiction and nonfiction. One recent study reported that a group of first graders actually preferred informational books when asked to choose books they would like to own.[3] Many elementary school librarians have told me that children's choices are eclectic, but that there are a number of boys who would prefer an exclusive diet of "real" books. In recent years there has been an increased effort to foster reading of nonfiction, at least in schools. Given the number of attractive and high-quality informational titles published each year, more of them should be receiving award attention.

With few exceptions, nonfiction books published in series for the school and library market seldom appear on any list, although they are an important part of any public library collection. Designed with curricular use in mind (even at the preschool level) they don't usually have the marriage of text and illustration that constitutes an informational picture book as defined for this collection or for most review journals. They are seldom sold in brick-and-mortar bookstores and are often more expensive than the usual children's hardback or paperback book. The quality of text and illustrations in these books has come a long way in recent years. Most of the books described in this bibliography are books that have received honors and have been mentioned on notable book lists, often in a variety of contexts, but I have included occasional examples of well-done series. Librarians, parents, and teachers should make it their business to seek out some of the better informational book series as well, especially ones that coincide with a young reader's particular interests. The annual *Booklist* Top 10 Series Nonfiction lists would be a good place to start.[4]

THE BOOKS IN THIS LIST

These annotations include books on a broad range of subjects—some with inherent child appeal and some that may need some introduction but are of interest and value to children. In reading for this selection, I've discovered that biographies and books about the natural world are publishers' and professionals' favorites. It was much more difficult to find excellent books—books that had garnered some measure of critical acclaim or even review attention—in more abstract subjects like math or money, or even about historical events or ideas. In part, this is appropriate to the age. Children enjoy reading about animals and about people they can admire. But why would it be difficult to find commendable informational titles about children and families, health, hobbies, places, and pets? I suspect this is because publishers have left those topics to the series bookmakers, publishers who look to support curricula and who sell their titles in sets to the school and library market. As I mentioned, I've included some books in exemplary series, but these titles, which get spotty attention at best, may be more difficult to find.

I have tried to include books that represent the broad range of people who live in this country. I have been less effective at finding international breadth. The number of books published in this country that reflect the world beyond our borders is quite small; of those actually written in another country and later published here, there are few that are informational. In a world that is increasingly connected, there should be global connections in children's reading as well.

Some subjects suddenly attract the attention of several authors and publishers, resulting in two or three books on the same subject appearing within a short space of time. Sometimes the subjects come from stories in the news. Pale Male, the red-tailed hawk that nested on Fifth Avenue in New York City, was one such story in this five-year span. Kenyan Nobel Peace Prize winner Wangari Maathai's tree planting was another. Books may mark anniversaries such as the 200th birthdays of Darwin and Lincoln and the fortieth anniversary of the *Apollo 11* moon landing. When there are several books on the same subject, comparing one book with another will widen and deepen a reader's understanding of a subject. For parents and teachers, looking at a pair of books with young readers and listeners provides an outstanding opportunity to talk about authors, illustrators, editors, and designers and the different choices they make—in selection of details, stance, organization, voice, perspective, style, pacing, colors, composition, balance, and so much more. For that reason I have not limited my selections to one per topic, and I encourage librarians, teachers, and parents to offer the possibility for comparison, contrast, and further exploration.

Though there are certainly gaps, this list includes plenty of splendid reading, listening, and looking. It is a distillation—there are many more good books than I could include or even mention in passing. Indeed, the hardest decisions were not the books I included but the books I had to leave out. Reading and rereading to make these selections has given me great pleasure. It has also reminded me how much reading pleasure there is for children to enjoy.

NOTES

1. Jean Craighead George, *The Wolves Are Back* (New York: Dutton Children's Books, 2008), n.p.
2. Carole Boston Weatherford, *Before John Was a Jazz Giant* (New York: Henry Holt, 2008), n.p.
3. Kathleen A. J. Mohr, "Children's Choices for Recreational Reading: A Three-Part Investigation of Selection Preferences, Rationales, and Processes," *Journal of Literacy Research* 38, no. 1 (2006): 81–104.
4. "Top 10 Series Nonfiction: 2011," www.booklistonline.com/Top-10-Series-Nonfiction-2011-Daniel-Kraus/pid=4701699, last accessed April 4, 2012.

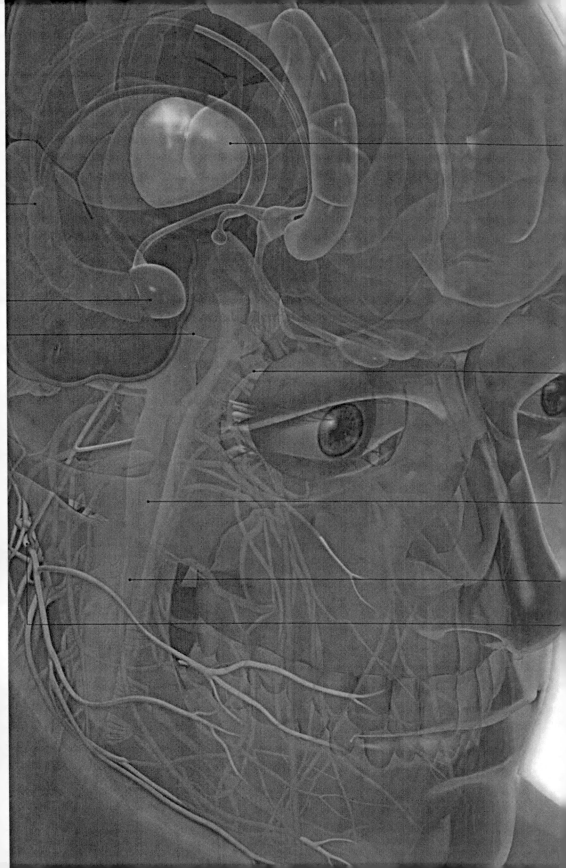

3
Ourselves and Our World at Home and School

TEACHERS KNOW IT IS important to start with what learners know. Social studies curricula start at home, with the child, the family, and the neighborhood. There are many outstanding picture books about children's home and family lives, but I found relatively few that were also factual. Those that are true or mostly true usually have a broader social studies theme. The best informational picture books about pets are also about famous people. Books about the human body and about health are more often aimed at older readers, although bodies are intensely interesting to children of all ages. This is an area that deserves more publishing attention.

FAMILIES

AJMERA, MAYA, SHEILA KINKADE, AND CYNTHIA PON

Our Grandparents: A Global Album

Illustrated with photographs
Watertown, MA: Charlesbridge, 2010
ISBN: 978-1-570-91458-4 | **AGES 3–7**

With charming photographs from thirty-four countries around the world, this album illustrates the roles grandparents play in children's lives. An intriguing opening spread offers names for Grandpa and Grandma in eighteen languages—written in the Roman alphabet so young readers can sound them out. Archbishop Desmond Tutu's forward describes grandparents'

FACING PAGE ART FROM

Human Body by Linda Calabresi, part of the Insiders series responsibilities, but the images that follow stress the joy of the grandparent-grandchild connection. Each double-page spread contains several photos and a single sentence with one word highlighted: *love, listen, explore, play, teach, learn, celebrate, share,* and *care.* "With our grandparents we feel happy, safe, and loved." Not only do the pictures come from around the world, they also suggest the diversity within countries. In England, a small boy helps his grandmother light a menorah; a white American holds her biracial granddaughter; an older girl leans against her Native American grandmother clad in a beautiful woven blanket; another American family makes tamales; and in Canada, a child admires a beautiful pair of fur and leather boots perhaps made by his First Nations grandmother. A world map shows which countries the pictures come from. Ideal for family sharing, the book ends with suggestions for things to do with your grandparents.

KUKLIN, SUSAN

Families

Illustrated with photographs by Susan Kuklin
New York: Hyperion Books for Children, 2006
ISBN: 978-0-786-80822-9 | **AGES 4–10**

Children between ages 4 and 14 present their families in their own words, describing what's important and choosing photographic settings that represent them. Each double-page spread contains a photograph of the family at home, a picture of the children, and a snapshot from family history, as well as the children's statements. For some children, what's important is their position—only child, twin, younger or older sibling; for some, their racial, ethnic, or religious heritage; and for some the variety of adults—grandparents, single parents, same-sex parents, parents who differ in race or religion, parents who are divorced or seldom home. Fifteen families are represented. The range is wide, suggesting the variation that might be found in an American classroom. A number of children have immigrant parents or grandparents; one child has Down syndrome; two mention adoption. Several chose to include pictures of parents or grandparents long ago as well. The substantial text suggests a book for older children, but the illustrations carry the story. Younger readers may well skim through, stopping only occasionally. This appealing photo essay, an ALSC Notable and CCBC Choice, effectively illustrates a broad range of family situations today, making it particularly useful for classroom use.

ONYEFULU, IFEOMA

Grandma Comes to Stay

Illustrated with photographs by Ifeoma Onyefulu
London: Frances Lincoln Children's Books, 2010
ISBN: 978-1-845-07865-2 | **AGES 3–7**

Excited by her grandmother's upcoming visit, Stephanie helps with the preparations. Then, when her grandmother comes, they show each other all the things they can do. Grandma reads Stephanie's favorite book and shows her how to tie a wrapper and a headdress. Stephanie shows Grandma how to kick a ball, ride a bike, do the ironing, and play with dolls. With an exceptionally simple text, illustrated with photographs of Stephanie taken at her home in Accra, Ghana, this photo essay affirms the universal pleasure in a family visit. Stephanie's activities will be familiar. She likes to draw, and Grandma brings her a box of pencils. She shows her grandmother how she can play an African drum; Grandma takes her to a festival to see real-life drummers and dancers and tells her a story about a magic drum. Onyefulu's photographs confirm the affection between the two. Grandma wears traditional clothing, but Stephanie's house is modern; this introduction to life in present-day Ghana demonstrates that city life is not too different around the world. The author-illustrator's *Deron Goes to Nursery School* (2010) is another title in this First Experiences series about daily life in Africa, and there are more to come.

PEETE, HOLLY ROBINSON, AND RYAN PEETE, WITH DENENE MILLNER

My Brother Charlie: A Sister's Story of Autism

Illustrated by Shane Evans
New York: Scholastic Press, 2010
ISBN: 978-0-545-09466-5 | **AGES 4–7**

Callie describes her twin brother Charlie, much like her but with words and feelings often locked inside because he has autism. Though fictionalized to the extent that names and details have been changed, the afterword makes clear that this was purposefully written by a mother-daughter pair about the girl's twin brother. Callie makes clear some of the issues: Charlie is quiet, has difficulty showing emotion, and does what he wants, even if it's dangerous. He's also smart, knows a lot, and has a way with animals. Even if he doesn't often say, "I love you," he can show it in play with his sister and his dog. Evans's mixed-media illustrations spread across both pages, using bold colors and large figures; they would work well for group sharing. The surfaces are textured with brushstrokes and the background is often a pale blue sky with stylized clouds, a pattern repeated on the endpapers, giving unity to the book. Holly Robinson Peete is an actress and autism activist. This celebrity family's story has been told for adults in Oakland Raiders quarterback Rodney Peete's *Not My Boy! A Father, a Son, and One Family's Journey with Autism* (Hyperion, 2010).

SCHOOL

MARX, TRISH, AND ELLEN B. SENISI

Kindergarten Day USA and China / Kindergarten Day China and USA

Illustrated with photographs by Ellen B. Senisi
Watertown, MA: Charlesbridge, 2010
ISBN: 978-1-580-89219-3 | **AGES 4–7**

Drawing and coloring, working with words and numbers, having lunch, celebrating birthdays, and playing on the playground are all activities common to kindergarteners in both China and the United States. Starting from one side, readers can visit a school in Schenectady, New York; flip the book over to visit one in Beijing. An introduction shows a child from each class pointing to China, one on a globe and the other on a Pacific-centered world map. The simple text stresses the similarities while describing a typical day. Well-reproduced photographs show smiling teachers, children working and playing on their own and in small groups, and even, sometimes, not getting along. On each spread, an analog clock shows the passage of time, giving the time in both countries (conveniently, twelve hours apart). Simple Chinese words are introduced in characters and accented pinyin. These classrooms are clean and nicely appointed; the work appears to be challenging. The Chinese children even hear a story read aloud in English! American readers will surely enjoy looking for similarities and the differences (the lunch menu is an obvious one) in this Global Fund for Children–sponsored book.

WINTER, JEANETTE

Nasreen's Secret School: A True Story from Afghanistan

Illustrated by Jeanette Winter
New York: Beach Lane Books, 2009
ISBN: 978-1-416-99437-4 | **AGES 6–10**

An Afghan grandmother tells how a secret neighborhood school for girls opened the world for her granddaughter after her parents disappeared. Winter begins with an author's note explaining the purpose of the sponsors, the Global Fund for Children, and the rule of the Taliban in Afghanistan from 1996 to 2001, and reminding readers that danger remains today. Children will skip that for the story of the traumatized child and her school. The text is sparse, a line or two on the generous white space of each page. Tight borders surround acrylic illustrations, whose intense colors and stylized shapes show dark clouds hanging over the Taliban-governed country and the grieving child. The dark colors of the early pictures lighten up as the year progresses—shades of pink appear in the borders and background as Nasreen finds a friend, then green as she learns more about the world. Blue skies gleam beyond the dark clouds. The intended audience may need help with the background, but they will recognize the healing role of friendship and enjoy identifying the stories Nasreen learns. This was a CCBC Choice; it made the Amelia Bloomer and CBC/NCSS Notable lists and won a Jane Addams Award.

PETS

CALMENSON, STEPHANIE

May I Pet Your Dog? The How-to Guide for Kids Meeting Dogs (and Dogs Meeting Kids)

Illustrated by Jan Ormerod
New York: Clarion Books, 2007
ISBN: 978-0-618-51034-4 | **AGES 4–7**

This step-by-step guide to meeting—and sometimes petting—strange dogs is narrated by a talented dachshund named Harry. Always ask permission: "May I pet your dog?" Offer your hand for a sniff. Don't reach over a dog's head. Be gentle. And so forth. These sensible guidelines are explained in the text and demonstrated in Ormerod's clear watercolor and pen-and-ink illustrations, which show a small boy and his wonderfully enthusiastic, long-haired short-legged dog. Speech bubbles add comments from the adults holding each dog the boy encounters. They meet Twigs, a jumpy puppy, Chester, a gentle giant with a favorite petting spot, and Bessie, who is uncomfortable with strangers. Harry demonstrates the tricks he can do. They avoid a dog guarding a car, and they admire (but don't bother) a dog who is working. An afterword offers additional helpful tips including how to behave if a dog frightens you. The last page includes a photo and description of the real Harry. The variety of dogs shown is appealing, and the advice is reasonable, not overwhelming. This is a necessary title for most collections.

CROSBY, JEFF, AND SHELLEY ANN JACKSON

Little Lions, Bull Baiters, and Hunting Hounds: A History of Dog Breeds

Illustrated by Jeff Crosby and Shelley Ann Jackson
Toronto, ON: Tundra Books, 2008
ISBN: 978-0-887-76815-6 | **AGES 6–12**

Opening with a brief description of how wolves became dogs and breeds were developed, this absorbing picture book reference introduces forty-two different dog breeds, from Afghan hounds to Boston terriers. These are organized by the breed's original purpose—hunting, herding, working, and human companionship—and presented in the order they likely appeared in history. Each section begins with carefully labeled and explained illustrations of a varied selection of dogs bred for a specific purpose. The individual descriptions that follow include a physical description, the place and purpose for their development, and how these dogs look and behave today. Where necessary, pronunciation is provided. Paintings of each breed, often full-bleed and even double-page spreads, show them in characteristic activities in the time and place where they developed; inset maps show the country of origin. Sidebars add additional information. The authors/illustrators, a husband-and-wife team, include a description of "mixed breed" dogs, and conclude with suggestions for choosing a pet. An extensive bibliography provides both books and websites for further exploration. Appealing to readers and browsers, this title was a Cybils finalist and CCBC Choice.

JENKINS, STEVE

Dogs and Cats

Illustrated by Steve Jenkins
Boston: Houghton Mifflin, 2007
ISBN: 978-0-618-50767-2 | **AGES 4–10**

Jenkins introduces these familiar pet families as two books packaged in one. Open from the cover with the appealing kitten and you see a book about cats, with tiny thumbnails reminding you that you can turn it over to read something similar about dogs. Open from the cover with the dog, and you find the same format. In either case, he includes equivalent descriptions of origins, breeds, physical appearance, behavior, babies, special characteristics, and amazing facts. In the center, a page titled "Friends or enemies?" describes the two animals together. Each topical double-page spread includes several paragraphs of text, a large illustration, and smaller ones with captions including even more information. Jenkins's customary cut- and torn-paper collages, on a plain white background, highlight the colors and shapes of each breed; show typical poses and significant details effectively; and even suggest texture through special papers. Young readers curious about these common pets will surely find the presentation intriguing and the parallels eye-opening. Text-heavy for reading aloud, this CCBC Choice is nonetheless both a book that can be appreciated by prereaders for its pictures alone, and a treasure trove of fascinating facts.

KENNEDY, EDWARD M.

My Senator and Me: A Dog's-Eye View of Washington, D.C.

Illustrated by David Small
New York: Scholastic Press, 2006
ISBN: 978-0-439-65077-9 | **AGES 4–9**

Splash, a Portuguese water dog, explains how his owner became a senator, how he became Ted Kennedy's dog, and what he does all day in Washington, DC, while the senator has meetings, rides the underground tram, holds a press conference on the Capitol steps, and speaks on the Senate floor. Splash goes along—except into the Senate chambers. Like any well-trained pet, he waits patiently and quietly, although a well-timed "WOOF! WOOF!" can move things along in a meeting. While this can serve as a quick introduction to the seat of American government in Washington, DC, and even includes an addendum on how a bill becomes a law, this is actually, as the late senator says in his dedication, a tribute to his dog, "a constant presence in the Capitol." David Small's caricatures, familiar from his Caldecott-winning illustrations for Judith St. George's *So You Want to Be President?* (Penguin, 2000), not only show the senator at work, they provide a quick summary of important Washington buildings. But mostly they show Splash being a dog, home with the Kennedy's new puppy, investigating his toys in the senator's office, and playing fetch on the Capitol grounds. A CBC/NCSS Notable.

VAN STEENWYK, ELIZABETH

First Dog Fala

Illustrated by Michael Montgomery

Atlanta: Peachtree, 2008

ISBN: 978-1-561-45411-2 | **AGES 5–9**

In 1940, President Franklin Roosevelt acquired a black Scottish terrier who became his best friend and constant companion. This endearing "first pup" story is set in the time of World War II. The author weaves in some historical events and something about the life and work of the president, but the dog is the focus. His antics are described with gentle humor. The author describes one of Roosevelt's fireside chats: "Fala couldn't come since he wouldn't promise to be quiet." When reporters and photographers excitedly waited for Fala to take a bite of his fourth-birthday cake, he wouldn't touch it until everyone left. Narrowly framed oil paintings in subdued hues offer a sense of time and place; irresistible tiny pencil sketches of the dog accompany the text. The endpapers repeat some sketches, showing the small dog walking sedately on a leash, running, playing, riding in a car, and eating his cake. An afterword explains that Fala lived out his life with Mrs. Roosevelt and was buried in the rose garden near the president's grave. A photograph of the Roosevelt Memorial in Washington shows the dog, sculpted in bronze, next to his owner. An IRA Teachers' Choice. Staake's *The First Pup: The Real Story of How Bo Got to the White House* (Feiwel and Friends, 2010) describes today's White House dog.

OUR BODIES

CALABRESI, LINDA

Human Body

Illustrated by Argosy Publishing

New York: Simon & Schuster Books for Young Readers, 2007

ISBN: 978-1-416-93861-3 | **AGES 7–12**

This introduction to human anatomy—including its workings, organs, systems, and senses—is presented through amazing cutaway, close-up, and even microscopic illustrations and informational bits. It is these striking, computer-generated illustrations that provide the "wow" factor for readers and browsers. From the textured cover showing the inside of a human head—with brains, nerves, and muscles—through the bionic man with replacement joints, limbs, and organs, a cutaway swimmer and diagrams of the workings of different joints, to microscope-like images of the many things in the air we breathe, the variety and scope are amazing. Each double-page spread covers a different topic (cells, heart, reproductive system, touch) introduced with a short paragraph. Most of the information is presented in labels, picture captions, and sidebars. One spread offers a time line of medical knowledge; another, inside-the-body views with ultrasound, MRI, X-rays and a pill camera. This is not easy reading, but a determined child will learn a great deal. There is a glossary and index in this entry in a *Booklist* Top 10 series, but, as with other Insiders books, no sources for the information are provided.

CLEMENTS, ANDREW

The Handiest Things in the World

Illustrated with photographs by Raquel Jaramillo
New York: Atheneum Books for Young Readers, 2010
ISBN: 978-1-416-96166-6 | **AGES 4–8**

Pictures and simple rhymes work together to make this appealing concept and puzzle book about hands and tools. On double-page spreads, a pair of photographs, each with a single line of text, show hands performing a task and, opposite, a tool doing it more easily and efficiently: two small hands dribble water over a pot with a tiny plant while a young girl waters a larger plant with a watering can. "Two wet hands can hold and pour. / This will pour a whole lot more." Boys and girls of varying ages and skin colors are shown in indoor and outdoor activities from eating (with fingers and chopsticks) to keeping ears warm on a snowy day. The book ends with a comforting idea: "For sharing love with tenderness . . . / the hand itself is handiest" and one of the hands shown is larger and older than the other. The end papers show seventy-two more images of hands and tools, some referring to activities shown in the book, others introducing new ideas. The whole could easily be used as a guessing game and a spur for children to make hand pictures of their own.

COCOVINI, ABBY

What's inside Your Tummy, Mommy?

Illustrated by Abby Cocovini
New York: Henry Holt and Co., 2008
ISBN: 978-0-805-08760-4 | **AGES 3–9**

Month by month, this fascinating title shows stages of fetal development in actual size in a flexible, oversized format that allows comparison with an actual abdomen. A time line of days and weeks runs along the bottom of each double-page spread. Text and text boxes on the left-hand side describe the baby's development while on the right are life-sized drawings of the growing child. (A note under the publication data reminds adult readers that sizes may vary.) Beyond the narrative, text boxes add further information. One series compares the unborn baby's changing size to familiar food objects, from a grain of rice to a pumpkin. Another offers intriguing facts: at month 4, the baby pees fifteen times a day; by month 7 it can blink its eyes. Throughout, the author uses the words *tummy* and *baby* although a note on the title page points out that the baby actually grows in a womb. The final foldout page shows a full-size fetus, ready for the mother to "Push! Push! Push! Push! Push!" Simple and tasteful, this English import is ideal for expectant mothers to share with their toddlers and even school-age children.

RAU, DANA MEACHEN

My Bones and Muscles / Huesos y músculos

Illustrated with photographs and diagrams
New York: Marshall Cavendish, 2007
ISBN: 978-0-761-42479-6 | **AGES 4–7**

This bilingual introduction to major bones and muscles inside the human body is part of a leveled reading program. The "What's Inside Me?" series, comfortably sized for the small hand, is designed for "fluent readers," but the illustrations will attract even nonreaders. The opening left-hand page shows a small boy with a backpack. Opposite, a diagram of a human body in the same posture shows the skeleton inside. Skull, rib cage, backbone, pelvis, and joints are labeled in both English and Spanish. Going on, text and photos describe these in detail, and include an X-ray and a bone in cross-section. Muscles described include the face muscles (for smiling), the tongue, and the heart. Photos of active children, a diverse range of boys and girls, demonstrate what the bones and muscles do. The science is simple but accurate, and new words are printed in italics, their meanings clear from context and defined in a bilingual glossary. The index is in both Spanish and English. This is the bilingual edition of a book originally published in 2005, when it made the AAAS/Subaru SB&F Best Books list. Other titles in the series introduce the brain, heart and blood, lungs, skin, and stomach.

RISSMAN, REBECCA

We All Move

Illustrated with photographs
Chicago: Heinemann Library, 2009
ISBN: 978-1-432-92150-7 | **AGES 4–7**

Photographs of climbing, dancing, jumping, racing, riding, running, skiing, swimming, swinging, and walking show a variety of people from around the world moving for exercise and fun in spite of disabilities and differences. Part of a series designed for early readers and distributed mostly to schools and libraries, this small book makes its point almost entirely through the images. Each page has one simple sentence and a well-reproduced photograph. The range of these pictures is imaginative. They show amputees with and without prostheses; a family out for a walk, including a boy with a cane; a boy on a scooter accompanied by his father in a wheelchair; women dancing and even racing in wheelchairs; a boy with an adaptive tricycle; a group of Chinese people doing tai chi; girls from unidentified but obviously third-world countries jumping ropes; and boys with special needs playing basketball. A "Words to Know" section at the end describes and shows a cane, a prosthesis, and a wheelchair, using illustrations from the book. The small trim size of this volume invites personal exploration and reflection. For adults, the lack of information about the places and people shown is unfortunate, but the unusual nature of the subject makes this valuable for any collection.

ROTNER, SHELLEY, AND SHEILA M. KELLY

Shades of People

Illustrated with photographs by Shelley Rotner
New York: Holiday House, 2009
ISBN: 978-0-823-42191-6 | **AGES 2–7**

Crisp, clear, mostly close-up photographs of children at home and school, in the city, on the playground, at the park or beach, and with their families demonstrate the splendid variety of skin tones humans may have. The authors' message is direct: "Our skin is just our covering, like wrapping paper. And, you can't tell what someone is like from the color of their skin." But it is the array of cheerful faces that will captivate readers far too young to decode the text. They may be just as fascinated by the variations in eyes and hair—even among people in the same family. Part of a long series of photo collections, the simple premise—"people come in many different shades"—is both obvious and important to discuss. Some pages have as many as six photographs, others only one or two, and there is a double-page spread of a grandly mixed group racing across a field of clover. Variations in design and composition will keep readers' attention. They will want to choose a name for their own skin shade. And the final photograph of seven different hands in a circle is sure to inspire imitation in a preschool setting.

OUR HEALTH

BECCIA, CARLYN

I Feel Better with a Frog in My Throat: History's Strangest Cures

Illustrated by Carlyn Beccia
Boston: Houghton Mifflin Books for Children, 2010
ISBN: 978-0-547-22570-8 | **AGES 6–10**

This intriguing collection of historical cures is presented with humor and engaging illustrations, setting the treatment in time and place and explaining that some may, in fact, have worked. Beccia draws readers in with a multiple choice format. For each malady—cough, cold, sore throat, wound, stomach ache, fever, headache, or "every sickness"—she presents a set of remedies, asking readers to guess which ones worked. The next few pages offer a paragraph of explanation for each cure, suggesting how they might have been successful, if they were, and how they're used in medicine today. Occasional historic records are included: an entry from Ulysses Grant's diary describes his use of mustard plasters; an eighteenth-century engraving shows a doctor drilling a hole in a patient's head. Boxed illustrations created with digital mixed media help set the cures in their historical context, with appropriate costumes and furnishings and plentiful humor. Live frogs crawl from a boy's frog soup; maggots feast on a wound with fork and knife. Comically caricatured figures look appropriately disgusted by the curious treatments. At the end, mothers' kisses work wonders throughout time. The author includes a selected bibliography. A Parents' Choice Silver Honor book.

COBB, VICKI

Your Body Battles a Skinned Knee

Illustrated by Andrew Harris with photomicrographs by Dennis Kunkel
Minneapolis: Millbrook Press, 2009
ISBN: 978-0-822-56814-8 | **AGES 7–12**

When you skin your knee, nerve cells let your brain know. Then other cells work together to stop the bleeding, stave off infection, and heal the injury. Lively cartoonlike illustrations show superhero cells (Platelet, Skin Cell, Blood Cell, Nerve Cell, and Macrophage) pitted against the evil germs. These are combined with clearly labeled scanning electron microscopic photographs of actual human body cells to show the healing process. Addressing the reader directly, this experienced science writer explains healing step-by-step in words that, for the most part, will be familiar to elementary school readers. This is just one of the Body Battles series, which includes titles on healing a tooth cavity, a broken bone, a cold, an earache, and a stomachache. Each features a few sensible suggestions for avoiding the problem or hastening remediation. The end matter for each volume includes a glossary, suggestions for further reading, websites and an index. A note at the beginning explains Kunkel's scanning electron microscope photographs and how to interpret the magnification information, noting that the color is artificial. These photomicrographs have been used in a number of books for young readers and offer a special appeal.

SINGER, MARILYN

I'm Getting a Checkup

Illustrated by David Milgrim
New York: Clarion Books, 2009
ISBN: 978-0-618-99000-9 | **AGES 3–7**

In jaunty rhymes, a child describes getting a standard physical examination, complete with a booster shot, while an accompanying text identifies and explains the use of the appropriate tools. Milgrim has added an additional layer to this helpful narrative by showing three different children and their parents in the waiting room of a modern medical practice and following them all through their experiences, as if the reader were looking into the different practice rooms. There are several different doctors (with white coats) and nurses (in scrubs) in the practice. These digital oil pastel illustrations show an appropriate range of ages, sexes, and ethnicities. A playful group of rabbits and a bird and the cartoonlike illustrations add a bit of fantasy in an otherwise very realistic depiction. At the end, an additional page of informational text explains that getting a checkup is important and briefly mentions other possible tests: urine, blood, vision, and hearing. Singer acknowledges that the experience can be worrying: "I'm feeling pretty brave, though I'm still a little scared. / But knowing what each tool is for helps me feel prepared." The gentle humor and smiling faces help defuse the tension. Engaging and useful.

SIY, ALEXANDRA

Sneeze!

Illustrated with microphotographs by Dennis Kunkel
Watertown, MA: Charlesbridge, 2007
ISBN: 978-1-570-91653-3 | **AGES 7–12**

From sweet-smelling hay to sudden sunlight, nine different triggers causing sneezes in young people are the springboard for this scientific explanation of the sneeze, illustrated with photographs from a scanning or transmission electron microscope. Kunkel's clearly identified, highly magnified, and thoughtfully colorized images are the attraction here. A dust mite fills one page; the many threads and spores of mildew fill another. Deep inside a human body, skeletal muscles and tendons are attached to bone. The endpapers repeat the image of highly magnified neurons, the cells that carry sneeze messages. The design, with its white type on black pages opposite the micrographs, reinforces the idea that the reader is venturing deep inside the human body. In no more than a few paragraphs per page, the author first describes nine possible triggers and then explains the sequence of events that lead to the explosive sneeze reflex. Black-and-white photographs of young people throughout help connect this information with the child reader. An explanation of how micrographs are made is part of the package. The end matter suggests resources and include websites, and a glossary serves as index of this CBC/NSTA Outstanding Science Trade Book. This author-illustrator pair also produced *Mosquito Bite* (Charlesbridge, 2005).

4
The Natural World around Us

ASKED ABOUT THE NONFICTION books her students enjoy, Laura Amy Schlitz, elementary school librarian and storyteller at the Park School near Baltimore, Maryland, wrote "I think that what children are after most is something that piques the imagination—something wondrous, beautiful or dangerous" (pers. comm.). Books in this section are full of wonders, terrors, and beautiful things. This is by far the largest category of informational picture books and surely the most striking in their illustrations. Science books routinely win awards, and they deserve them. From dinosaurs to pill bugs, from the oceans to the stars, from heredity to number theory, these are subjects that interest some of the best writers and illustrators working today.

DOTLICH, REBECCA KAI

What Is Science?

Illustrated by Sachiko Yoshikawa
New York: Henry Holt, 2006
ISBN: 978-0-805-07394-2 | **AGES 3–7**

A single poem, accompanied by fanciful illustrations of a group of children and their dog exploring the world and beyond, recounts the many subjects of science, asking and answering the title question: "What is science? / So many things." Rhyming couplets read aloud easily and would lend themselves to performance. "So into the earth and into the sky, / we question the how, the where, when, and why." First published in a poetry anthology, the poem makes a splendid picture book text, encouraging the kind of imagination science inquiry requires. This imagination is evident in

FACING PAGE ART FROM

Nic Bishop Spiders by Nic Bishop

the colorful humorous illustrations, done in acrylic, pastels, and paper collage on double-page spreads. From varying angles and perspectives, close-up and at a distance, two girls and a boy read books; use equipment; dig in the earth and swim in the sea; climb trees and mountains; ride bikes, a camel, and a train; fly a spaceship and an airplane, and more, usually with big smiles and occasionally with expressions of awe. This appealing introduction to a vast field of knowledge belongs in every school library. An AAAS/Subaru SB&F Prize finalist.

LOOKING AT NATURE

ARNOSKY, JIM

Wild Tracks! A Guide to Nature's Footprints

Illustrated by Jim Arnosky
New York: Sterling, 2008
ISBN: 978-1-402-73985-9 | **AGES 6–10**

For his one hundredth book, naturalist Arnosky returned to the subject of animal tracks. Here, he shows how these marks in snow, sand, or mud can identify the animal and reveal behavior. Running deer spread hoofs wide for stability; their back toe prints show. A skunk's running pattern is diagonal, while fox keep all four feet in line. Each chapter illustrates and describes the tracks of a different animal family—deer, other hoofed animals, bear, small animals, felines, canines, and reptiles and birds together. The illustrations include selections from a nature journal, pencil sketches with handwritten labels and measurements framing a few paragraphs of explanatory text. Opposite, a full-bleed acrylic painting shows a member of that animal family in its natural habitat. Life-size paintings of the tracks of these animals appear on double-page spreads, including four gatefolds. The table of contents will make it easy for budding trackers to return to the numbered pages to find the animal they seek. Though oversized for a field guide, this is sure to appeal to young readers curious about the world around them and may send them out to do some tracking and sketching themselves. Winner of a Bergh Award, this was also an ALSC Notable.

BARDOE, CHERYL

Gregor Mendel: The Friar Who Grew Peas

Illustrated by Joseph A. Smith
New York: Abrams Books for Young Readers, 2006
ISBN: 978-0-810-95475-5 | **AGES 7–10**

Born in the early nineteenth century, Gregor Mendel was clever, but poor. After finishing school he became a friar, living and working in an abbey with a well-stocked library. Here, he had time for careful research, planting generations of peas looking for patterns. His report of his findings in 1865 was the first scientific description of the workings of heredity, through dominant and recessive genes. Although his conclusions were ignored until 1900, he is now recognized as the world's first geneticist. The relatively lengthy text of this science biography reflects the friar's need for patience as he planted his seeds year after year. But the author understands what might intrigue her audience: the boy's grumbling stomach, the question of why children in the same family look different. What happens to apparently lost traits? Realistic watercolors, some stretching across the gutter, bring the story to life; detailed drawings explain his experiments. In an afterword the author points out how Mendel used the scientific method and also provides a selected bibliography. Published in conjunction with Chicago's Field Museum, this received an Orbis Pictus honor, was an AAAS/Subaru SB&F Prize finalist, and was deemed notable by both ALSC and IRA.

BOND, REBECCA

In the Belly of an Ox: The Unexpected Photographic Adventures of Richard and Cherry Kearton

Illustrated by Rebecca Bond
Boston: Houghton Mifflin Books for Children, 2009
ISBN: 978-0-547-07675-1 | **AGES 5–9**

Missing the Yorkshire countryside of their childhood, the Kearton brothers took to going out from London, where they worked, to photograph birds' nests in the early mornings. Traveling around the country and finding ever more elaborate ways to conceal themselves, they produced the first photographic guide to nests, eggs, and birds in their natural surroundings in 1895. Their story is gently, poetically told in short lines that are a pleasure to read aloud and in watercolor illustrations done with a quiet palette and graceful lines. Bond varies the size and placement of her illustrations, telling their story just as clearly in her pictures. She offers a charming glimpse into that late nineteenth-century world: horse carts and bowler hats in the city, a country boy's rough jacket and boots, and the bulky camera. Details are added with pen and brown ink. Two pages at the end show a selection of their photographs set on a black background like an old-fashioned photo album. Bond includes a bibliography and source notes for the direct quotations. The last page summarizes the later life of these two remarkable early naturalists. This ALSC Notable is an appealing addition to any environmental collection.

LASKY, KATHRYN

John Muir: America's First Environmentalist

Illustrated by Stanley Fellows
Cambridge, MA: Candlewick Press, 2006
ISBN: 978-0-763-61957-2 | **AGES 7–10**

Born in Scotland in 1838, environmentalist John Muir came to the States as a child and fell in love with its natural world, which he was instrumental in preserving through promoting the establishment of national parks and founding the Sierra Club. Lasky emphasizes his travels, often on foot. From Scotland to Wisconsin, to Canada during the Civil War, Florida, California, Alaska, and back to California's

Yosemite, he explored the countryside. He experimented with inventions, wrote up his observations, and convinced politicians to set up measures to protect the wilderness. The straightforward, chronological exposition is presented on a background of acrylic paintings showing the boy and gradually aging man, often in his beloved natural world. Double page spreads demonstrate the glory of northern lights in Wisconsin, the magnitude of the Sierra peaks, the danger of a narrow ice bridge across a glacial crevasse in Alaska, as well as the comforts of camp and dog. Insets focus on specific details. Additional sketches suggest his preoccupation with recording what he saw. The bibliography includes a suggestion for further reading as well as the author's sources, and a description of the Sierra Club is appended. An Orbis Pictus honor and CBC/NCSS Notable, this also appeared on the John Burroughs list.

MCGINTY, ALICE B.

Darwin: With Glimpses into His Private Journal and Letters

Illustrated by Mary Azarian
Boston: Houghton Mifflin Harcourt, 2009
ISBN: 978-0-618-99531-8 | **AGES 7–12**

This beautifully illustrated biography of the noted naturalist for middle grade readers describes his life from childhood through his famous *Beagle* voyage to his eventual success. The author emphasizes Darwin's passion for collecting and experimentation. She addresses but does not dwell on his hesitations to publish his controversial ideas, so at odds with church teachings. The writing is clear and conversational, presented with generous margins and extensive leading making the text invitingly accessible. Quotations from Darwin's own writings, presented in script on scraps of yellowed paper, supplement the narrative; the combination is effective. Azarian's detailed woodcuts, hand-tinted with watercolors, accompany and extend the story as vignettes, full-page pictures, and even double-page spreads. The subtitle is echoed in the cover, which imitates one of Darwin's own leather-bound journals. Through a hole, the reader can glimpse the young scientist making notes aboard ship. The exemplary end matter includes an author's note, specific sources for each of the quotations, and some additional adult resources. From the many Darwin titles published to mark his anniversary, this Orbis Pictus honor book and CBC/NCSS Notable is particularly appealing.

SHELDON, DAVID

Into the Deep: The Life of Naturalist and Explorer William Beebe

Illustrated by David Sheldon
Watertown, MA: Charlesbridge, 2009
ISBN: 978-1-580-89341-1 | **AGES 5–9**

From childhood, William Beebe liked exploring nature. He got a job collecting birds for the New York Zoological Society but soon realized he'd rather study them in their natural habitat. A trip to the Galapagos Islands ignited his interest in sea life, and he is most famous today for his record-breaking deep-sea dive in 1934. For this purpose, an engineer colleague, Otis Barton, invented a diving vessel they called a bathysphere, in which they descended over 3,000 feet into unexplored depths of the ocean. The author-illustrator's acrylic paintings capture the feeling of their dive. In dim blue light the two men peer out from the capsule; then, from outside, the tiny vessel is surrounded by toothy animals and mysterious dots of light in the inky blackness of the deep sea. Throughout the book, double-page illustrations filled with plants and animals in all kinds of environments convey this early ecologist's excitement about the natural world. A final scene shows him teaching children at his research station in Trinidad. For curious readers, this CBC/NSTA Outstanding Science Trade Book also includes more about of the bathysphere, some quotations from Beebe, a glossary, and a list of resources.

YACCARINO, DAN
The Fantastic Undersea Life of Jacques Cousteau
Illustrated by Dan Yaccarino
New York: Alfred A. Knopf, 2009
ISBN: 978-0-375-85573-3 | **AGES 5–9**

From a sickly boyhood in which swimming was therapeutic, Jacques Cousteau grew up to love the sea, exploring it extensively, inventing new tools and equipment, and sharing his discoveries through books, films, and TV. With a simple text, no more than a paragraph a page, Yaccarino highlights the oceanographer's career, ending with his realization of threats to his beloved underwater world and his founding of the Cousteau society. Unsourced but appropriate quotations from his writings appear in occasional bubbles. Yaccarino uses swirling lines and a palette of blues, greens, gold, and orange for his stylized illustrations. They provide much to look at: sea creatures on the endpapers; cartoon-like drawings of the scrawny, tinkering boy, as well as Cousteau and his crew sampling 2,200-year-old wine, double-page underwater spreads (one zooming in on Cousteau's face, another showing Antarctica's water teeming with life), a busy set of lights, cameras and equipment, and the variety of creatures he encountered in the underwater world. Airbrushing softens the texture and layers give the sense that the reader is looking through the water. A bibliography and chronological list of events complete this enthusiastic introduction to a renowned scientist, which was a CBC/NSTA Outstanding Science Trade Book. Jennifer Berne's *Manfish* (Chronicle Books, 2008) has similar appeal.

ENVIRONMENTS AND ECOSYSTEMS

ARNOSKY, JIM
Babies in the Bayou
Illustrated by Jim Arnosky
New York: G. P. Putnam's Sons, 2007
ISBN: 978-0-399-22653-3 | **AGES 3–7**

From alligators to raccoons, turtles, and wood ducks, there are babies in the bayou whose mothers guard them, shepherd them around, and protect them from danger.

This nicely circular description of the ecological chain of connections in a southern waterway introduces that world to the youngest readers and listeners. Naturalist Arnosky's text has a lovely rhythm and repetition, patterned in a way that encourages reading aloud. One by one, each family is introduced; at the end of its segment, there is a hint, in words or pictures, of the creature to come. The mood is calm and reassuring. In spite of sharp teeth and claws, in spite of lurking enemies, these babies' mothers will keep them safe. For his lifelike illustrations, Arnosky used muted shades of transparent acrylics, with opaque touches of black and white. Beyond the creatures mentioned in the poem, knowledgeable readers will recognize white ibis, brown pelicans, a kingfisher, and other birds; a snake; a salamander; and some tiny fish, as well as a variety of plants and flowers. A greenish light filters through the trees; the endpapers match. Beautifully presented, this AAAS/Subaru SB&F Prize finalist was also a CCBC Choice.

GEORGE, JEAN CRAIGHEAD

The Wolves Are Back

Illustrated by Wendell Minor
New York: Dutton Children's Books, 2008
ISBN: 978-0-525-47947-5 | **AGES 5–12**

Eliminated in the lower forty-eight states by 1926, gray wolves have been reintroduced and successfully reestablished in the Lamar Valley in Yellowstone National Park, restoring the natural web of life. Two noted children's nature writers produced books about this piece of environmental good news in 2008, the year wolves were taken off the endangered species list in that part of the United States. They supplement each other nicely. George introduces a single wolf pup, demonstrating its role in the ecosystem through its daily activities. She flashes back to the time when there were no wolves. Her gentle, lyrical prose uses variations on the title as a repeated refrain. The repetition supports reading aloud and remembering. Wendell Minor's lushly detailed, expressive paintings, done in watercolor and gouache, have texture and depth. They show individual species—moose, raven, vesper sparrow, buffalo, beaver, badger, bear, and more—in the context of the spectacle of that vast wilderness. For reading aloud and reading alone, this book can be read over and over. Pair with Patent's *When the Wolves Returned* (below). This title was a CBC/NSTA Outstanding Science Trade Book, appeared on the CBC/NCSS Notable list, was a finalist for the AAAS/Subaru SB&F Prize, and received a Bergh Award.

GUIBERSON, BRENDA Z.

Life in the Boreal Forest

Illustrated by Gennady Spirin
New York: Henry Holt, 2009
ISBN: 978-0-805-07718-6 | **AGES 5–12**

Across a vast stretch of Alaska, Canada, Scandinavia, and Russia, the great northern forest—home to a web of interconnected wildlife—is threatened, as are many other natural places, by human development. Short columns of text introduce the animals of the area: warblers, cranes and other migrating birds; beaver, lynx, fox, and ermine; tiny voles and their enemy, the great horned owl; and more—as well as trees and even the lichen that nourish the moose in the winter. Guiberson demonstrates their interdependence and the effect of periodic population swings. Though the text is lengthy, the language makes this a treat to read aloud. Onomatopoetic words and phrases capture the sounds: the "Plish, ploosh!" of the diving loon, the "Crackle! Thwak!" as trees tumble, and the "Whoom, whoosh!" of the dog sled, as well as expected songs, calls, and howls. Spirin's beautiful, detailed paintings spread across three-quarters of each double-page spread, inviting young readers to pore over them to identify the creatures mentioned in the accompanying column of text. With a color palette of whites, greens, browns, and tans and occasional spots of red, he demonstrates the changing seasons. This was an Orbis Pictus recommended book, and CBC/NSTA Selectors' Choice.

JENKINS, STEVE

Down, Down, Down: A Journey to the Bottom of the Sea

Illustrated by Steve Jenkins
Boston: Houghton Mifflin Harcourt, 2009
ISBN: 978-0-618-96636-3 | **AGES 5–8**

Jenkins's signature paper collage illustrations take the reader on an imaginary journey from the surface to the depths of the Pacific Ocean. Along the way he presents a wide variety of creatures from an albatross flying above and Portuguese man-of-war floating at the surface, through sea turtles and vampire squid, down to the hag fish and sea lilies of the abyssal plain he calls the "ooze," and to hydrothermal vents and the bottom of the Marianas Trench. On a background of steadily deepening blue to the black of the depths, a few creatures appear on each double-page spread, not shown to scale. A relatively difficult paragraph or two of text adds information, including explanations of krill and the food chain, filter feeding, soft bodies, bioluminescence, "marine snow," sulfur-loving bacteria, and ocean pressures. Each double-page spread serves as a chapter. Extensive end notes provide more detail about the creatures illustrated; silhouettes show their relative size in comparison to a human body or hand. The author includes a bibliography and an illustration of human explorations against a bar graph of depth similar to that on previous pages. This was an ALSC Notable. Jenkins's website, www .stevejenkinsbooks.com, offers an interesting description of his bookmaking process.

PATENT, DOROTHY HINSHAW

When the Wolves Returned: Restoring Nature's Balance in Yellowstone

Illustrated with photographs by Dan and Cassie Hartman
New York: Walker, 2008.
ISBN: 9780802796868 | **AGES 6–10**

When Yellowstone National Park was established over one hundred years ago, geologic wonders were the attraction. It didn't seem unreasonable to eradicate wolves in favor of the elk and deer early tourists and hunters enjoyed. But with wolves removed, the balance of nature was disturbed. Through their reintroduction in the 1990s, that balance is being restored. Patent's thoughtfully organized approach to this ecological good news meets children's informational needs on two levels. In boxes on the left-hand page, short, simple sentences describe issues and outcomes. On the right, these ideas are developed more fully. Striking modern photographs by the Hartmans, a father-daughter team, as well as pictures from the past are displayed against a black background, giving the book the look of a photo album. Patent gives detailed examples of the effects of the reintroduction on different parts of the ecosystem, emphasizing its complexity. A bibliography and index make this useful for research, and the final endpapers offer a review. Pair this with George's more literary *The Wolves Are Back* (above) to offer something on this topic for every reading taste. This was an Orbis Pictus honor book, a Selectors' Choice on the CBC/NSTA list, and an ALSC Notable.

ROOT, PHYLLIS

Big Belching Bog

Illustrated by Betsy Bowen
Minneapolis: University of Minnesota Press, 2010
ISBN: 978-0-816-63359-3 | **AGES 5–9**

This is a beautiful appreciation of a little-known wilderness in northwestern Minnesota, a "big buggy blooming bog of butterflies and burrowers and birds." This quiet place holds many secrets: strange, sometimes carnivorous plants, curious, specialized animals, ancient trees, and ghostly trails of long-gone caribou. Listening carefully, you might hear mysterious sounds. But the biggest secret of all—the escape of methane from below the sphagnum moss through the slow-moving brown water—has never been heard. Root's lyrical text is full of interesting detail and quiet suspense, but also full of alliteration and repetition, a joy to read aloud. A hermit thrush leads the reader into and through the bog in Bowen's bold, framed woodcuts, painted with a dark, shadowy palette and heavy, dark lines. The boxed text on one page faces the illustration on the opposite at first. Deeper into the bog, the painting fills a double-page spread. End pages include miniature images of bog plants and animals, encouraging readers to go back to identify details in the pictures and also adding further information, including Latin names. There are two pages of bog facts as well. This oversized volume merits a place in any nature collection.

SERAFINI, FRANK

Looking Closely along the Shore

Illustrated with photographs by Frank Serafini
Toronto, ON: Kids Can, 2008
ISBN: 978-1-554-53141-7 | **AGES 4–7**

"Look very closely. What do you see? A flower? A fossil? What could it be?" This guessing game asks a child to choose what the close-up image, in a small circle on the opposing page might represent. The next two pages show the big picture, along with two paragraphs of additional information. The riddle is suitable for a young child—especially one with some seashore experience. The details in the explanation are geared to an early elementary school student. Everything pictured—sand dollar, gooseneck barnacle, lined shore crab, ochre sea star, coconut palm, blue mussel, queen conch, green sea anemone, and smoothly worn coastal rocks—can be found on some North American coast, although not together. The author-photographer's stated intent is to encourage children to look more closely at the world around them. This IRA Teachers' Choice is part of a series that also explores the desert, forests, and the garden. A drawback to the series is that no locations are given for any of the photographs; indeed, the seashore pictured on the final pages is in Fiji, far from home. Still, the interactive nature of the presentation will appeal to young naturalists. *Looking Closely in the Rain Forest* (Houghton Mifflin, 2010) made the CBC/NSTA list.

SIDMAN, JOYCE

Dark Emperor and Other Poems of the Night

Illustrated by Rick Allen
Boston: Houghton Mifflin Harcourt, 2010
ISBN: 978-0-547-15228-8 | **AGES 6–10**

Beginning and ending with scenes of the woodland at sunset and dawn, this beautiful combination of poetry, facts, and art celebrates the night world. After an opening welcome song, each poem introduces a different creature. Great horned owls, spiders, crickets, and bats are familiar, but some are not—like the primrose moth and wandering eft. "I am a baby porcupette" tells how a young porcupine is left on the ground while its mother sleeps in trees during the day. They are reunited at night. Sidman also describes the nocturnal activities of mushrooms and oak trees. Raccoons are introduced in the explanations. Careful observers will find them and even more creatures hiding in the intricate illustrations, printed from a series of carved linoleum blocks and colored with gouache. Their soft, hazy colors fit the subject. These twelve poems vary in style and form; all work well for reading aloud. Set with a spot illustration on the left side of a double-page spread, they face a larger illustration and a column of exposition, in much smaller print, on the right. A glossary completes this Newbery honor book and CBC/NSTA Outstanding Science Trade Book. Sidman's earlier collection, *Butterfly Eyes and Other Secrets of the Meadow* (Houghton Mifflin, 2006), was on an earlier CBC/NSTA list.

STEWART, MELISSA

Under the Snow

Illustrated by Constance R. Bergum
Atlanta: Peachtree, 2009
ISBN: 978-1-561-45493-8 | **AGES 4–8**

In winter, when snow covers fields, forests, ponds, and wetlands, a hidden world of animals lies underneath. Using examples including ladybugs in a stone wall, centipedes and a bumblebee queen in a rotting log, bluegills, a frog and a turtle buried in mud, and a wetland beaver family inside their lodge, Stewart describes how some animals spend their winters in hibernation or frozen solid, while others are resting, slowly swimming, or active as always. The lyrical text packs a lot of information, describing a broad range of environments, animals, and activities. Appropriately for the intended audience, the narrative begins and ends with humans enjoying the winter and getting ready for spring. Bergum's muted watercolor illustrations often show activity on two levels, above and below the snow and ice. Pages with only humans are shown full-bleed; the other pictures are in two or even three panels stretching across the double-page spreads. Some frames within frames enlarge the image. Animals are shown close-up and in realistic detail. This charming read-aloud or read-alone was a CBC/NSTA Selectors' Choice and CCBC Choice and won a Zolotow Award for its picture book text.

PLANTS

ASTON, DIANNA HUTTS

A Seed Is Sleepy

Illustrated by Sylvia Long
San Francisco: Chronicle Books, 2007
ISBN: 978-0-811-85520-4 | AGES 5–9

This follow-up to Aston and Long's AAAS/Subaru SB&F Prize–winning *An Egg Is Quiet* (Chronicle Books, 2006) looks at the plant world, explaining the many varieties of plant seeds, their appearance, method of distribution, composition, and development. The text is on two levels. For reading aloud, there is a series of descriptive sentences: a seed is sleepy, adventurous, inventive, generous, and more. Each sentence is followed by a very short explanation in a similar script font. Another paragraph, hand-lettered, adds further information for older readers or more patient listeners. Here the author doesn't hesitate to use more scientific words, such as *photosynthesis*, *monocots*, and *gymnosperms*, defining them in context. Labels are clear. The careful seed drawings—many highly magnified—and beautiful, accurate illustrations of plants and flowers done with ink and watercolors and set mostly on a white or pale-colored background deserve lengthy attention. Readers may want to look for matches among the seeds on the double-page spread that opens the book and the plants on the similar one at the end. The scale of these drawings varies widely and is never given. But overall, this IRA Teachers' Choice is a fine introduction to basic botany.

CHIN, JASON

Redwoods

Illustrated by Jason Chin
New York: Roaring Brook Press, 2009
ISBN: 978-1-596-43430-1 | AGES 7–10

In this interesting combination of fantasy and science fact, an Asian American boy reading a book about redwoods on the subway imagines it so vividly it comes to life around him. The author weaves in many facts about redwoods, ending with an afterword about their endangered status. The straightforward expository prose is not the book's strength; the excitement is in the imagery, which carries the narrative arc as well as adding information. The imagination in these detailed watercolors sets this book apart. In the opening illustration, before the title page, the boy finds a book. In that book, the title page shows a girl who appears at the end of his story, picking up his book to read; he is reading her story. Details of the boy's real life interrupt but don't stop the vision he sees in his mind as he reads it. Watch for the reappearing flying squirrel. Although the author tells us in an afterword that he was inspired by his reading of Richard Preston's *The Wild Trees* (Random House, 2007), he does not offer young readers any place to go to find out more, a surprise given the informational nature of the text. An AAAS/Subaru SB&F Prize finalist, this was also a CBC/NSTA Selectors' Choice and NCTE Notable.

FLORIAN, DOUGLAS

Poetrees

Illustrated by Douglas Florian
New York: Beach Lane Books, 2010
ISBN: 978-1-416-98672-0 | **AGES 6–10**

The sideways cover reveals what's unusual about this book. It must be turned so that the trees pictured can stretch up to their full height, crossing the gutter of each double-page spread. Eighteen poems describe interesting species of trees from around the world, as well as their seeds, roots, rings, leaves, and bark. Some will be familiar—oak, giant sequoia, paper birch, and weeping willow. Others, like the baobab, scribbly gum, and monkey puzzle, may be new and intriguing. As always, Florian makes use of a variety of poetic forms and arrangements of letters and words on a page. Puns abound: "The bark's a thing to bark about"; "Yew may find yews near a grave—"; a Japanese Cedar seed is "ex-seed-ingly small." The book ends with a "Glossatree" providing more information about the subject of every poem. All this is illustrated in Florian's characteristic scribbly style using gouache watercolors, decorated with colored pencil, rubber stamps, oil pastels, and collage on primed brown paper bags. The trees are recognizable if not particularly realistic. This is a delight to the eye and the ear, but it also conveys interesting information, and the author has included his bibliography. This playful poetry collection was a CBC/NSTA Outstanding Science Trade Book.

GERBER, CAROLE

Winter Trees

Illustrated by Leslie Evans
Watertown, MA: Charlesbridge, 2008
ISBN: 978-1-580-89168-4 | **AGES 4–9**

Walking in a snowy winter woods, a boy and a dog identify seven common eastern North American trees by shape, bark, twigs, buds, and occasionally needles and leftover leaves: "They stand distinct as skeletons. / We clearly see the form of each: / the egg shape of the maple tree; / the taller oval of the beech. . . ." The quiet tone of this rhyming introduction to winter trees is supported by its clean, simple illustrations, done with linoleum block prints, watercolor, and collage, and digitally enhanced. Sugar maple, American beech, paper birch, yellow poplar, bur oak, Eastern hemlock, and white spruce are the trees shown, their heavy lines contrasting with the white space of the snow. A single four-line poem appears on each double-page spread; both text and appearance are suitable for the early elementary school reader, but the book could be read aloud to even younger children. The end matter includes a little more information and illustrations of each tree mentioned. More celebration of winter than field guide, this will have a variety of classroom uses, but the gentle poem might make good bedtime reading as well. This CBC/NSTA Outstanding Science Trade Book also made the John Burroughs list.

ANIMALS

COLLARD, SNEED B.

Wings

Illustrated by Robin Brickman
Watertown, MA: Charlesbridge, 2008
ISBN: 978-1-570-91611-3 | **AGES 3–10**

Birds, bats, and some insects have wings that come in a variety of shapes, sizes, colors, and numbers. Covered with feathers, skin, or scales, they work in a variety of ways for flying and other uses. This straightforward description of the remarkable variety of wings includes an example, a simple phrase in a large font, and a fairly detailed paragraph of explanation on each page or double-page spread; overall, a surprising amount of information. But it is the pictures that will draw readers in, right from the galah cockatoo, leaf-nosed bat, and sunset moth on the cover. Brickman's three-dimensional illustrations are made of paper, painted and sculpted. The feathers look almost real, and the paper airplane at the end may prompt imitation. The range of animals from around the world is impressive, and some pages even include extras; each one is labeled. There is a simple explanation of lift provided by the shape of a curved wing and a diagram of the figure-eight motion of hummingbird and dragonfly wings. A glossary and a book and web resource list complete the package. This companion to Collard and Brickman's *Beaks* (Charlesbridge, 2002) was named a CBC/NSTA Outstanding Science Trade Book and an AAAS/Subaru SB&F Prize finalist.

HUGHES, CATHERINE D.

Little Kids Big Book of Animals

Illustrated with photographs
Washington, DC: National Geographic, 2010
ISBN: 978-1-426-30704-1 | **AGES 3–8**

Organized by biome, this introduces thirty iconic animal species in double-page entries featuring photographs, fast facts, short paragraphs, info bits, and a question connecting the animal with young readers' own lives. Designed for adults to share with children, this has lively graphics and relatively simple text accompanied by illustrations ranging from double-page spreads to colorfully framed close-ups. From grassland and ocean through desert, forest, and polar areas, the organization subtly helps children make the appropriate connection between an animal and its environment. Cheetah, dolphin, camel, tiger, penguin—most species are well-known. In an excellent concluding section of tips for parents, a trip to a zoo is a recommended supplement. But the author also mentions animals that might be seen in one's own yard: a black-and-yellow garden spider or raccoon. A simple map shows the continents where the animals described can be found. Frankly a reference and teaching tool, this CBC/NSTA Outstanding Science Trade Book is also a browser's delight. Each page is clearly labeled according to biome, and the pattern and color of the background make it easy to find the pages appropriate to a particular animal, even if the reader is too young to use the index.

JENKINS, STEVE

Bones: Skeletons and How They Work

Illustrated by Steve Jenkins
New York: Scholastic Press, 2010
ISBN: 978-0-545-04651-0 | **AGES 6–10**

Cut-paper collages illustrate this introduction to the arrangement of bones and the way they work in humans and other mammals, birds, reptiles, amphibians and most fish. Jenkins's intriguing images, slightly textured yellow-gray bones on solid background, demonstrate the similarities in vertebrate skeletons, showing comparative sizes, and adaptations. The scale is usually indicated. The minimal text—simple titles and short paragraphs of explanation—is presented in large, heavily leaded type. Humor and questions for the reader add further interest. One spread demonstrates the similarity of the pieces of the arms and hands of humans, moles, spider monkeys, gray whales, turtles, and fruit bats; another shows symmetry in the skeleton of a bullfrog; and a third illustrates all 206 bones of the human body. Behind a gatefold, the same bones are assembled into a human skeleton. An earlier gatefold shows nearly 200 ribs of a small python, at actual size. Yet another foldout page compares ten animal skulls with a human skull, again, all at actual size. The back matter includes many more facts but no sources or suggestions for further research. Readers will want to know more. This Parents' Choice Silver Honor book was an ALSC Notable, and a Cybils and AAAS/Subaru SB&F Prize finalist.

JENKINS, STEVE, AND ROBIN PAGE

How to Clean a Hippopotamus: A Look at Unusual Animal Partnerships

Illustrated by Steve Jenkins
Boston: Houghton Mifflin Harcourt, 2010
ISBN: 978-0-547-24515-7 | **AGES 7–10**

Animals large and small form mutually beneficial partnerships, illustrated here with examples from around the world. Once again, this experienced husband-and-wife team has found an engaging way to present accurate information about the natural world. Their broad subject is presented in a comic book–like layout with small panels, each including (but not always enclosing) a cut-paper illustration, and snippets of text. Each page also has a headline: "Have beak, will travel"; "That tickles!" "Who's in charge here?" The authors define symbiosis early on in the text and again, in more detail, in the back. Relationships shown may support grooming; warning; providing or finding food or making it more accessible; camouflage; defense; and protection. The pages are not numbered, but the end matter includes a small reproduction of each double-page spread with more information about the animals pictured including size, habitat, and diet. A short bibliography will lead readers, intrigued by these quick summaries, to sources for further information. The graphic format of this CBC/NSTA Outstanding Science Trade Book and ALSC Notable may appeal to older readers than those who loved their highly acclaimed *How Many Ways . . . Can You Catch a Fly?* (Houghton Mifflin, 2008), and *Move!* (Houghton Mifflin, 2006).

JENKINS, STEVE, AND ROBIN PAGE

Sisters and Brothers: Sibling Relationships in the Animal World

Illustrated by Steve Jenkins
Boston: Houghton Mifflin, 2008
ISBN: 978-0-618-37596-7 | AGES 4–9

Here's another example of the effective ways Jenkins and Page present the natural world to young browsers. Here, Jenkins's cut- and torn-paper illustrations accompany concise descriptions of a variety of sibling relationships across the animal world. Dealing first with numbers—singletons, twins, identical quadruplets, and teeming hordes—they go on to describe behaviors. Bears, hyenas, and black widow spiders fight. Cheetahs and falcons help each other hone their skills. Some siblings live and work together for life; others part company early. A Nile crocodile mother hides her babies in her mouth; shrew babies follow their mother in a long connected line. Cichlids and myna birds have stepsiblings. These images appear on a white background with a heading, a big label suitable for the youngest reader or listener, and just a paragraph or two of text for the more determined reader. The back matter adds further facts but includes no page numbers. Though the authors don't identify their sources precisely, they may have been the encyclopedic titles suggested for further reading. This was an AAAS/Subaru SB&F Prize finalist and, like Jenkins's *Living Color* (2007), both a Cybils finalist and Orbis Pictus recommended book.

POSADA, MIA

Guess What Is Growing inside This Egg

Illustrated by Mia Posada
Minneapolis, MN: Millbrook Press, 2007
ISBN: 978-0-822-56192-7 | AGES 3–8

This guessing game for the very young introduces the eggs of penguins, ducks, alligators, spiders, octopus, and sea turtles. The format is simple and repetitive: a couplet or two of description and the title's challenge are superimposed on a double-page spread showing the eggs in their nest or natural surroundings and just a small portion of the parent. On the next page is the answer in large print, plus another paragraph of explanation, on a picture of the emerging tiny creatures: ducklings with their mother, sea turtles aiming for the water; tiny spiders floating away. These realistic illustrations, done in watercolor and collage, add texture to the scenes. The rhyming couplets don't scan well, but the facts are clear and easy to understand. At the end, a double-page spread shows the actual size of these eggs, and a second shows four stages in the development of ducklings inside through cross sections. Simple, straightforward, and effective, this would be a welcome accompaniment to egg-hatching activities as well as an interactive, informative read-aloud. This was a CBC/NSTA Outstanding Science Trade Book, Cybils finalist, and IRA Teachers' Choice.

SCHAEFER, LOLA M.

Just One Bite

Illustrated by Geoff Waring
San Francisco: Chronicle Books, 2010
ISBN: 978-0-811-86473-2 | **AGES 4–10**

This large, square book illustrates in actual size what eleven creatures can eat in the titular "just one bite." The simple text takes a back seat to striking illustrations spreading across two, three, and four fold-out pages. A butterfly probes deep into a hibiscus flower. A giraffe's tongue curls around a thorny acacia branch. The large shapes have been rendered with clean edges using brush, crayon, and computer. The focus is the mouths, tongues, and teeth of these animals and their food. The worm, butterfly, frog, octopus, parrot, rabbit, komodo dragon, snake, bear, giraffe, elephant, and sperm whale are identified generically in the text but more specifically (Asian elephant, hyacinth macaw) in two pages of back matter describing mouths and eating habits in more detail. This additional material uses appropriate but probably unfamiliar vocabulary well within the range of older elementary readers. The book is cleverly designed for its broad readership. The back matter appears on the trifold page that includes the optional conclusion: "microorganisms . . . can eat even the largest animal until it becomes part of the earth that feeds us all, large and small." This CBC/NSTA Outstanding Science Trade Book works equally well for group and individual reading.

SCHWARTZ, DAVID M., AND YAEL SCHY

Where in the Wild? Camouflaged Creatures Concealed—and Revealed: Ear-Tickling Poems

Illustrated with photographs by Dwight Kuhn
Berkeley: Tricycle Press, 2007
ISBN: 978-1-582-46207-3 | **AGES 5–12**

Each double-page spread of this highly interactive puzzle book features a poem and a photograph of an animal almost invisible in its natural surroundings. Lift a flap to find the partially grayed-out picture revealing the animal and some additional information. From coyote to killdeer eggs, crab spider to red-spotted newt, the animal world is represented in its astonishing variety, and the point is clear: camouflage is a common technique for both predator and prey. The full-color photographs are remarkable; even a sharp-eyed adult may have trouble finding some creatures. The poems feature alliteration, a variety of forms, and enough information for an educated guess. Developmental changes are explained, metamorphosis defined, and the gradual darkening of English pepper-moths described without the use of the phrase *natural selection*, although the concept is referred to in the teacher's guide available on the publisher's website. A delightful read-aloud and read-alone, this was a CBC/NSTA Outstanding Science Trade Book and a finalist for the AAAS/Subaru SB&F Prize, and appears on the John Burroughs list. Equally intriguing sequels, *Where Else in the Wild* (2009) and *What in the Wild* (2010), also made the CBC/NSTA list.

SEIDENSTICKER, JOHN, AND SUSAN LUMPKIN

Predators

Illustrated with CGI and 3-D model imagery
New York: Simon & Schuster Books for Young Readers, 2008
ISBN: 978-1-416-93863-7 | **AGES 6–14**

Who can resist a book about nature's killers? Especially one with a tiger's open mouth embossed on the cover? This splendid introduction to the animal world focuses on creatures at the top of the food chain—cats, bears, dogs and wolves, sharks, crocodilians, and birds of prey. The information is presented in bite-sized chunks on double-page spreads organized into two sections. The first explains the food chain, describes some predators of the past and some prey defenses, and goes on to give examples of natural weapons, senses, and methods. The second section describes animals and habitats more specifically. Two final pages present animal classification. The digitally created illustrations are as irresistible as the facts. Through exaggerated focus and perspective, they seem to leap off the paper, a stunning effect the producers of the Australian Insiders series call 3-D. Crossing the gutters, a gigantosaurus stalks its prey, an anaconda squeezes a tapir, an owl swoops down with talons extended. One after another, the king species are shown catching and killing their prey. Chock-full of information, this CBC/NSTA Outstanding Science Trade Book also includes small world maps, boxes of fast facts and sidebars, a glossary, and an index, but no sources or suggestions for further reading.

SIDMAN, JOYCE

Ubiquitous: Poetry and Science about Nature's Survivors

Illustrated by Beckie Prange
Boston: Houghton Mifflin Harcourt, 2010
ISBN: 978-0-618-71719-4 | **AGES 8–14**

Poems in a variety of forms accompany expository informational paragraphs about varied life forms that have survived and flourished on our planet. From bacteria to humans, Sidman has arranged her poems in the order each example appeared, and carefully matched form to subject: a diamante for the bacteria, a shape poem for the shark, and a breathless romp of a "Tail Tale" for the squirrel. Her explanations are equally interesting, and the many sources for her information are detailed in an author's note that stresses the changing nature of scientific fact. Prange's intriguing linocuts, tinted with watercolors on double-page spreads, sometimes serve as a base for the poem and always add to the visual experience. The endpapers are striking, a curved and coiled time line conveying a sense of the vast stretches that passed after the formation of the earth before the first appearance of life, as bacteria; and the even longer span between bacteria and the far more recent mollusks, lichens, sharks, beetles, diatoms, geckos, ants, grasses, squirrels, crows, dandelions, coyotes, and finally humans. An Atlantic-centered representation of the globe, a full-page glossary, acknowledgements, and illustrator's note complete this exemplary informational poetry collection, which was a CBC/NSTA Outstanding Science Trade Book and ALSC Notable.

SINGER, MARILYN

Eggs

Illustrated by Emma Stevenson
New York: Holiday House, 2008
ISBN: 978-0-823-41727-8 | **AGES 7–12**

In this beautifully illustrated title, Singer focuses on the container that protects the embryo of birds and spiders, most insects, fish, amphibians, and even a few mammals. Rather quickly, she covers the necessary general information: fertilization, the role of the yolk, oxygen, and temperature, and environment in its development, and the differences between fish, amphibian, reptile and bird egg coverings. Stevenson's detailed gouache paintings help to demonstrate variations in texture, size, form, and color. The two go on to explain and illustrate where and how often different animals lay eggs, whether and how they care for them, and how the newborn creature gets out of its protective covering. Full pages of comparative images highlight particular points. Text transitions are clear, and words defined in the glossary are printed in italics. The text is moderately difficult, suitable for upper elementary readers, but the pictures may appeal even to nonreaders curious about this aspect of the natural world. This would be an excellent follow-up read to Aston's *An Egg Is Quiet* (Chronicle Books, 2006). Singer includes a description of her research, an extensive bibliography and acknowledgments, and a list of organizations for further information. This was a CBC/NSTA Outstanding Science Trade Book and both a Cybils and AAAS/Subaru SB&F Prize finalist.

STEWART, MELISSA

Why Are Animals Blue?

Illustrated with photographs
Berkeley Heights, NJ: Enslow Elementary/Enslow Publishers, 2009
ISBN: 978-0-766-03251-4 | **AGES 5–9**

From great blue heron and blue shark to peacock and blue darner dragonfly, this simple topic book shows that animals' colors serve to hide them, to warn or surprise predators, to attract mates, and to help them keep an even body temperature. Frankly educational, it begins with a table of contents and short pronunciation glossary of words to know, helpful for beginning readers. These words are bold-faced the first time they appear in the text. A definition of *animal* and examples of animal colors are given in the opening chapter. Continuing, each double-page spread includes a clear close-up photograph of a creature, a label, and, except as part of the final "guessing game," an explanation of the function the blue coloring serves for the creature. Sometimes only part of the animal is blue, as in the blue-footed booby, but the author has chosen her examples well. Maps at the end suggest where each animal might be found in the wild. Both books and websites about animal coloration and camouflage appear on the "Learn More" pages. There is an index to the simple science vocabulary but not to the animals described. This CBC/NSTA Outstanding Science Trade Book is part of a series called Rainbow of Animals.

FISH

BUTTERWORTH, CHRISTINE

Sea Horse: The Shyest Fish in the Sea

Illustrated by John Lawrence
Cambridge, MA: Candlewick Press, 2006
ISBN: 978-0-763-62989-2 | **AGES 4–8**

This beautifully understated picture book describes the characteristics of sea horses, using the example of Barbour's sea horses. In terms appropriate for primary grade listeners, the author explains their appearance, habitat, behavior, mating and reproduction, and development of young. The text is set in two sizes of type on background illustrations made from vinyl engravings, watercolor washes in appropriately muted colors, and printed wood textures. Larger type provides a simple description of the actions of the main character, told in a lively, appealing manner. "Every day at sunrise, Sea Horse swims slowly off to meet his mate. They twist their tails together and twirl gently around, changing color until they match." Smaller type adds further scientific information for independent readers, such as defining its Latin name *Hippocampus* and terms like *camouflage*. A note on the index in the back reminds readers to look at both levels of text. End papers show other sea horse species. No sources are given for the information but the help of a British sea horse expert is acknowledged. Distinctive for the amount of information it manages to convey to very young reader, this USBBY Outstanding International Book was a CCBC Choice and appeared on the John Burroughs list.

MCMILLAN, BEVERLY, AND JOHN A. MUSICK

Sharks

Illustrated with CGI and 3-D model imagery
New York: Simon & Schuster Books for Young Readers, 2008
ISBN: 978-1-416-93867-5 | **AGES 7–12**

The first section of this striking introduction to an ocean superpredator describes their physical characteristics, history, lives, and relationships with other animals and human beings. The second focuses more closely on seven species and their relatives: the great white, Greenland sleeper, bull shark, hammerhead, whale shark, wobbegong, and cookie cutter shark. The jazzy design and eye-catching illustrations of the Insiders series are perfectly suited for this topic. Sharks lunge out from the page, jaws agape; cutaways show their internal organs; a time line charts the evolution of sharks and bony fish over millions of years; and a map plots their migrations in the world's oceans. In the In Focus section, locator maps, fast facts and a depth bar add information about each species described. Sizes are compared to a 10-year-old boy. The information is delivered in single paragraphs, one describing the main subject of the double-page spread and the others as picture captions. This reading isn't easy, but the reader drawn in by the astonishing (sometimes scary) graphics will be likely to puzzle it out or insist that an adult provide the explanations. The end matter of this CBC/NSTA Outstanding Science Trade Book includes a shark family tree, glossary, and index but no sources.

STOCKDALE, SUSAN

Fabulous Fishes

Illustrated by Susan Stockdale
Atlanta: Peachtree, 2008
ISBN: 978-1-561-45429-7 | **AGES 2–7**

"Fish that swim in numbers / fish that swim alone / no matter what they look like, / they call the water home." Rhyming couplets and bright acrylic illustrations introduce a wide variety of colorful fish to make this simple point. Page by page the author/ illustrator shows different species, in their usual environment, describing either behaviors or appearance. "Striped fish, / spiked fish, / fish that leap and glide." The pattern of images supports the reader. Acrylic paintings framed in blue accompany the first two phrases in each line; a full-bleed double-page spread encourages slowing down on the longer, third phrase. The sharp edges and clear patterns of the shapes look almost like collage; they are easy to recognize and remember. The last spread shows a diver with mask and snorkel as well. In the back matter, in the order of presentation, thumbnail illustrations accompany the English name of each fish, an interesting fact, and where it might be found. Except for the discus, all are saltwater fish, but most might well be seen in an aquarium. This CBC/NSTA Outstanding Science Trade Book and Cybils finalist is an ideal accompaniment to a field trip, but it is also a grand read-aloud and early introduction to marine life at any time.

AMPHIBIANS AND REPTILES

ARNOSKY, JIM

Crocodile Safari

Illustrated by Jim Arnosky
New York: Scholastic Press, 2009
ISBN: 978-0-439-90356-1 | **AGES 7–10**

Survivors from the age of dinosaurs, crocodiles live all over the world, including 2,000 of them here in the United States. Having researched their alligator cousins, naturalist Arnosky and his wife decided to canoe through Southern Florida mangrove swamps to photograph, paint, and count crocodiles for themselves. Arnosky opens with an introduction to these large wild reptiles and explains how to tell them apart. (When its mouth is closed, a crocodile's teeth still show). Then slowly, cautiously, he begins to describe their crocodile encounters. There were three who daily visited a trailer park creek, a pile of four at the tip of the Everglades, one longer than their twelve-foot canoe who surfaced alongside, and even a baby on a sandbar. Along the way he weaves in information about crocodiles' characteristics, their lives, and the habitat they share with other dangerous animals and plants. Detailed acrylic paintings show crocs close-up along with some of their neighbors. Often, these spread across the gutter, bounded with vines and saplings. The softly colored backgrounds vary, as does the changing light in the swamps. Like any good naturalist, Arnosky includes details of time, weather, and tide for each picture. Slightly menacing and wonderfully informative, this CBC/NSTA Outstanding Science Trade Book includes a DVD and a song.

BISHOP, NIC

Lizards

Illustrated with photographs by Nic Bishop
New York: Scholastic, 2010
ISBN: 978-0-545-20634-1 | **AGES 4–10**

Clear text, crisp, colorful design, and astonishing photographs characterize this introduction to lizards from all over the world. Opening with a photograph of a gliding gecko parachuting from branch to branch, the biologist/photographer captures one revealing moment after another. The centerfold shows a brown leaf-tailed gecko curled up on a leaf and almost invisible. This opens on both sides to four shots of a basilisk walking upright on water. Bishop shows tiny details—the ear opening that distinguishes lizards from snakes, a chameleon's body-long tongue in action, the spiky skin and tiny claws of the desert-dwelling Australian thorny devil. A well-organized, lively text describes lizard habitats, egg-laying and lack of child-rearing, specialized bodies and behaviors, feeding and mating. Solid colored page backgrounds complement the colors of the photographs, and differing font sizes easily distinguish topic sentences (for simple read-aloud) from text and captions. As always, the back matter includes an explanation of Bishop's research methods and photography, done in the wild and at home of lizards he's raised, as well as an index to the numbered pages, a list of further reading, URL, and a glossary. A CBC/NSTA Outstanding Science Trade Book, this was also an ALSC Notable and AAAS/Subaru SB&F Prize finalist. Bishop's *Frogs* (Scholastic, 2008) was even more highly lauded. There is further information about all of Bishop's natural history titles on his website: www.nicbishop.com.

CHRUSTOWSKI, RICK

Turtle Crossing

Illustrated by Rick Chrustowski
New York: Henry Holt, 2006
ISBN: 978-0-805-07498-7 | **AGES 5–8**

A familiar "turtle crossing" road sign on the cover and dedication page can serve as the child reader's entry point for this attractive story of a turtle's life cycle. A painted turtle hatchling leaves her nest in the spring, traveling quickly to the nearest water, a pond where she stays for several years. The author-illustrator shows her life there: what she eats, how she avoids predators like the large snapping turtle, how she burrows in the mud to spend the cold winters and basks in the spring and summer sun. Lush colored pencil and watercolor-wash illustrations—mostly double-page spreads—accurately show the turtle in and out of water as well as birds and flowers around the pond. Finally, after five years, with a now toughened shell nearly impervious to predators, she's ready to mate, and to recross the road to deposit her own eggs. The child connection is made again when a car stops and a boy helps her across the road back to the pond. (His mother watches for traffic.) An afterword explains further about safe ways to help these ancient reptiles follow their traditional routes, but there is no documentation. This appealing and informative introduction was a CBC/NSTA Outstanding Science Trade Book.

MARKLE, SANDRA

Hip-Pocket Papa

Illustrated by Alan Marks
Watertown, MA: Charlesbridge, 2010
ISBN: 978-1-570-91708-0 | **AGES 5–8**

In Australia, the tiny hip-pocket frog provides an example of paternal child-rearing in this attractive large-format title. Markle's text follows a father frog through the process, from guarding his eggs to watching his froglets crawl away. Although male and female guard their "pearl-like eggs" together, after they hatch, the female leaves. The tadpoles "wiggle" up the male's legs to pockets on his hips. For nearly thirty days, with his tadpoles safely hidden as they develop, the male travels the forest floor, searching for water and food and avoiding his natural enemies. Other creatures from this Australian environment—antechinus, quoll, currawong, and more—may be unfamiliar to American readers, but who they are is clear from the illustrations and described more fully in an animal glossary at the end. Marks's pen, pencil, and watercolor paintings, done in the greens and browns of the forest floor, are full of details and varying perspectives. They show well from a distance, and Markle's lyrical text begs to be read aloud. A final page includes an author's note, a few further facts, and suggestions for readers wanting to know more. This CBC/NSTA Outstanding Science Trade Book and ALSC Notable is a good companion to Marks and Markle's koala story, *Finding Home* (Charlesbridge, 2008).

MARKLE, SANDRA

Slippery, Slimy Baby Frogs

Illustrated with photographs

New York: Walker, 2006

ISBN: 978-0-802-78062-1 | **AGES 5–10**

This striking photo essay shows the development of baby frogs from conception to adult froghood, using examples from around the world. Opening with an explanation of frogs' double lives—tadpoles have gills to live in water; adults have lungs and breathe air—Markle then starts at the beginning, showing a pair of hourglass tree frogs and then a group of foam nest frogs mating. Photographs taken in the wild show a variety of methods that different species use to protect developing eggs and keep them moist. She follows the hatched frogs growth to adult form. Some are soon independent; others continue to have a parent's care. While the photographs will attract even quite young naturalists, the surprisingly informative text of this CBC/NSTA Outstanding Science Trade Book and CBC/IRA Children's Choice is not easy. But the author has chosen details that will intrigue her audience. Some words are defined in context; a glossary doubles as an index. A world map indicates where particular frogs live and there are even instructions for raising tadpoles. This series, also describing *Tough, Toothy Baby Sharks* (Walker, 2007) and *Sneaky, Spinning Baby Spiders* (Walker, 2008), is the next step for young readers and listeners whose curiosity has been whetted by Nic Bishop's simpler introductions.

SAYRE, APRIL PULLEY

Turtle, Turtle, Watch Out!

Illustrated by Annie Patterson

Watertown, MA: Charlesbridge, 2010

ISBN: 978-1-580-89148-6 | **AGES 5–9**

Repeating the title as a refrain, the narrator describes the life of a sea turtle from egghood to egg-laying motherhood, pointing out many predators and hazards she may meet along the way and many hands that help her. Turtle's story is simple and straightforward, told as a series of suspenseful encounters and escapes. Night herons, cats and raccoons, cars on the beach, and bright lights in the wrong direction are threats to the hatchling; gulls, sharks, plastic bags masquerading as jellyfish, and a shrimper's net are potential hazards in the water. Watercolor, gouache, and pastel paintings on double-page spreads emphasize the blueness of the nocturnal and underwater worlds.

The brown baby turtle, realistically depicted and gradually increasing in size, stands out. The illustrations, the structure, and the language of the text lend themselves well to reading aloud. This is an ideal introduction to sea turtle life, now so dependent on the helping hands of humans. A short afterword offers examples of this work around the world and a website for further exploration. A second lists and describes sea turtle species and explains that the turtle shown is a loggerhead. This reillustration of a title first published in 2000 was a CBC/NSTA Outstanding Science Trade Book.

BIRDS

KELLY, IRENE

Even an Ostrich Needs a Nest: Where Birds Begin

Illustrated by Irene Kelly
New York: Holiday House, 2009
ISBN: 978-0-823-42102-2 | **AGES 5-9**

From emperor penguins and others that make no nest at all, through the communal sociable weaver's nest to the complicated courting constructions of bowerbirds, this introduces the astonishing variety of methods birds use to keep their eggs warm around the world. As might be expected from the title, the focus is mainly on different nest building materials and construction techniques. Curiously, though the birds covered range from American dipper to the yellow-rumped thornbill of Australia, the ostrich isn't one of them. This probably won't worry readers, who will pore over the detailed drawings and the text, which gives the appearance of hand-printed notes. One to three birds are shown on a page; at the end, a map gives a general idea of where these birds might be found across six continents. Watercolor, gouache, acrylic, and pen and ink combine to make illustrations that include detailed small sketches of birds, nests, and some surprising materials: clothespins, dollar bills, bark, trash bags. Young readers are encouraged to offer feathers, bits of yarn or string and animal fur for birds in their own neighborhoods. Like her earlier *It's a Butterfly's Life* (Holiday House, 2007), this was a CBC/NSTA Outstanding Science Trade Book.

KIRBY, PAMELA F.

What Bluebirds Do

Illustrated by Pamela F. Kirby
Honesdale, PA: Boyds Mills Press, 2009
ISBN: 978-1-590-78614-7 | **AGES 4-10**

From a blind in her North Carolina yard, photographer Kirby observed and photographed the Eastern bluebirds she introduces to young readers, carefully distinguishing male from female and both from other blue birds one might encounter. This photo essay describes their courtship behavior, nest box, eggs, and feeding of five nestlings. A scrawny newborn chick with a collar of down is shown in a human hand, and we see all five nestled together in their small quarters, after their first brown spotted feathers have grown. Both parents feed the babies, first in the nest box and then outside as they gradually move away and learn to find food on their own. The author even points out the difference between the words *fledgling* and *fledging* for her young, not necessarily proficient readers. The simple sentence structure will help the fledgling reader; her sharply reproduced photographs also tell the story. Extensive back matter includes more detailed information about the three kinds of North American bluebirds, further information about the birds and about inviting them to your yard, acknowledgments, a bibliography (including websites and sources for live mealworms), and a glossary. This AAAS/Subaru SB&F Prize finalist also appeared on the CBC/ NSTA and John Burroughs lists.

MARZOLLO, JEAN

Pierre the Penguin: A True Story

Illustrated by Laura Regan
Ann Arbor: Sleeping Bear Press, 2010
ISBN: 978-1-585-36485-5 | **AGES 4–7**

In a San Francisco museum, an African penguin that lost his feathers was given a wetsuit to keep him warm until they could grow back again. A straightforward, simple text in rhyming couplets tells this satisfying true story chronologically, focusing entirely on Pierre the penguin and his keeper, Pam. No more than a few lines per page are set on double-page spreads of large-scale, realistic paintings. An opening spread shows the museum's African hall, with the penguin exhibit at the end, but quickly the viewer moves inside the penguins' world. Readers and listeners will learn intriguing details of museum work, like the secret door behind the exhibit through which Pam enters to feed the penguins twice a day. Although Pierre has a name, he is not given other human characteristics; still, his body language is expressive. The idea for his wetsuit came from the raincoat Pam's dog wears in the cold Northern California rains, and Pam and a colleague are shown designing and carefully fitting this costume which the penguin wore until his own coat regrew. A series of questions and answers about the story and a link to a webcam conclude this CBC/NSTA Outstanding Science Trade Book.

SAYRE, APRIL PULLEY

Vulture View

Illustrated by Steve Jenkins
New York: Henry Holt, 2007
ISBN: 978-0-805-07557-1 | **AGES 4–7**

This playful, poetic introduction to carrion-eating turkey vultures would be a delight to read aloud to a group of preschool children. "Wings stretch wide / to catch a ride / on warming air. / Going where?" Flying high, the vultures turn up their noses at the live animals they see; they look for foods that "REEK." After dining on a "stinky dead deer" the vulture washes and preens, soars high in the sky again, coming to rest in the evening to sleep in groups, "like families." Simply presented, the text has just three big ideas: the flying, eating, and sleeping habits of these distinctive birds. Jenkins's cut-paper collages on solid backgrounds show well at a distance, highlighting the black birds' purpley-red faces, heavy gray beaks, and white wing edges. The end matter provides more information about turkey vultures, a website, and locations of vulture celebrations. No sources are given but several scientists are thanked for their review help. A Geisel honor book and ALSC Notable, this was a finalist for the Cybils Award and the AAAS/Subaru SB&F Prize.

SCHULMAN, JANET

Pale Male: Citizen Hawk of New York City

Illustrated by Meilo So
New York: Alfred A. Knopf, 2008
ISBN: 978-0-375-84558-1 | **AGES 7–12**

When a pale red-tailed hawk found a home near the roof of a fancy New York City apartment house, the building's human occupants tried to evict them. Bird watchers from Central Park and all over the country rallied successfully in his support. Happily, Pale Male has now raised numerous families. Some descendants have chosen to nest in the city as well. Two things distinguish Schulman's version of this highly publicized story: the extensive bird-watching detail and the way the author uses the example of one bird to present a larger environmental issue to young readers. How can humans and animals occupy the same area? Beautiful watercolor and color pencil illustrations demonstrate the variety of bird and human life that can be found in and around Central Park, an "oasis" in the middle of the city. An author's note brings the story up to date and makes a personal connection. Endpapers show the hawk's widespread red tail feathers, a stunning display. The extensive text and suggested further reading and viewing sources make this suitable for older readers than either Winter's *Tale of Pale Male* (Harcourt, 2007) or McCarthy's *City Hawk* (Simon & Schuster Books for Young Readers, 2007). One of the *New York Times* Best Illustrated Books of its year, this book also appeared on ALSC and CBC/NCSS Notable lists.

STEWART, MELISSA

A Place for Birds

Illustrated by Higgins Bond
Atlanta: Peachtree, 2009
ISBN: 978-1-561-45474-7 | **AGES 6–10**

Focusing on eleven specific species, Stewart describes how birds thrive in a particular environment, how those environments have changed, and what humans have done and can do to protect and encourage them. The two-level text features a general statement about bird and human behavior, and a sidebar about a specific species. Piping plover, for example, nest directly on the beach, so people are fencing off areas where nests have been found. Some birds are found through much of the country or their stories are well known—eastern bluebird, northern cardinal, grasshopper sparrow, hermit thrush, bald eagle, and spotted owl. Others are unusual—Hawaii's crested honeycreeper, the Florida scrub jay, Kirtland's warbler, and common murre. Acrylic paintings, spreading across the gutter, show birds in their habitat. These finely detailed illustrations make the birds easy to identify; as a bonus they also show nests and eggs or chicks. Range maps on the endpapers include thumbnails of the birds described, mostly on their nests. Finally, the author describes why and how young people can help birds flourish. The selected bibliography highlights books for young readers. Spread by spread, introducing a problem and offering a solution, this CBC/NSTA Selectors' Choice provides an unusually positive approach to environmental issues.

MAMMALS OTHER THAN HUMANS

ARNOLD, CAROLINE

A Platypus' World

Illustrated by Caroline Arnold
Minneapolis: Picture Window Books, 2008
ISBN: 978-1-404-83985-4 | **AGES 5–8**

This appealing introduction to the curious Australian egg-laying mammal follows a female platypus into the water, where she hunts for food, and into a new land burrow, where she lays eggs and raises a pair of babies who eventually come outside and learn to hunt on their own. Simple cut-paper illustrations fill the double-page spreads. Their dark, shadowy colors reflect the animal's nocturnal world, and some of the papers have some texture. A straightforward narrative, ideal for reading aloud, appears directly on the illustration. Other animals in the platypus's world are included in the pictures and identified in text boxes. Arnold's Animals series also includes titles about bald eagles, kangaroos, killer whales, koalas, moose, pandas, penguins, polar bears, walruses, wombats and zebras. All feature an opening fast-fact page (including scientific names) and a gentle story focused on child rearing. They end with a map, fun facts, glossary, index, and suggested books and websites for further research, and each acknowledges the advice of experts. Carefully researched and attractively presented, they provide exactly the kind of information young readers want to know, nicely connected to their universal interest in animal babies. This title was a CBC/NSTA Outstanding Science Trade Book.

ARNOSKY, JIM

Slow Down for Manatees

Illustrated by Jim Arnosky
New York: G. P. Putnam's Sons, 2009
ISBN: 978-0-399-24170-3 | **AGES 4–7**

A sun-drenched Florida canal is home to the manatee that naturalist Arnosky follows in this gentle fictionalized story based on a recent incident. Injured by a boat, the huge, slow-moving mammal was seen by passing fishermen and removed with heavy equipment to an aquarium where visitors followed her recovery. After her calf was born, both were returned to the canal. Arnosky focuses on the experience for the manatee—her wide watery world narrowed to a small tank and then reopened. The book's design supports the subject: a wavy ribbon separates text from pictures that cross the gutter, opening to double-page spreads at key moments: the injury, the birth of her calf, nursing the baby, and their return to the canal. Arnosky's pastel acrylic wash paintings are perfectly suited for this watery environment and full of environmental detail. On the text side, a tiny inset focuses on a single image, suggesting what to look for. In an afterword, the author lays no blame on the boater, saying that "accidents do occur," but also points out the expertise necessary to rescue and rehabilitate these animals. This CBC/NSTA Outstanding Trade Book goes well with Arnosky's *All about Manatees* (Scholastic, 2007) and *A Manatee Morning* (Simon & Schuster Books for Young Readers, 2000).

DOWSON, NICK

Tracks of a Panda

Illustrated by Yu Rong
Cambridge, MA: Candlewick Press, 2007
ISBN: 978-0-763-63146-8 | **AGES 4–8**

This appealing introduction to this likable Chinese bear follows a panda baby and its mother from birth through several years as the two find food, move to a more productive location, and move again to avoid approaching humans. Brush and watercolor paintings on double-page spreads, done in a Chinese style in black, white, some green and occasional hints of red, close in enough to show details of panda paws and claws and back off to show the landscape. Information is given on two levels: fast facts are set off in a smaller font from the imagined story of their journeys. The presentation is attractive as well. Brown endpapers have a bamboo design; there's a traditional landscape on the back cover and boards, a red spine, and a charming mother and baby on the front. Refreshingly, the gentle text says nothing about saving the species although a short paragraph of back matter points out that few are left in the wild. Page numbers and an index allow even the very young intended reader to find a particular piece of information, and there is no anthropomorphization. There are, however, no sources or suggestions for further research. Pair this ALSC and CBC/NCSS Notable with titles about the panda kindergarten described below.

GIBBONS, GAIL

Elephants of Africa

Illustrated by Gail Gibbons
New York: Holiday House, 2008
ISBN: 978-0-823-42168-8 | **AGES 5–9**

Physical characteristics, family life, and habits are the major topics of this introduction to the elephants of Africa. Gibbons begins by putting this species in context, mentioning their savanna and forest world, and showing where they live on a general map of the continent. A brief mention of elephant ancestors is followed by more extensive explanation of their lives through something a child reader can easily understand: how they use their body parts. Watercolor-and-ink illustrations on double-page spreads show the elephants in families, finding food and water, and facing danger. Close-up insets show more detail. These rather busy pictures have titles and some captions, supplementing a text running along the bottom of each page. Some words have been defined in context, but the intended audience may find this surprisingly difficult to read. This prolific Vermont author-illustrator has published more than 135 topic books for children since she began in 1975. Science of all sorts, holidays, the foods we eat, and the things we do—her range is broad. Always colorful and informative, the books are fine classroom resources. This title was a CBC/NSTA Outstanding Science Trade Book.

GUIBERSON, BRENDA Z.

Ice Bears

Illustrated by Ilya Spirin
New York: Henry Holt, 2008
ISBN: 978-0-805-07607-3 | **AGES 4–9**

During their first year, twin polar bear cubs learn about their tundra world, waiting through a lean summer until the ice returns and they can fatten up on seals. Words and pictures combine here to give a sense of the Arctic environment. Onomatopoetic words in italics describe sounds they might hear: the "Slurpslurp" of their nursing, the "Chuffchuff" of their mother's warning when a male threatens them, "Crunch, crik!" as the ice breaks up. The cubs are introduced to new foods, mostly seal, but also lemming and a portion of a beached whale. The well-written text is framed in a small box on each double-page spread where Spirin's watercolors emphasize the myriad shades of blue and green, gray and white of this polar world, picturing it in sharp detail. Young readers and listeners will enjoy the story, but its message is contained in the back matter. An "Arctic Ice Report" notes the effects of global climate change and the melting of polar ice on the bears and other animals who share their world. A list of environmental organizations is included, but no sources or acknowledgments. This Orbis Pictus recommended book would be a good springboard for discussion of climate issues.

HATKOFF, JULIANA, ISABELLA HATKOFF, AND CRAIG HATKOFF

Winter's Tail: How One Little Dolphin Learned to Swim Again

Illustrated with photographs
New York: Scholastic Press, 2009
ISBN: 978-0-545-12335-8 | **AGES 8–12**

Found badly entangled in a crab trap rope, a baby Atlantic bottlenose dolphin is rescued, rehabilitated, and provided with a prosthetic tail that allows her to swim normally. Illustrated with photographs including remarkable pictures of the actual rescue, this heartwarming tale highlights the work of the Clearwater Marine Aquarium and Kevin Carroll of Hanger Prosthetic and Orthotics in Florida. Woven into the story are details of dolphin life, in the wild and in aquariums. This is another story of healing as well as the story of an animal. One photograph shows Kevin Carroll in his workshop; others show a boy and a girl, each with a different style of artificial leg, meeting and even petting the dolphin calf, now named Winter. The human connection is clear, and readers learn that the special silicone gel developed for the dolphin's prosthesis now has wider use. An extensive endnote provides further information about Winter's journey, the aquarium, bottlenose dolphins, dolphin training, and Hanger Prosthetic and Orthotics. Like other books the Hatkoffs have written about rescued baby animals, including *Owen and Mzee* (Scholastic, 2006), *Knut* (Scholastic, 2007), and *Looking for Miza* (Scholastic, 2008), this CBC/NSTA Outstanding Science Trade Book should have broad appeal.

JENKINS, MARTIN

Ape

Illustrated by Vicky White
Cambridge, MA: Candlewick Press, 2007
ISBN: 978-0-763-63471-1 | **AGES 5–9**

This beautiful introduction to four rare great apes species—orangutan, chimp, bonobo, and gorilla—reminds readers of their similarities to a fifth, much more common species: the human. One member of each species stands for the whole: "Orangutan swings with her baby." "Gorilla lounges, chewing on bamboo stems and chomping on leaves." In a few sentences, the author describes common behaviors children will understand: Chimp's gang sometimes gets into fights; in the trees, Bonobo plays with her friends. Captions offer a bit more detail. What distinguishes this oversized album are the striking pencil and oil illustrations by a talented former zookeeper. These realistic and expressive close-ups, black with a bit of brown on an expanse of white on the double-page spreads, show the animals in action. They won a Henry Bergh Award. The book concludes with the gentle reminder that humans have taken up so much space in the world, there is little room left for other great apes. A map of the eastern hemisphere shows where these four species live in a band across central Africa, and on the islands of Sumatra and Borneo. There is an index to behaviors and a few suggested websites for organizations working to save these fascinating creatures.

LUNDE, DARRIN P.

Hello, Bumblebee Bat

Illustrated by Patricia Wynne
Watertown, MA: Charlesbridge, 2007
ISBN: 978-1-570-91374-7 | **AGES 3–7**

No larger than a bumblebee, the world's smallest bat is only an inch long. This endangered species from Thailand flies at dawn and dusk, eats insects, and folds its wings to sleep hanging upside down in its cave. With brown fur, a pig nose, and long, pointy ears, this tiny creature looks anything but fierce in Wynne's illustrations, which give him a cheerful smile and show his diminutive size by including other creatures. The format is predictable and reassuring. A simple question such as "Bumblebee Bat, how do you see at night?" and the bat's first-person answer appear in large white text on a dark blue left-hand page. Opposite, a detailed pen-and-ink drawing, colored with watercolors and color pencil, shows the bat in action. Often some detail from the illustration crosses the gutter, connecting it more closely with the text. Finally, the words "Good Night, Bumble Bat!" appear on a double-page spread showing bat and siblings asleep in a cave. In lieu of an afterword, a spread showing the cave from the outside underlies a few simply written paragraphs of additional information. This Geisel honor book is not only an early reader; it would be a perfect bedtime book for a preschool naturalist.

MARKLE, SANDRA

How Many Baby Pandas?

Illustrated with photographs
New York: Walker, 2009
ISBN: 978-0-802-79783-4 | **AGES 5–9**

Baby pandas, most from the China's Wolong Giant Panda Breeding Center, are shown from birth through cubhood, in this introduction to this endangered species as well as counting book. Beginning with the first-page question, "How many baby pandas have just been born?" and an illustration of the tiny pink, almost unrecognizable newborn, each left-hand page shows more and more pandas growing and developing until we reach six, shown on both pages as "three on the playground . . . plus three in the yard." The counting continues to eight; a final page shows the sixteen born in one banner year. The photographs are appealing, but the design is confusing, and in a library binding some pictures seem to run into each other. Photo credits reveal that one actually shows Tai Shan, then at the National Zoo in Washington, DC. The strength of this title is its developmental approach, which will intrigue elementary school readers. Markle finishes with fast facts, a glossary/index defining words italicized in the text, a note about the earthquake effects on the breeding center, and suggested bibliography and websites. This was an Orbis Pictus honor and a CBC/IRA Children's and IRA Teachers' Choice. Younger listeners may prefer Joanne Ryder's *Panda Kindergarten* (HarperCollins, 2009) illustrated with photographs by Dr. Katherine Feng, a regular tour escort at the center.

MARTIN, JACQUELINE BRIGGS

The Chiru of High Tibet: A True Story

Illustrated by Linda S. Wingerter
Boston: Houghton Mifflin Harcourt, 2010
ISBN: 978-0-618-58130-6 | **AGES 5–10**

In the high northern plains of Tibet, chiru—antelope-like creatures with valuable soft wool—were hunted almost to extinction. Naturalist George Schaller first took up their cause. He hoped to find their remote calving grounds and then ask the Chinese government to protect the area, but the trip was too difficult. Later, four experienced trekkers did make their way across the plains, through mountains and a canyon to discover this secret place. Martin spins the tale of their journey in lyrical prose, emphasizing its length, its difficulty, and the distinct possibility it would be fruitless. Her circular narrative begins and ends with description: "There is a place so cold, it takes the fleece of five sheep to keep one person warm...."The text is set on or opposite softly textured acrylic paintings. The extensive landscapes are done in icy blues; the oranges and pinks of sunrise fill one striking spread, showing the men and their tiny tents on a vast, misty plain. Other animals from the area appear, and there are mandala-like designs. A map sets the story geographically and some photographs from the expedition conclude this CBC/NSTA Outstanding Science Trade Book, winner of a Parents' Choice Silver Honor.

MASON, ADRIENNE

Skunks

Illustrated by Nancy Gray Ogle
Toronto, ON: Kids Can, 2006.
ISBN: 9781553377337 | **AGES 5–9**

Found almost everywhere in the continental United States and southern Canada, striped skunks and their relatives are nocturnal mammals distinguished by their defensive weapon: a strong-smelling oil spray. Spread by spread, this introduction to an animal family more often smelled than seen describes their habitat, behavior, child rearing, and relationship to human beings. This slim but informative title also includes sign (tracks and diggings) and a spread showing skunks of the world. The text, presented in paragraphs and fact boxes, is accessible to fledgling readers. All four native species are pictured and identified. Realistic, finely detailed paintings, both double-page spreads and vignettes, show the animals in a variety of contexts and poses: on a meadow, in the woods, curled up in an underground den in winter, facing a fox, and even with kits. These images emphasize the skunk's claws; though small, this is a formidable animal. With a table of contents, glossary, and index, this topic book demonstrates the conventions of nonfiction exposition through a subject endlessly fascinating to young naturalists. A CBC/NSTA Outstanding Science Trade Book, this is part of the publisher's long-standing Wildlife Series.

SIMON, SEYMOUR

Horses

Illustrated with photographs
New York: HarperCollins, 2006
ISBN: 978-0-060-28945-4 | **AGES 6–9**

The author of over 250 science books for children here provides a simplified overview of horses and ponies: how they came to be, their physical characteristics, communication, gait, colors and breeds, and uses. It is the illustrations—striking color photographs—that will capture horse-loving readers and listeners. From the endpapers showing a herd of horses and the black horse galloping across the double-page title spread, Simon goes on to show horses working, horses jumping, cowboys riding the range, a double-page spread of mother and child, two horses nuzzling, and close-ups of horse heads. These photographs are described generally in the text, but have no captions or clear identification. The text is relatively difficult for the likely reader and the generalizations, particularly about coat colors and breeds, may leave some false impressions. This is a book to whet a child's appetite; while it offers no sources or suggestions for further reading, a good library can offer many possible titles from years past. The author received an AAAS/Subaru SB&F Lifetime Achievement Award for his lasting contribution to children's science literature; this title made the CBC/NSTA list and was a CBC/IRA Children's Choice.

INSECTS AND SPIDERS

BAKER, NICK, MARGARET PARRISH, AND DK PUBLISHING INC.

Bug Zoo

Illustrated with photographs
New York: DK, 2010
ISBN: 978-0-756-66166-3 | **AGES 5-10**

TV Naturalist Nick Baker provides instructions for capturing and keeping thirteen different species. He opens with a short chapter on "zoo tools" and general techniques, most of which involve easily obtainable supplies. Then, chapter by chapter, on double-page spreads, he introduces each creature. The first spread describes the animal and suggests ways to catch it; the second gives instructions for constructing housing, feeding, and observing your creature. Paragraphs of explanation and plenty of photographs, some enlarged for clarity, are arranged on graph paper in a relatively orderly way. Arrows with titles help: "Creature features," "Building an enclosure," "Things to look for." There is an extraordinary amount of solid, if unsourced, information; there is also humor and play with words as well: "The louse house," "Aphids . . . the hungry herds," "Making an earwiggery." The pictures are attached with tape or paper clips; hand-written additions give a notebook effect. Though researched in England, Baker makes clear that these creatures—wood lice, slugs and snails, aphids, caterpillars, worms, earwigs, ladybugs, spiders, crickets and katydids, pseudoscorpions, mosquito and dragonfly larvae, and backswimmers—can be found worldwide. While adults may frown at the idea of keeping bugs, child readers will be intrigued and entranced.

BISHOP, NIC

Spiders

Illustrated with photographs by Nic Bishop
New York: Scholastic, 2007
ISBN: 978-0-439-87756-5 | **AGES 5–10**

The heart of this extraordinary look at some of the most successful predators in the natural world is a series of fascinating close-up photographs. From the green lynx spider, found in southern backyards, to the cobalt blue tarantula from Thailand, Bishop demonstrates the variety of spider life, shows and describes their body parts and sensory apparatus, and explains their hunting methods and eating. In one photograph a black-and-yellow garden spider extrudes silk from its spinnerets, wrapping its prey for a later meal. A gatefold opens to show the leap of a jumping spider. Bishop spies on spider courtship, and shows young spiderlings carried on the back of a wolf spider or, dwarfed by moss plants, searching for a first meal. Three levels of clear text describe each picture: an identifying caption and a paragraph of explanation with one sentence boldfaced for younger readers or listeners. This first of an award-winning series builds on the work Bishop did earlier for Montgomery's *Tarantula Scientist* (Houghton Mifflin, 2004), but goes far beyond. His research expeditions and home spider care are described in an author's note and on his website. This was both a Sibert and Orbis Pictus honor book, a finalist for the AAAS/Subaru SB&F Prize, and an IRA Teachers' Choice. Bishop's *Butterflies and Moths* (Scholastic, 2009) and *Marsupials* (Scholastic, 2009) as well as titles described earlier have similar appeal.

FROST, HELEN

Monarch and Milkweed

Illustrated by Leonid Gore
New York: Atheneum Books for Young Readers, 2008
ISBN: 978-1-416-90085-6 | **AGES 3–10**

Simple poetic lines describe the relationship between monarch and milkweed, showing changes in both over time. The milkweed grows. A north-flying monarch butterfly discovers it and lays an egg. A caterpillar hatches, eats its leaves, cocoons, and breaks out as butterfly, which flies toward Mexico while the milkweed seeds develop and float away from the pod, finding a new place to grow. This title about the often-studied butterfly is unusual in that it gives equal attention to the host plant. Acrylic and pastel paintings, done with a speckled effect, show both, from afar and in detailed close-ups. As the butterfly emerges it fills a striking, wordless double-page spread. End papers, redrawn from monarch watch maps, show the butterfly migration path, and an author's note makes clear that it takes several generations of butterflies to complete each journey. These illustrations show well, and the simple text is a delight to read aloud. "Rain comes / snow comes, / rain comes again. / Sun warms the earth. / Earth warms the seed, / and under the dirt, it opens." This CCBC Choice and CBC/NSTA Outstanding Science Trade Book has broad appeal. Stephen Swinburne's *Wings of Light* (Boyds Mills Press, 2006), an AAAS/Subaru SB&F Prize finalist, shows a yellow sulphur butterfly making a similar migration.

MORTENSEN, LORI

In the Trees, Honey Bees

Illustrated by Cris Arbo
Nevada City, CA: Dawn Publications, 2009
ISBN: 978-1-584-69114-3 | **AGES 4–7**

From "Morning light, / Warm and bright" to "Chilly night, / Cluster tight," simple rhyming couplets and photo-realistic full-bleed illustrations introduce the lives and work of honeybees to the youngest readers and listeners. At the bottom of each spread, a short paragraph of explanation adds information. This cheerful introduction contains no hint of the honeybee issues described in *The Buzz on Bees* (below), but it will give younger children a solid understanding of what bees do. Arbo's detailed paintings show close-ups of the inside of a hive where worker bees dance a wiggle dance, bring pollen back to the hive, and care for their queen, and nurse bees feed larvae in the combs. Two double-page spreads shows bees collecting nectar and pollen; others back off to show the garden of a farm where the honeybees live in a tree. A "bear attack" adds humor. The afterword of this CBC/NSTA Outstanding Science Trade Book adds another level of information and offers suggestions for further learning.

ROTNER, SHELLEY, AND ANNE LOVE WOODHULL

The Buzz on Bees: Why Are They Disappearing?

Illustrated with photographs by Shelley Rotner
New York: Holiday House, 2010
ISBN: 978-0-823-42247-0 | **AGES 6–10**

Scientists and beekeepers alike are working to solve a scientific mystery now called honeybee colony collapse disorder. Opening with a professional beekeeper's discovery that thousands of his bees have disappeared, this photo essay describes the problem and explains its importance in a conversational narrative, extensively illustrated with Rotner's photographs. A middle section provides more detail about pollination, bee species, and the industry that trucks bees around the country for specific crops. Readers see honeybees pollinating flowers and the variety of foods, plants, and products that depend on their work. A series of images on one double-page spread show that birds, other insects, even wind and water may carry pollen. Captions on another identify a few of North America's 4,000 pollinating native bee species. And a third spread contrasts a healthy hive and a hive with CCD. Finally the authors list some of the factors that may be causing the problem, describe what scientists are doing, and suggest things for readers to do themselves. Rotner's photographs are bright, but the authors' message is chilling. Websites, intriguing facts, and short descriptions of bee experts who contributed to the authors' research complete this CBC/NSTA Outstanding Science Trade Book.

VOAKE, STEVE

Insect Detective

Illustrated by Charlotte Voake
Somerville, MA: Candlewick Press, 2010
ISBN: 978-0-763-64447-5 | **AGES 3–7**

"LISTEN—over by the fence. Can you hear a scratching sound?" Here's a gentle invitation to step outside and explore the insect world, looking for insects that live alone or together, that camouflage themselves, hide in leaves and under stones, or fly over a pond. The text organized by the kind of insect described—paper wasp, ant, solitary bee, Herald moth, leaf-miner caterpillar, earwig, ground beetle, and dragonfly—and presented on two levels. In large type is the invitation: "Lift up a stone and you might see an earwig scuttle out." Additional facts are added in a smaller font. The author includes the kinds of details that intrigue young listeners, but along the way he makes the major points: they have six legs and three body parts; they begin as eggs; and most undergo metamorphosis. His calm text is accompanied by ink-and-watercolor sketches, beginning with the insect-filled meadow on the end covers, just right for an identification game, and a line of ants wandering through rocks on the title page. Though the palette is pale, these pictures will show to a small group because the book is large-sized. This inviting, intriguing introduction, an AAAS/Subaru SB&F Prize finalist, would be an appropriate read-aloud for a quite young child curious about the world.

WADSWORTH, GINGER

Up, Up, and Away

Illustrated by Patricia Wynne
Watertown, MA: Charlesbridge, 2009
ISBN: 978-1-580-89221-6 | **AGES 4–7**

From egg sac to egg-laying and new generation, the life and death of a garden spider is chronicled in simple text and detailed illustrations. Most of this story follows a "sister spider" whose efforts to escape hungry siblings and a variety of predators are shown close-up. The illustrator zooms out to show the broad landscape and the sky through which the baby spiders soar, carried by their own silk threads. These illustrations, in watercolor, gouache, ink, and colored pencil, are done with a draughtsman's care. There is much for a young reader to ponder. The text, set in short phrases, looks accessible for early readers but employs a lively language, enjoyable to read aloud: "Her legs tickle the tips of tulips / until the thread lifts her / up, up, and away with the warm wind." Although the spider "decides to stay" in her new farm home, for the most part the author sticks to description that can come from careful observation. The author and illustrator's dedications acknowledge the influence of both E. B. White and Garth

Williams, and teachers may well want to have this book on hand when they introduce students to the most famous spider of all. This also made the CBC/NSTA list.

OTHER INVERTEBRATES

CAMPBELL, SARAH C.

Wolfsnail: A Backyard Predator

Illustrated with photographs by Sarah C. and Richard P. Campbell
Honesdale, PA: Boyds Mills Press, 2008
ISBN: 978-1-590-78554-6 | **AGES 4–7**

Unlike most garden snails, who chew on plants, the rosy wolfsnail of the southern United States eats other snails and slugs. Close-up photographs document a wolfsnail's slow journey up a hosta plant, its discovery of another snail's slime trail, its consumption of the smaller land snail, the empty shell left behind, and the carnivorous snail's return to rest. The large font text is written relatively simply but uses appropriate vocabulary (*mucus, radula*) defined in context or in the glossary. The animal is shown from a variety of angles. The steady pace of its journey is occasionally interrupted by a different picture: an expanse of hosta leaf, a threatening bird, a worm. Further facts at the end of the book include its scientific name and distribution, its reproductive behavior, and its threat to native Hawaiian snails as an introduced predator. The author took all but one of the photographs herself, but acknowledges the help of experts in her research process, which included keeping snails alive. The suspenseful narrative arc, clear text, and supportive illustrations are ideal for early readers who may be inspired to look more closely in their own backyards. This was a Geisel honor book and ALSC Notable.

TOKUDA, YUKIHISA

I'm a Pill Bug

Illustrated by Kiyoshi Takahashi
La Jolla, CA: Kane/Miller Book Publishers, 2006
ISBN: 978-1-929-13295-9 | **AGES 2–5**

A pill bug, a curious nocturnal scavenger, introduces itself to very young naturalists, describing where it lives, what it eats, how it reproduces, grows, and hibernates in winter. Illustrated with simple, flat shapes done through paper collage, this Japanese import provides the necessary facts in sentences addressed to the reader and simple enough to be understood by a toddler. "By the way, you don't think we're insects, do you?" The illustrations show the creature's actual size several times, once in a small child's hand. The text gives instructions for keeping one for observation, temporarily. *Roly-poly* is another common name for this creature, found throughout this country and fascinating to small children, perhaps because of its habit of rolling up into an armored ball when threatened. In a series of pictures, the illustrator demonstrates this for the child "reading" the pictures; another series shows the way they shed their shells, first back and then front, over a period of two days. "And we never forget to eat the old shell! Yum! Very nutritious." This charming introduction to an unsung part of the natural world was a *Booklist* Editor's Choice.

EXTINCT ANIMALS

FLORIAN, DOUGLAS

Dinothesaurus: Prehistoric Poems and Paintings

Illustrated by Douglas Florian
New York: Atheneum Books for Young Readers, 2009
ISBN: 978-1-416-97978-4 | **AGES 5–8**

From *Brachiosaurus* to *Spinosaurus*, short, witty poems describe the age of dinosaurs and eighteen examples. The last poem summarizes current theories about their extinction. There is joyful wordplay but also detail to help young enthusiasts remember identifying characteristics. "This creature was seen / In times called Cretaceous. / Its jaws were horrific. / Its profile distinct. / I find it terrific / That it's T-rex-tinct." Florian's illustrations are both childlike and sophisticated. From gouache, collage, and colored pencils, to stencils, dinosaur dust, and rubber stamps, his varied materials provide surprising effects. Drawn, painted, and pasted on brown paper bags whose color shows through the different colored backgrounds, each double-page spread presents a different genus, with an easily understood pronunciation guide as well as the meaning of the Latin name. The humor extends to the illustrations: an iPod hangs from the neck of the *Tyrannosaurus rex* skeleton; *Gigantosaurus* eats cell phones and computer parts. Each page rewards close attention. A "glossarysaurus" at the end provides further information, and the author also provides a list of museums and fossil sites as well as suggestions for further reading. A must for any enthusiasaurus, this was an NCTE Notable and a CCBC Choice.

JUDGE, LITA

Born to Be Giants: How Baby Dinosaurs Grew to Rule the World

Illustrated by Lita Judge
New York: Flash Point/Roaring Brook Press, 2010
ISBN: 978-1-596-43443-1 | **AGES 7–10**

Every giant dinosaur was once a baby. New scientific discoveries and clues from modern animals suggest how these babies grew and were cared for from egg to nestling to adult. This gateway title provides a relatively simple, engaging overview of a complex field. Judge uses and defines in context scientific terms such as *paleontologist, altricial,* and *precocial* and makes clear the difference between speculation and scientific findings. At one point she describes the discovery of thousands of closely packed fossilized eggs, some still with dinosaur embryos inside. "A herd of *Saltasaurus* mothers must have gathered by the riverbank to bury the eggs in the sand." Watercolor illustrations show large-eyed dinosaur babies, sometimes in comparison to their enormous parents (on the title page, a newly hatched *T. rex* is smaller than its mother's clawed feet). Occasionally, dinosaurs and modern animals appear on the same page to demonstrate a point. The end matter includes further description of the eight species, including pronunciation and an illustration in comparison to a human, a glossary, a bibliography, an author's note (with a photograph of the author doing dinosaur bone field study), and acknowledgments. The author's website includes some pencil and painted versions of her illustrations.

LONG, JOHN A.

Dinosaurs

Illustrated with CGI and 3-D model imagery
New York: Simon & Schuster Books for Young Readers, 2007
ISBN: 978-1-416-93857-6 | **AGES 6–12**

This first volume in the eye-catching Insiders series provides an overview of the field and a more focused look at eleven dinosaurs. Each double-page spread combines a paragraph of introduction with more detailed information in labels explaining parts of the computer-generated illustrations. The text is divided into two sections. The introduction includes an illustrated time line from the Paleozoic to the Cenozoic eras, explaining three parts of the Triassic era in more detail, and going on to describe general dinosaur anatomy, survival and extinction, flight, care of the young, fossils, and the work of paleontologists. The dinosaur evolution is shown, and the change over time of imagined reconstructions of iguanodons demonstrates the way scientists continue to reinterpret fossil findings. The In Focus section describes particular genera, setting them in time and illustrating most in scenes with vegetation appropriate to the era. Each is compared to the size of a 10-year-old boy. There's no explanation for the dinosaur colors chosen, and there are no sources or suggestions for further reading, but the facts are consistent with current understanding. With an embossed cover, striking illustrations, intriguing information, and appropriate comparisons, this has terrific child appeal. A *Booklist* Top 10 series.

O'BRIEN, PATRICK

Sabertooth

Illustrated by Patrick O'Brien
New York: Henry Holt, 2008
ISBN: 978-0-805-07105-4 | **AGES 5–8**

The fearsome cat on the cover will draw readers into this pictorial description of a creature that lived as long as thirteen million years ago. Named for long canine teeth that look something like a curved sword, this is a sabertooth, now extinct, but surely one of the most dramatic of the fossil animals being re-created from discoveries in the La Brea Tar Pits in California. Beginning with pictures of modern cats, the author/illustrator quickly moves to their distant cousins, the sabertooths. A double-page spread shows a Smilodon leaping out of the page, with a smoking volcano behind. These watercolor and gouache paintings will captivate even nonreaders, but they also carry information. The text is set as extended captions. One spread shows a complete skeleton; notes explain the differences from modern cats. Another set of illustrations show life-size canine teeth of a Smilodon, and a modern tiger, and point out human canines as well. O'Brien demonstrates that fossil discoveries don't reveal what these animals looked like by painting different possibilities. And, he shows some of their prey and two different human species who lived with them until they died out 10,000 years ago, perhaps because of a prehistoric global warming event. A CBC/NSTA Outstanding Science Trade Book.

RAY, DEBORAH KOGAN

Dinosaur Mountain: Digging into the Jurassic Age

Illustrated by Deborah Kogan Ray
New York: Frances Foster Books/Farrar Straus Giroux, 2010
ISBN: 978-0-374-31789-8 | **AGES 8–11**

Instructed by Andrew Carnegie to find "something big" for his new science museum, paleontologist Earl Douglass explored parts of a rich Jurassic rock formation in Utah where he found a nearly complete *Apatosaurus* and fossil remains of nine other species of dinosaurs, in what became Dinosaur National Monument in 1915. An extensive text, set on sand-colored pages or directly on Ray's full-bleed paintings, provides background and describes the process of excavation and the long, patient work leading to Douglass's most important discovery. Dusty tans and icy blues of her palette echo the desert landscape. Opening with an image of a mounted skeleton, viewed by a large crowd, she grounds this story in the enthusiasm for dinosaurs that swept the country. Later illustrations mostly show men at work. An *Apatosaurus* skeleton graces the endpapers, a double-page map of today's National Monument shows where the story took place, and small side sketches add pictorial interest and information. Sidebars include quotations, often from Douglass's own writings. At the end of this CBC/NSTA Outstanding Science Trade Book and Cybils finalist is a list and description of dinosaur species discovered in the quarry, some further information about major players, a glossary, and a bibliography.

SERENO, PAUL C., AND NATALIE LUNIS

Supercroc: Paul Sereno's Dinosaur Eater

Illustrated with photographs
New York: Bearport, 2007
ISBN: 978-1-597-16255-5 | **AGES 5–10**

On a fossil-hunting expedition in the sands of the Sahara Desert, paleontologist Sereno uncovered a gigantic skull, fossilized remains of a dinosaur-eating crocodile. Measuring nearly six feet and complete, it was accompanied by bones of enough other crocodiles that a model of this Cretaceous period reptile could be constructed. Using data from modern animals, scientists deduced the animal's lifestyle, calculated its incredible bite force, and determined its probable size—about that of a city bus. The life-sized model is now on tour. Presented in double-page spread chapters accompanied by photographs, this has the appearance of an old scrapbook. The methods of scientific inquiry are evident. Information is presented clearly, in two or three paragraphs of text for each chapter; unfamiliar words are bolded and defined in a glossary. Photographs are captioned; taped-on notes add extra information. The end matter includes a description of three dinosaurs that lived alongside the Supercroc, a bibliography, suggested reading and browsing, and an index. Part of the Fossil Hunters series designed for schools and libraries, this CBC/NSTA Outstanding Science Trade Book has the trim size of a schoolbook, but the illustrations—many provided by Sereno's expedition—make this accessible to the nonreader as well.

SHELDON, DAVID

Barnum Brown: Dinosaur Hunter

Illustrated by David Sheldon
New York: Walker, 2006
ISBN: 978-0-802-79602-8 | **AGES 5–10**

Named in the expectation that he would do great things and intrigued by fossils from childhood, Barnum Brown grew up to become one of the most successful dinosaur hunters of all time. Exploring in the western badlands for New York's American Museum of Natural History, he was the first to discover *Tyrannosaurus rex*. In Canada, competing with a Canadian team, his knack for finding bones led to a splendid variety of new discoveries for the museum's collection. The text includes details of the process. Sheldon's gently humorous paintings, done with acrylics, gouache, and India ink, show a bespectacled Barnum, often at work in the field with the dinosaurs he imagines looking on and sharing the same sun. Mostly double-page spreads, they contrast the sandy badlands with the greens and browns of the workers clothing and the bones they find. Museum scenes show the director putting the skeletons together and crowds admiring the result. On the endpapers a tyrannosaur poses as modern researchers imagine. Back matter adds further information about the rivalries among paleontology teams and new understandings about dinosaur posture. A list of museums and resource guide highlighting books for young readers will encourage further exploration. A CBC/NSTA Outstanding Science Trade Book.

HOW THE EARTH WORKS

BANG, MOLLY, AND PENNY CHISHOLM

Living Sunlight: How Planets Bring the Earth to Life

Illustrated by Molly Bang
New York: Blue Sky Press, 2009
ISBN: 978-0-545-04422-6 | **AGES 4–10**

In Bang's highly regarded *My Light* (Blue Sky Press, 2004), the sun explained energy and electricity. In this glorious companion book, the sun goes on to explain how its light energy becomes the energy for life on earth. Plants use sun energy and carbon dioxide to build sugar (glucose); they breathe out oxygen. Humans and animals get sun energy by eating plants. We breathe in oxygen, and breathe out water and carbon dioxide, which plants breathe in. This is the circle of life on Earth. Bang illustrates this with vibrant, colorful paintings full of curves and swirls. Tiny yellow dots (representing photons) surround forms and appear in waves in the sky. Illustrations and text are precisely designed for young readers. They will delight at the variety of animals shown. The process of photosynthesis is depicted in squares, which represent close-ups of each step. A more detailed explanation is given in notes at the end of the book. The endnotes also point out, probably for adult readers, the places where the narrative simplifies some scientific facts. The combination of Bang's experience and MIT ecology professor Chisholm's expertise has produced a highly original and thought-provoking introduction to a fundamental scientific concept. This won the AAAS/Subaru SB&F Prize.

CASSINO, MARK, AND JON NELSON

The Story of Snow: The Science of Winter's Wonder

Illustrated by Nora Aoyagi with photographs by Mark Cassino
San Francisco: Chronicle Books, 2009
ISBN: 978-0-811-86866-2 | **AGES 4–10**

Highly magnified photographs of snow crystals form the heart of this excellent introduction to that weather phenomenon. The text explains snowflake formation, illustrates the variety within the three basic forms—stars, plates, and columns—and gives instructions for catching and observing them yourself. The text is presented on three levels: a simple sentence with the main idea for reading aloud, a more detailed paragraph of explanation, and captions for the illustrations. The font is clear and easy to read, and Aoyagi's drawings, in watercolor and ink, help make the explanations clear. But readers will be most fascinated by the endless variations in Cassino's spectacular photographs. While the book encourages readers to follow up by exploring snow crystals themselves, the publisher's website offers a particularly well-thought-out teacher's guide and the author's own website (www.storyofsnow.com) has more information and additional snow crystal photographs from his ongoing investigations. Notable not only for its subject but for the author's obvious enthusiasm, this should be a part of every weather collection and offers a nice complement to Jacqueline Briggs Martin's biography of the man who pioneered snowflake photography, *Snowflake Bentley* (Houghton Mifflin, 1998). This AAAS/Subaru SB&F Prize finalist also made the CBC/NSTA list.

COLE, JOANNA, AND BRUCE DEGEN

The Magic School Bus and the Climate Challenge

Illustrated by Bruce Degen
New York: Scholastic Press, 2010
ISBN: 978-0-590-10826-3 | **AGES 7–10**

The redoubtable Ms. Frizzle retools her magic school bus to explore global climate change. In the now-hybrid bus, her class travels around the world to see causes and effects of climate change and explore energy alternatives. They start saving energy at school and at home, put on a play, and get the whole town involved. Even a visiting South Korean student gets drawn in; this is a worldwide phenomenon. This author-illustrator pair has been presenting science topics through the Magic School Bus series since 1986. But this may be their most challenging subject yet. As always, their explanations are clear, simple but accurate, and entertaining. Much of the information is conveyed by Degen's cartoon illustrations, speech bubbles, text boxes, and handwritten student reports. The students view ice melt in the Arctic, circle the world, and explore the atmosphere, sliding down sunbeams and watching greenhouse gases through "special microscope-goggles." They learn about a variety of energy alternatives and simple changes anyone can make. The concepts aren't new, but the presentation is sure to attract more readers. The ending "online chat" addresses some of the controversy and also distinguishes between Ms. Frizzle's fantasy world and the facts. This won the AAAS/Subaru SB&F Prize.

SCHAEFER, LOLA M.

An Island Grows

Illustrated by Cathie Felstead
New York: Greenwillow Books, 2006
ISBN: 978-0-066-23930-9 | **AGES 4–7**

"Magma glows. / Volcano blows. / Lava flows / and flows / and flows. / An island grows." Simple rhyming couplets and stylized illustrations combine here to introduce the process of volcanic island formation from undersea eruption to the island's eventual colonization by plants and people. While the text includes some appropriate scientific terms that will be unfamiliar, it has been set invitingly with only a phrase or two on a page, in large type. The illustrations vary in size and placement on the pages; some grow like the island, and some stretch across the spread. Done in cut-paper collage with the look of folk art, these document the process and change from seascape to thriving community with farms, markets, and celebrations. "Busy island in the sea, where only water used to be." An afterword describes the process in more detail, but still simply enough for primary students to understand and the author includes suggested titles for further research. Geology is an unusual subject in the picture book world. This Cybils finalist and CCBC Choice is a good beginning. It also received a Zolotow commendation for its picture book text.

WELLS, ROBERT E.

Why Do Elephants Need the Sun?

Illustrated by Robert E. Wells
Chicago: Albert Whitman, 2010
ISBN: 978-0-807-59081-2 | **AGES 6–9**

A series of engaging pen-and-acrylic illustrations of monkeys frolicking around a large elephant illustrates this relatively simple explanation of the importance of the sun in elephant's lives—and our own. Touching on photosynthesis, the water cycle, gravity, the sun's composition and the way it generates energy, as well as the many ways humans use solar energy, the text of this appealing AAAS/Subaru SB&F Prize finalist breaks down some important scientific concepts and connects them to a child's life and imagination. With one to three sentences on each double-page spread, information is well paced. The book must be turned vertically to appreciate some illustrations, another way to keep the child reader engaged. The scientific terms are not easy to read and there is no glossary; this book seems particularly intended for reading aloud. Wells concludes with further intriguing facts about the sun and a "thank you note to the world's scientists" for discovering so much about how the sun works, but provides no sources or suggestions for further exploration. Other titles in Wells's useful and attractive series of informational books include *What's So Special about Planet Earth?* (2009), *Did a Dinosaur Drink This Water?* (2006), and *Can You Count to a Googol?* (2000).

STARS AND THE UNIVERSE

FOX, KAREN C.

Older Than the Stars

Illustrated by Nancy Davis
Watertown, MA: Charlesbridge, 2010
ISBN: 978-1-570-91787-5 | **AGES 4–9**

"These are the blocks that formed from the bits that were born in the bang when the world began." A catchy, cumulative "House that Jack Built" rhyme is the entry point for learning some solid science here, current theories about the origin of the universe. Pointing out that we are all made of star stuff, the author concludes, "You are as old as the universe itself," a wonderfully mind-blowing concept for a young reader or listener. Each verse of the poem is hand-lettered on a double-page spread, illustrated with vibrant pencil, cut-paper, and potato prints digitally combined. Sidebars offer a fuller explanation of the stage presented in the rhyme, still using vocabulary appropriate to the intended audience; a glossary at the end defines concepts like *atom, proton*, and *universe*. The combination of lettering and pictures support the gradual coalescence of the random bits and blocks into the universe we now recognize. A final time line, not to scale, summarizes the growth of the universe from something smaller than a speck of dust to the expanding one we continue to learn about today. Energetic and imaginative, these appealing illustrations and memorable text beg to be shared.

KUDLINSKI, KATHLEEN V.

Boy, Were We Wrong about the Solar System!

Illustrated by John Rocco
New York: Dutton Children's Books, 2008
ISBN: 978-0-525-46979-7 | **AGES 6–9**

This quick history of scientific theories about the solar system emphasizes changes in our understandings since the time of the Greeks and Romans from the discovery that the earth was round and not the center of the system to the recognition that Pluto is not a major planet but part of a group of dwarf planets. The author also makes a point of describing changes in the tools scientists use. The naked eye yielded to the telescope; records were kept over time revealing the recurrence of comets; radio telescopes, space exploration, and the Hubble Space Telescope all have contributed to our increasing knowledge. Rocco's computer-enhanced caricatures add humor, showing astronomers through the ages and even a group of future children at a space museum on the moon. Varied in size, shape, and placement on the page they keep the eye engaged. Further names and dates are provided in a back matter time line, and the author also includes a bibliography and some suggested further resources, including the NASA kids website. This reminder that science is not a collection of static facts to be memorized is a companion to Kudlinski's AAAS/Subaru SB&F Prize finalist, *Boy, Were We Wrong about Dinosaurs!* (Dutton Children's Books, 2005).

MATHEMATICS

CAMPBELL, SARAH C., AND RICHARD P. CAMPBELL

Growing Patterns: Fibonacci Numbers in Nature

Illustrated with photographs by Sarah C. and Richard P. Campbell
Honesdale, PA: Boyds Mills Press, 2010
ISBN: 978-1-590-78752-6 | **AGES 5–10**

In the natural world, many flowers and plants with parts arranged around a stem show a pattern known to ancient mathematicians called *Fibonacci numbers*. The Campbells demonstrate this sequence through photographs of flowers arranged in an ever increasing spiral representing not only the numbers 1, 1, 2, 3, 5, 8 but also a curving line much like the golden ratio. Then, intriguingly, for older readers most likely to be curious about the math, they go on to show how these numbers turn up in the pinecone bracts, sunflower heads, and the sections of a pineapple skin. Tinted rows and numbers allow for easier counting. Finally, they show a cutaway of chambered nautilus shell, demonstrating the spiral in the animal world. Not all plants and animals show this pattern; readers are invited to take a closer look outside. This text is deceptively simple at the beginning. Readers may be drawn unawares into surprisingly sophisticated mathematical thinking, and the explanation is clear. Back matter provides more information about number series and the golden spiral, along with a glossary. This clever presentation of an important mathematical concept made both the ALSC Notable and CBC/NSTA lists.

D'AGNESE, JOSEPH

Blockhead: The Life of Fibonacci

Illustrated by John O'Brien
New York: Henry Holt, 2010
ISBN: 978-0-805-06305-9 | **AGES 6–10**

Born in Pisa at a time when people still calculated with Roman numerals, young Leonardo was fascinated by numbers. Inattentive to his other schoolwork, he was called "blockhead." His father wanted him to be a merchant and took him to North Africa where he learned the Hindu/Arab number system we use today and came home to promote its use. Humor in both the fine-line illustrations and the colloquial text adds interest to this accessible story of a man who loved math. The narrative includes the famous reproducing rabbit problem, the Fibonacci number sequence, and the spiral they create. Although no one actually knows if Fibonacci understood the significance of the sequence he discovered, the author posits an imaginary friend to whom he explains its meaning, pointing out its significance in the natural world. A page of biography at the end places this thirteenth century mathematician in history, and the book ends with puzzle questions asking the reader to find examples of the numbers and the spirals in the text. This is an excellent introduction to this mathematical sequence for young readers, and also provides an unusual and appealing look at the medieval world.

FRANCO, BETSY

Zero Is the Leaves on the Tree

Illustrated by Shino Arihara
Berkeley: Tricycle Press, 2009
ISBN: 978-1-582-46249-3 | **AGES 2–7**

This gentle, poetic picture book introduces the concept of zero using examples from school and play, spanning the seasons from fall to summer. With an opening description of its egglike shape and the statement "Zero is a number," Franco goes on to explain this abstract idea in concrete terms. Although some examples refer to school life, many will be familiar even to very young listeners, just learning to count: "Zero is . . . / the sound of snowflakes / landing on your mitten. 0 sounds." Each double-page spread repeats the pattern. The contemplative mood extends to Arihara's gouache paintings. In muted colors, against an expansive background of land and sky, she shows children, sometimes singly and sometimes in groups, engaged in a variety of activities including playing ball, walking a dog, trudging through mud season, swimming in a pool, helping in the garden, building a sand castle, and looking at night stars. Within the mixed groups of children, individuals are identifiable, adding another layer of interest. This unusual title can extend a child's mathematical understanding but appeals to the senses as well. With its calm repetition and nighttime ending, it might even become part of a bedtime routine. This was a CCBC Choice.

ROBBINS, KEN

For Good Measure: The Ways We Say How Much, How Far, How Heavy, How Big, How Old

Illustrated with photographs by Ken Robbins
New York: Roaring Brook Press, 2010
ISBN: 978-1-596-43344-1 | **AGES 7–12**

In this intriguing title, units of measurement common in American English (and some from literature) are defined with illustrative, explanatory photographs, and their likely etymology described. A male model demonstrates units built on the human body: a foot, a hand, a yard, a fathom. Overhead photographs show a mile, a league, an acre, and a section. The objects are familiar: a soccer ball weighs a pound, five quarters are roughly an ounce, ice cream and strawberries come in pints (wet and dry), and so forth. Most of the photographs were taken by the author/illustrator but there are drawings from elsewhere including da Vinci's "Vitruvian Man" on the title page. For the most part, each page introduces a single unit. Some text may be difficult for young readers and listeners, but the pictures make the meaning clear. A sidebar in the introduction explains the metric system, and metric equivalents are provided in the book. Math and science teachers may notice omissions and some imprecision, but will welcome the title for the way it connects measurement concepts to a student's everyday world. This was an Orbis Pictus recommended book.

5

The World We Make

H UMANS ARE NATURALLY CURIOUS and inventive, and young children are fascinated by tools, equipment, and explorations of all kinds, in the home and in the world. Some can name every kind of construction vehicle; others play endlessly with cars and trucks. They want to know about things that go, from farm tractors to airplanes. While few children today have even visited a real farm, most have watched road builders, and many have watched rocket launches. They wonder about origins, and they dream about driving and flying themselves. From farming to space travel, this section includes books to inspire budding cooks, gardeners, inventors, pilots, and engineers.

FOOD AND FARMING

ARGUETO, JORGE

Sopa de frijoles: Un poema para cocinar / Bean Soup: A Cooking Poem

Illustrated by Rafael Yockteng
Toronto, ON: Groundwood Books/Libros Tigrillo/House of Anansi Press, 2009
ISBN: 978-0-888-99881-1 | **AGES 5–9**

This celebration of the act of cooking offers a gentle, free-verse recipe for making a "loving lovely bean soup" with beans, garlic, onion, and salt. "Thank you for your lovely taste," you say to the onion as you cut it up; you bury the peel and garlic skins "so Mother Earth keeps on growing

FACING PAGE ART FROM

Roadwork by Sally Sutton

flavors." The Spanish comes first on the page and is more lyrical, but both versions work. Yockteng's earth-toned paintings, framed with a slightly irregular white border, perfectly support the anticipation of the narrative. In one picture the small cook winks at his mother, who occasionally appears in a supervisory way but whose face is never shown. He dances around the kitchen, enjoying the aroma. In the text, "The water boils and sings. / The beans dance / together." Served with tortillas to his waiting family, it provides a yummy meal. An asterisk marks steps where adult supervision is necessary. The recipe does not mention presoaking the beans, but is otherwise perfectly workable. This USBBY Outstanding International Book and CCBC Choice is a tasty treat. Argueto's joyful *Arroz con leche / Rice Pudding* (Groundwood Books, 2010), illustrated by Fernando Vilela, is equally delicious.

BARASCH, LYNNE

Hiromi's Hands

Illustrated by Lynne Barasch
New York: Lee & Low Books, 2007
ISBN: 978-1-584-30275-9 | **AGES 5–9**

Hiromi Suzuki, Japanese American daughter of a sushi chef, grew up to be an *itamae-san*, a sushi chef herself, thanks to the larger possibilities for women in the United States. Her imagined first-person narrative opens with her parents' return to visit family in Japan, where her father had grown up poor, trained to choose and slice fish and make perfect rolls, and left when sent to New York by his restaurant owner. There he flourished, opening his own restaurant and, later, training his daughter at her insistence. The story includes details about Japanese culture, but what will probably most engage its readers are the details of making the sushi in its many varieties. Barasch illustrates this story about her daughter's childhood friend with watercolor-and-ink sketches filled with details of fish markets, different kinds of fish, and different sushi preparations. In front, a single endpaper and half-title show a variety of sushi ingredients; in back, opposite the glossary and pronunciation guide, varied forms are displayed on traditional plates. Disappointingly, the Japanese characters shown are not real, and some conversations and feelings are imagined; the unusual factual content outweighs these shortcomings. This won an APALA honorable mention for its illustration and made the Amelia Bloomer list.

COOPER, ELISHA

Farm

Illustrated by Elisha Cooper
New York: Orchard Books, 2010
ISBN: 978-0-545-07075-1 | **AGES 5–10**

This charming picture book describes life on a modern midwestern farm, from tilling the soil in April, through planting and harvesting corn, until the land can rest in November, waiting for next year. Cooper opens with the farm's ingredients: people, buildings and heavy equipment, animals. In straightforward sentences, he chronicles their activities and even the feel of the changing seasons. "March is mud month." On May nights, "everyone itches." In August, "it's so steamy the horizon shimmers." The effect is calm and almost poetic. The slightly distant tone begins on the endpapers where a checkerboard of roads, fields, and farms forms the abstract pattern you might see from an airplane. Some animals have names, but not the farmer, the second farmer, the boy, or the girl whose year we follow. The tiny featureless figures in Cooper's watercolor paintings, unframed vignettes on a slightly oversized page, emphasize the vast Midwest landscape. Occasional scenes stretch across the gutter, and two full-bleed, double-page spreads provide a real change of pace: the farm at night under a starry sky and after a storm. The text of this ALSC Notable is lengthy for a read-aloud but informative. Cooper provides a similarly appealing account of a day at the shore in *Beach* (Orchard Books, 2006).

GOLDISH, MEISH

Bug-a-Licious

Illustrated with photographs
New York: Bearport, 2009
ISBN: 978-1-597-16757-4 | **AGES 7–11**

More than 1,700 kinds of insects are eaten in over one hundred countries worldwide, according to the author of this undeniably appealing—or perhaps disgusting—picture book. From leaf-footed bugs on Mexican pizza to crickets in lollipops in the United States, each double-page spread includes a two- or three-paragraph description (on a paper napkin background) and a photograph of the food, plus an inset photo of the animal and an additional fast fact. The text includes descriptions of how the insects are caught and prepared, and, from time to time, their taste and nutrient value. The author makes clear (and the cover reiterates) "one eater's 'yuck!' is another eater's 'yum!'" Crackers with wasps from Japan, water bugs fried or boiled in Thailand, termites raw in Uganda, roasted in Nigeria or fried in Ghana, dried stinkbugs in South Africa—the author provides nine examples and includes a world map. A glossary of words bolded in the text, an index, and a bibliography support the text. Part of the publisher's Extreme Cuisine series, a website offers links to additional information. Other titles describe meals of spiders, unusual mammals, reptiles and amphibians, and surprising seafood. One of *Booklist*'s top new nonfiction series for youth and a CBC/IRA Children's Choice.

GOODMAN, SUSAN E.

All in Just One Cookie

Illustrated by Timothy Bush
New York: Greenwillow Books, 2006
ISBN: 978-0-060-09092-0 | **AGES 6–10**

As Grandma puts together the dough, her dog and cat discover where and how we get each ingredient, from butter and sugar through to the chocolate chips. They watch as the baking turns each one into a chocolate chip cookie. This clever concept is appealingly illustrated with muted watercolors in a variety of panels. From hand washing to serving, Grandma's step-by-step activities are shown framed in light wood with carved hearts. Other information is provided in insets of various sizes and shapes using a different font. The cat and dog, and sometimes other animals, provide side comments. Their cheerful cartoon faces echo Grandma's enthusiasm, and likely that of the reader. The cat is the researcher, using a variety of sources from library and Internet to Grandma's encyclopedias. The bouncy dog can hardly wait to eat; there is a special chocolate-free, bone-shaped treat for him. While the cookies are cooling, all three admire a world map showing where the ingredients came from; many are produced in various parts of the world. Who could resist Grandma, with her pink sneakers and her plateful of cookies? A recipe is included. An ALSC Notable.

MORA, PAT

Yum! ¡Mmmm! ¡Qué rico! Americas' Sproutings

Illustrated by Rafael López
New York: Lee & Low Books, 2007
ISBN: 978-1-584-30271-1 | **AGES 7–10**

From the blueberry to vanilla, foods that originated in the Americas are celebrated in fourteen haiku, while sidebars explain the likely origin of each ingredient. This interesting and versatile combination of poetry and information will appeal to a variety of readers and tastes. López illustrates each double-page spread with fanciful acrylic paintings done on wood panels. A father breathes fire from his green chile. A grinning girl licks chocolate from her lips. People fly through the air, a lizard munches a prickly pear, and a pineapple dances. The poetry celebrates sensations and sounds as well as taste: cranberries pop, peanut butter is smeared, pecan shells must be cracked, and red tomatoes "burst in your mouth." The book opens with a simple, unlabeled map of the Americas; the variety of backgrounds suggests the range of natural environments in which each food grows. Sources for the author's information are provided on the verso and an author's note combines all fourteen ingredients into a jump rope rhyme at the end. This was an Americás Award winner and an ALSC Notable. It has also been published in Spanish and in a bilingual edition.

PURMELL, ANN

Maple Syrup Season

Illustrated by Jill Weber
New York: Holiday House, 2008
ISBN: 978-0-823-41891-6 | Ages 5–9

In late winter, when the sap is running in the maple trees, it's maple syrup season. The whole extended family gathers to tap the trees, collect the sap, boil it down, and make syrup and delicious sugar-on-snow taffy. Although the family is fictional and the illustrations add some fanciful details (rabbits and a raccoon carrying a sap bucket away), this is a clear and informative explanation of the traditional syrup-making process. The text is relatively simple and straightforward, set on full-bleed illustrations done with gouache, artist's crayons, gesso, and plastic wrap. The naive art could represent almost any time period, but the setting is probably present-day New England. The characters are easily recognizable: Dad with his glasses and neatly trimmed beard, Hannah with her plaid shirt and braids, and Hayden with his green and yellow cap and mittens. A cat and dog follow the action, too. Two pages of "Maple Syrup Lore" and a "Maple Syrup Glossary" add more specific details about the process and the product. This sweet celebration was a CBC/NCSS Notable. Pair this with Purmell's earlier *Christmas Tree Farm* (2006).

REYNOLDS, JAN

Cycle of Rice, Cycle of Life: A Story of Sustainable Farming

Illustrated with photographs by Jan Reynolds
New York: Lee & Low Books, 2009
ISBN: 978-1-600-60254-2 | **AGES 8-12**

Since the ninth century, Balinese farmers have been apportioning water and growing rice according to a system that allows their fields to lie fallow long enough to regenerate, a system that turns out to be more productive than an experiment with the green revolution in the late twentieth century. This photo essay for middle grade and middle school readers describes the intricate relationship between the water cycle, the religion, and the agricultural practices of that Indonesian island. Their traditional system included a period when ducks grazed the stubble in the fields, eating insect pests and providing fertilizer. Priests and ritual gatherings allocated the water coming from the mountains to individual farms. The text explains the work of an American anthropologist and scientists who determined that the traditional system was more effective. The attraction for younger readers will be the beautiful photographs of rice fields, Balinese temples, citizens making offerings, and children working in the fields. The back matter includes an author's note about sustainable agriculture contrasting Balinese farming practices with those in the United States, a map, and a glossary. This attractive presentation appears on the John Burroughs and IRA Global Notable lists.

SIDDALS, MARY MCKENNA

Compost Stew: An A to Z Recipe for the Earth

Illustrated by Ashley Wolff
Berkeley: Tricycle Press, 2010
ISBN: 978-1-582-46316-2 | **AGES 4-7**

Aided by a goose and a spotted dog, four fictional children add ingredients to their pot of compost stew throughout the year in this cheerful, environmentally conscious book. The rhyming instructions for composting use an alphabet of ingredients from apple cores to zinnia heads. Textured papers, fabric, old calendar pages, and more are the materials for the collage and gouache illustrations that exemplify adaptive reuse.

The children represent a racial mixture; their pot is a large compost bin. Working inside and out, they collect materials, moisten, stir, and cover their concoction. The author has included some that readers might not have thought of themselves—hair clippings, dryer lint, paper shreds, and quarry dust. A note in the front adds further information and suggests a website. The rhymes and rhythm work and would be fun to read aloud; the author has broken up the alphabet along the way with her refrain: "Just add to the pot / and let it all rot / into Compost Stew." The illustrations are large enough to show a group but include intriguing details. The endpapers show earthworms working their way through the rich, brown result. Charming and kid-friendly.

CONSTRUCTION, EQUIPMENT, AND THINGS THAT GO

ABRAMSON, ANDRA SERLIN

Heavy Equipment Up Close

Illustrated with photographs
New York: Sterling, 2007
ISBN: 978-1-402-74799-1 | **AGES 7–12**

Imagine a machine more than twenty-two stories tall, another longer than two football fields! Imagine one able to carry the space shuttle! These are just a few of the machines pictured in this oversized album whose cover, with its equipment montage and jutting-out dump truck, is sure to appeal to construction equipment fans. Double-, triple-, and quadruple-page foldouts show giant trucks, mining machines, cranes, tree harvesters, pavers, and more. The accompanying text describes their size, weight, use, and some history, sometimes using technical language not defined. Some components (like the gears on a tracked vehicle) are shown actual size; many pictures include a human for scale. Frankly a book for browsing, the large-font text provides multiple entry points; most paragraphs have a headline. Extra information is provided in captions and text boxes. An index allows easy access to favorite pages. Most of the illustrations are stock photographs, and there is no documentation or follow-up reading suggestions—but the dog-eared condition of the library copy I read suggests that young browsers don't care. Fighter planes, fire engines, race cars, ships, and submarines are other topics written by this author for the Up Close series, one of *Booklist*'s Top 10 series.

COPPENDALE, JEAN

Fire Trucks and Rescue Vehicles

Illustrated with photographs
Buffalo, NY: Firefly Books, 2010
ISBN: 978-1-554-07621-5 | **AGES 4–8**

Designed to attract early readers, the easy-to-read text and bright photographs of this topic book describe a variety of rescue vehicles from firefighting ladder trucks to police cars and motorcycles. Each double-page spread features a large photograph of the vehicle; most also include an inset, boldly framed in color. The author describes the use of helicopters in forest fires, road and mountain accidents, and sea rescues; specialized equipment such as airport fire trucks, fireboats, and lifeboats; ambulances; and the use of a fleet of motorcycles for protection in a motorcade. A paragraph of simple text introduces each subject; captions explain each picture. A glossary defines words boldfaced in the text, such as *criminals*, *paramedics*, and even *vehicle*. There is a page of activities and an index. Some scenes are quite dramatic: a man and a dog hang in midair from a helicopter; fireboats are shown in action spraying the smoke-filled back of a ship; paramedics tend a highway victim. Photographs for this English import have come from all over the world, and the appeal of the series—which includes titles about cars, tractors, trucks, bulldozers, cranes, diggers, and loaders—is obvious. One of *Booklist*'s Top 10 Early Literacy series.

FLOCA, BRIAN

Lightship

Illustrated by Brian Floca
New York: Atheneum Books for Young Readers, 2007
ISBN: 978-1-416-92436-4 | **AGES 4–8**

The lightship *Ambrose* holds her place no matter what. With a simple, perfectly paced text, the author-illustrator conveys the hurry-up-and-wait life of the crew, anchored at sea to warn other ships by sight and sound of hazards below. The specific ship and its crew and cat are imagined, but the details of their lives are real: "The higher the waves, / the harder the work; / the harder it is to climb the stairs, / to check the charts / to drink the coffee, / to visit the head." The present-tense narrative adds immediacy to this piece of the past. Floca's watercolor-and-ink illustrations, from vignettes to double-page spreads, are full of tiny details. They show the ship inside and out, in all kinds of weather and throughout the year. The central double-page spread shows a near miss, as the SS *Ardizzone* comes too close. Floca's homage is explicit. On the endpapers, a labeled cutaway drawing of the ship includes the crew's gin rummy game and the terns flying by. An author's note adds more history, noting that the last lightship in this country ended service in 1983. This ALSC Notable won a Cybils Award in the nonfiction picture book category.

HOPKINSON, DEBORAH

Sky Boys: How They Built the Empire State Building

Illustrated by James Ransome
New York: Schwartz & Wade Books, 2006
ISBN: 978-0-375-83610-7 | **AGES 5–9**

Endpapers with photographs from the times will draw readers into this story of the construction of the Empire State Building in New York City, beginning in 1930. A fictional frame adds emotion to the story, told by a boy whose father is unemployed, like many during the Depression. His awe and admiration are clear. But the focus of this narrative is the building process. In clear, accessible free verse, Hopkinson describes the arrival of steel girders on "rumbling flatbed trucks." The skeleton is assembled; the sky boys "crawl / like spiders on steel, / spinning their giant web in the sky." Step by step she shows the riveting process and later, the addition of a skin. Oil paintings with varying perspectives, sequential frames, and full-page or spread illustrations (for one, you must turn the book sideways) add interest and information. There are dramatic skies and dizzying views of the ground below. Finally the boy and his father enter the completed building, ride up the long elevator, and see what the sky boys have seen. An afterword adds further information about the building and the author's research. This CCBC Choice and ALSC Notable won a Boston Globe–Horn Book honor.

HUDSON, CHERYL WILLIS

Construction Zone

Illustrated with photographs by Richard Sobol
Cambridge, MA: Candlewick Press, 2006
ISBN: 978-0-763-62684-6 | **AGES 5–9**

Step by step, photographs and simple text follow the construction of the Stata Center in Cambridge, Massachusetts, from architect drawings (including endpapers from the Gehry studio) to the finished building. The author presents the project as one of fitting together the pieces of a puzzle; the photographer shows the diversity of the people involved. The design of this book reinforces its subject. A question-mark road sign usually set off with yellow-and-black caution tape marks definitions for subject-specific words used and bolded on the page: words like *architect, rebar, crane, scaffolds, insulation, fixtures*. The color photographs, full of details to puzzle out, will intrigue a lap-sitter or independent reader. Their varied angles and thoughtful composition are more artistic than informational, but they do support the text. For two pictures of the nearly complete building, the designer has made use of the color in the photograph, setting the text of one against the yellow plastic wrapping that covered the building's metal skin, and another against a near-night sky. A photographer's note describes the potential danger of walking around a construction site and shares his enthusiasm for the process. Young construction buffs will also be enthusiastic about this Orbis Pictus recommended book, a CCBC Choice.

SUTTON, SALLY

Roadwork

Illustrated by Brian Lovelock
Cambridge, MA: Candlewick Press, 2008
ISBN: 978-0-763-63912-9 | **AGES 2–6**

"Tip the stones. Tip the stones. / Lift and slide and dump. / Lay the groundwork for the road. / Crash! ROAR! **THUMP!**" Step by step, this chronological description of road building is a celebration of sights and sounds, and a read-aloud winner. The rhythmic, repetitive language, perfect rhyme and scansion, and onomatopoetic words will have young listeners chanting along in no time. The vocabulary is simple and the text large, encouraging young readers. Each double-page spread features a single stanza, ending with three punchy words in increasingly larger, bolder type. The pictures are large and bright; they show well even to groups. They feature a variety of machines, identified on a back page of "Machine Facts," a kind of glossary in words and pictures. They also feature a diverse road crew, including women. Clean lines show details of each machine well, without cluttering the pages. These pigmented ink illustrations have the look of textured paintings, complete with bits of grit. The asphalt endpapers add to the effect. First published in New Zealand, where it won the picture book section of the New Zealand Book Award, this was a CCBC Choice in the United States.

INVENTORS AND INVENTIONS

BARRETTA, GENE

Neo Leo: The Ageless Ideas of Leonardo da Vinci

Illustrated by Gene Barretta
New York: Henry Holt, 2009
ISBN: 978-0-805-08703-1 | **AGES 8–12**

Sketches and mirror-written notes reassembled after his death show that hundreds of years ago Leonardo da Vinci thought up modern inventions including gliders, contact lenses, an automatic rotisserie, and more. A breezy text provides a short introduction to the man and then, on facing pages, describes and dates each invention's first appearance in the modern world (Neo) and shows Leonardo's version (Leo). The author-illustrator cleverly combines his brown-toned versions of the inventor's sketches with a backward script with additional description. Readers can puzzle it out or run for a hand mirror. Barretta sets his story in time with an opening double-page spread full of humorous allusions to the Italian Renaissance. The light tone continues throughout the book. Rather than an introduction to the man's life, this is a surprisingly sophisticated introduction to his ideas for readers with ideas of their own. An author's note at the beginning of this CBC/NCSS Notable and IRA Teachers' Choice describes da Vinci's notes; a bibliography of books, websites, and DVDs at the end offers suggestions for further exploration. Barretta wrote similarly about the inventions of Ben Franklin in *Now and Ben: The Modern Inventions of Ben Franklin* (Henry Holt, 2006), also honored by NCSS.

BARTON, CHRIS

The Day-Glo Brothers

Illustrated by Tony Persiani
Watertown, MA: Charlesbridge, 2009
ISBN: 978-1-570-91673-1 | **AGES 7–11**

Stories of inventions always appeal and this one highlights a particularly bright idea. An accident in 1933 led Bob Switzer to spend months recuperating in a dark basement, where his brother Joe was experimenting with light. Together they discovered the interesting effects of chemicals added to paints viewed under ultraviolet light. They continued to experiment with chemicals, light, and paint. Ultimately they discovered a combination that glowed in ordinary light as well. Day-Glo paints, used first in World War II, are everywhere today and used lavishly in the book. The cover illustration of a globe circled with Day-Glo orange sums up the story, and the endpapers, in orange, yellow, and chartreuse reinforce the effect. Persiani's whimsical cartoons begin in gray, adding muted color accents as the research progresses. When they finally succeed, the billboard breakthrough sprouts tongues of bright orange flame. In the end matter the author explains how regular and daylight fluorescence work; there is an animated demonstration and discussion guide on the publisher's web page. The author's note describes his research. As a biography, chronicle of invention, or spur for research, this should have appeal for both curious young and reluctant older readers. A Sibert honor book and ALSC Notable, this won a Cybils Award.

KRULL, KATHLEEN

The Boy Who Invented TV: The Story of Philo Farnsworth

Illustrated by Greg Couch
New York: Alfred A. Knopf, 2009
ISBN: 978-0-375-84561-1 | **AGES 7–10**

Born in 1906 on a farm in Utah, Farnsworth was mechanically gifted from early childhood, and fascinated by the new inventions using electricity. As a teenager, he came up with a way to broadcast images, discussing his idea with a teacher and, at 21, built the first successful TV. This biography shows other sides of this inventor: he played the violin, invented a washing machine, and courted and married a woman who helped him build his first models. The text appears in a rounded box along with a small image or two on one side of the double-page spread, opposite a full-page illustration created mostly in muted tones with acrylic wash and colored pencil. These often show the lanky boy with his head full of schematic diagrams. The endpapers, with their images of television sets through the years, are a nice touch. The author's note explains how Farnsworth was finally awarded priority of invention but no credit or money for his invention in his lifetime. The bibliography highlights books for young readers and suggests related websites and an archived television show. This Orbis Pictus recommended book also appeared on the CBC/NSTA list and won a Parents' Choice Gold Award.

MCCARTHY, MEGHAN

Pop! The Accidental Invention of Bubble Gum

Illustrated by Meghan McCarthy
New York: Simon & Schuster Books for Young Readers, 2010
ISBN: 978-1-416-97970-8 | **AGES 5–9**

In the Fleer chewing gum factory in the 1920s, accountant Walter Diemer grew interested in their quest to make a gum that could be used to blow bubbles. He continued to play around with mixtures after others had given up, finally discovering the magic formula for Dubble Bubble in 1928. Its signature pink color was accidental, too, the only color he had on hand. McCarthy surrounds her simple story of Diemer's invention with interesting facts about chewing gum's history. She includes quotations and brings her biography of the inventor right up through his rise to vice president of the company and retirement. "I've done something with my life. . . . I've made kids happy around the world." Short, simple text is printed on a background of humorous, mostly full-bleed double-page acrylic paintings in lively pinks, greens, and browns. McCarthy's round-faced, pop-eyed characters are particularly appropriate to her bubbling subject. Back matter adds more facts about the man, about the benefits of chewing gum, and about gum's history, including a photograph of a wall of gum deposits in Seattle. A bibliography provides the sources for her quotations. This Cybils finalist is a sweet treat.

MCCULLY, EMILY ARNOLD

Marvelous Mattie: How Margaret E. Knight Became an Inventor

Illustrated by Emily Arnold McCully
New York: Farrar Straus Giroux, 2006
ISBN: 978-0-374-34810-6 | **AGES 7–10**

Loving the process of inventing and making things, Margaret Knight (Mattie to her family) made toys for her brothers, a shuttle guard for the looms at the mill where she worked in Manchester, New Hampshire, and a machine that would make flat-bottomed paper bags for which, after a court case, she won a patent in 1871. The challenges she faced as a woman inventor are shown in the text, and made even clearer in an author's note that also explains that no one actually knows what the device was she invented, at the age of 12, to prevent further injuries by flying shuttles like the one that felled her neighbor. The author invents conversations throughout her text, but the facts of Knight's story are true and will appeal to today's young readers. McCully's pen-and-ink drawings of Mattie's ideas imitate those done for Knight's patent; they run along the bottom of many pages, which also include ink-and-watercolor illustrations for her story showing an endlessly curious Mattie. The short bibliography lists the author's sources, but there are no suggestions for further reading. This AAAS/Subaru SB&F Prize finalist and Outstanding Science Trade Book was a CCBC Choice and made the Amelia Bloomer list.

MORTENSEN, LORI

Come See the Earth Turn: The Story of Léon Foucault

Illustrated by Raúl Allén
Berkeley: Tricycle Press, 2010
ISBN: 978-1-582-46284-4 | **AGES 7–9**

In Europe, in the early 1800s, people accepted that Earth rotates on an axis, but no one had proved this scientific fact. The focus of this biography is the "beautiful experiment" designed by Léon Foucault, a slow, shy boy who grew up to be a clever inventor. Although he had had no formal scientific training, he was curious about microscopes, cameras, and the speed of light. One day, watching the movements of a steel rod in a lathe, he realized how a pendulum could show the turning of the earth. And in 1851 he demonstrated that to a group of Parisian scientists. The story of a scientist who fails in school but discovers great things is a familiar one, but perennially popular. Mortensen tells this one in a straightforward fashion, easy to digest even if the reader isn't quite clear about the actual science. Allen's pencil-and-watercolor illustrations, digitally finished, feature the brown tones assigned to historical times. Sometimes they show incidents in panels; sometimes they spread across both pages. Always, they convey a sense of the time and place. This CBC/NSTA Outstanding Science Trade Book includes a helpful pronunciation guide, glossary, and bibliography of the author's sources.

MURPHY, GLENN

Inventions

Illustrated with photographs
New York: Simon & Schuster Books for Young Readers, 2009
ISBN: 978-1-416-93865-1 | **AGES 7–12**

From the wheel to the Internet, this addition to the popular Insiders series profiles twenty-three inventions that have changed the way humans use and understand their world. Like others in the series, this opens with an introductory section. This defines *invention*, provides a time line, and describes the tools of our Stone Age ancestors. The bulk of the book consists of double-page spreads devoted to specific inventions. Each includes a descriptive paragraph and a variety of examples, with labels and short explanations. Busy pages of computer-enhanced imagery include a number of smaller pictures set on a double-page photograph. Some spreads require that you turn the book lengthwise. Along the bottom of each is a time line for that invention. For music players, for example, the time line runs from Edison's phonograph, through a gramophone using a flat disc, a Walkman, a compact disc player, and a digital audio player. A few inventions may surprise readers by their inclusion or their long history: the power station, locks and keys, and bionics for better bodies. Others are obvious: the printing press, the telescope, the automobile, and rocket. This CBC/NSTA Outstanding Science Trade Book includes an index and glossary but no sources. It's a treat for browsers and inventors-to-be.

FLIGHT AND SPACE TRAVEL

BROWN, TAMI LEWIS

Soar, Elinor!

Illustrated by François Roca
New York: Melanie Kroupa Books, 2010
ISBN: 978-0-374-37115-9 | **AGES 6–10**

Born in 1917, Elinor Smith's first plane ride at the age of 6 made her determined to become a pilot. She took flying lessons as a teen and by 16 was a licensed pilot. Her most famous feat was flying a tiny biplane under all four of the bridges spanning New York's East River, the event on which this biography focuses. The story is told with enthusiasm and no little drama. From the beginning, Smith heard that her dreams were impossible: she was too young to take lessons, too young to solo, and "not good enough" to fly under a bridge: "Airplanes are for men and boys." The author, a licensed pilot herself, measures out her information so that suspense builds to the culminating flight. She deftly weaves in quotations from her own interviews with the pioneering aviator as well as written sources. Bold oil paintings, mostly on double-page spreads, set the story in time and place. They often include a broad expanse of sky behind the human figures. Roca's static style adds to the sense of history. This Amelia Bloomer selection concludes with a note about Smith's later life, a few photographs, a narrative description of the author's research, and a list of sources.

BURLEIGH, ROBERT

One Giant Leap

Illustrated by Mike Wimmer
New York: Philomel Books, 2009
ISBN: 978-0-399-23883-3 | **AGES 5–9**

Simple poetic sentences and oil paintings recall the first moon landing in 1969 from the separation and descent of the *Eagle* through the astronauts' first steps and exploration, their journey back up to rejoin *Columbia*, and subsequent return to Earth. Burleigh's accessible text, usually one sentence per line, focuses on the three men. There are moments of tension as Collins waits to hear of the landing and then waits for their return, as Aldrin and Armstrong approach their landing watching their fuel dwindle, and later as they wait for their craft to ignite for liftoff. There are moments, too, of pure joy as the two step out to explore the silent world, collect rocks, and raise the flag, and finally all three triumphantly return to earth. The text is set in white on a dark background, shades of blue, green, brown, and black picking up colors in the painting on the facing page. Double-page spreads show the *Eagle* on the moon and, later, the men dancing across its surface. In both, a half-earth hangs silently above. For young readers who can't get enough of this story, this Orbis Pictus recommended book and Outstanding Science Trade Book is a good complement to Brian Floca's *Moonshot* (below).

DEMAREST, CHRIS L.

Hurricane Hunters! Riders on the Storm

Illustrated by Chris L. Demarest
New York: Margaret K. McElderry Books, 2006
ISBN: 978-0-689-86168-0 | **AGES 5–9**

As a hurricane approaches the Atlantic coast, members of the Air Force's 53rd Weather Reconnaissance Squadron take off in a specially equipped WC-130 Hercules turboprop airplane to fly into the eye and measure the storm. The simple text serves as captions for the double-page full-bleed illustrations, appropriately large-sized for the large-sized storm. Chalk pastel illustrations contrast the relaxation of beachgoers with the hardworking people at the National Hurricane Center. They show the plane taking off, the force of the winds on a small tropical island, the deployment of the crew among their many instruments, the dropsonde with its parachute descending into the storm, and civilian preparations below. One particularly effective spread contrasts the small size of the plane, shown in the hurricane's eye, with the huge and chaotic ocean swells. The book opens with a labeled line drawing of the plane and closes with an extensive author's note. References include one no-longer-working website, but the information is still accurate. Demarest, a volunteer firefighter, has written earlier books about men and women facing danger, including *Mayday! Mayday!* (Margaret K. McElderry Books, 2004), about the Coast Guard, and *Hotshots!* (Margaret K. McElderry Books, 2003), about firefighters. This was a CBC/NCSS Notable and CCBC Choice.

FLOCA, BRIAN

Moonshot: The Flight of Apollo 11

Illustrated by Brian Floca
New York: Atheneum Books for Young Readers, 2009
ISBN: 978-1-416-95046-2 | **AGES 4–7**

This celebration of the first moon landing, describing the process step-by-step with simple, poetic text and watercolor-and-ink illustrations, is an ideal introduction to that historic event. Floca begins with the destination and with the astronauts' suiting up. *Columbia* and *Eagle* are almost invisible atop a towering rocket that lifts off with a mighty shower of debris on a powerful double-page spread. The reader sees men working in control rooms, bystanders watching the launch. Illustrations emphasize the jumble of dials and floating objects inside the astronauts' quarters and the difficulties of ordinary life, including going to the bathroom. The *Eagle* lands, Armstrong and Allen walk away from their tiny craft and admire the earth glowing in the sky. A family watches on television. The splash of their return to earth comes as a relief. The text reads aloud beautifully; the illustrations are accurate and full of details. The front endpapers offer a description of the vehicles and stages; in back is a more detailed narrative history. One of the *New York Times* Best Illustrated Books; finalist for the AAAS/Subaru SB&F Prize, the Cybils Award, and Children's Choice; a Sibert honor book and ALSC Notable, this book is as breathtaking as the event itself.

PLATT, RICHARD

Moon Landing

Illustrated by David Hawcock

Cambridge, MA: Candlewick Press, 2008

ISBN: 978-0-763-64046-0 | **AGES 7 AND UP**

Elaborate pop-up engineering illustrates this fortieth anniversary celebration of the 1969 *Apollo 11* moon landing, providing both background and details of the flight equipment. Opening the first page reveals a Redstone rocket launching; the next has a Gemini spacewalk as well as a foldout illustration of the much larger Saturn 5. Lift the flaps to reveal its innards. Viewers can explore the sections of the moon shot spacecraft; pull a tab to see how the lunar module adapter cleverly folds up inside; and open 360 degrees to explore a moon globe. Another page reveals the workings of a spacesuit and a portable life-support system, and, finally, the *Eagle* pops up with Armstrong and Aldrin alongside. There is a great deal of information in the accompanying text, organized topically in five chapters: "Into Orbit," "Race to Space," "Moon Bound," "The Astronauts," and "Moon Landing." Two pullout books add more: a description of rocket pioneers and a collection of official pictures of Apollo crews. While the text is accurate, it's also relatively difficult to read; it's the intricate constructions that will appeal. The features of this CBC/NSTA Outstanding Science Trade Book are best explored on a large flat surface where the base of the book will be steady.

When he grew tired, he stretched out beside the Passaic River.
Gurgle, gurgle—swish, swish, swoosh!—gurgle, gurgle.

The water went slipping and sliding over
the smooth rocks, then poured in a torrent
over the falls, then quieted again below.
The river's music both excited and soothed Willie.
Sometimes, as he listened to its perfect tune,
he fell asleep.

6

The Things We Do

INFORMATIONAL BOOKS THAT TELL young children how to do things are few and far between. Such books are usually aimed at middle grade readers. But there is no lack of excellent books about how other people have done things. Biographies predominate in this section, stories of writers, artists, musicians, and performers of all kinds, as well as lives of famous athletes. In most cases, the child will never have heard of the man or woman; these are not stories of modern-day stars. Rather, they are introductions to people whose lives and works still have meaning in the twenty-first century.

WRITERS

BROWN, MONICA

My Name Is Gabito: The Life of Gabriel García Márquez

Illustrated by Raúl Colón
Flagstaff: Rising Moon, 2007
ISBN: 978-0-873-58934-5 | **AGES 7–12**

An imaginative child, born and raised in Aracataca, Colombia, where a ghost lady rocked their rocking chair and parrots could tell the future, Gabito grows up to be a famous storyteller. The flavor of the work of Garcia Márquez is captured in the offbeat imagery of both the words and the pictures in this charming biography. Beginning with a series of "Can you imagine" sentences to draw readers in, the simple text focuses on childhood experiences described in his memoir. The last paragraph tells reader that

FACING PAGE ART FROM

A River of Words by Jen Bryant

the small boy became a world-famous writer; more career details appear in an afterword. Colón's oil pastels soar across the pages. Fish and people fly. Plenty of white space around the details allows room for the reader's imagination as well. Tropical colors abound and the phrase *can you imagine* is repeated in script across some of the more magical images. This was an ALSC Notable, a commended title for the Américas Award, and a Pura Belpré honor book for its illustrations. Like its predecessors, *My Name Is Gabriela* (Luna Rising, 2005) and *My Name Is Celia* (Rising Moon, 2004), biographies of Gabriela Mistral and Celia Cruz, this is also available in a bilingual English/Spanish edition.

BRYANT, JEN

A River of Words: The Story of William Carlos Williams

Illustrated by Melissa Sweet
Grand Rapids: Eerdmans Books for Young Readers, 2008
ISBN: 978-0-802-85302-8 | **AGES 7–12**

In precise language characteristic of the poet, Bryant introduces the poet William Carlos Williams, who spent a lifetime delivering babies, treating children, and working on his poems. Her spare text and Sweet's masterful illustrations combine to show how much Williams's poetry was influenced by his early childhood experiences, his love of nature, and his remarkable attention to detail. Created in watercolor, collage, and mixed media, these illustrations have the air of pencil sketches, filled with ideas and words and often done on layers of lined paper or old textbooks. One page shows many different typed drafts of "so much depends." Another shows Williams napping beside an actual "river of words," the Passaic of his childhood. Nine poems or excerpts appear on the endpapers. The book concludes with three parallel time lines: dates highlighted poems appeared, life events, and world events. An author's note talks more about Williams' dual careers; the illustrator describes her research; and suggestions for further reading are appended. This won a Caldecott honor for its pictures and Zolotow honor for its text. It was an Orbis Pictus recommended book and an IRA Teachers' Choice, and was listed on the *New York Times* Best Illustrated Books, ALSC, NCTE, and CBC/NCSS Notable lists.

KERLEY, BARBARA

The Extraordinary Mark Twain (according to Susy)

Illustrated by Edwin Fotheringham
New York: Scholastic Press, 2010
ISBN: 978-0-545-12508-6 | **AGES 7–10**

Determined to "set the record straight" about her famous father, 13-year-old Susy Clemens wrote her own biography describing his appearance, his character, his good and bad habits, his childhood, and their good times at her aunt's farm in New York. The focus of this unusual, appealing biography is Susy's work. Through her eyes the reader is introduced to a loving father and billiards player, a man who enjoyed cats and was often distracted from his work, a philosopher who also told funny stories. Much of this comes from her original manuscript, now in the University of Virginia Library. Excerpts from her journal, with their original misspellings, have been printed in script and tipped in between the oversize pages, providing an intimate picture of America's most famous author. Stylized, digitally created illustrations spread across the double pages, filled with curly lines representing the sound of Twain's voice or words from his pen. They also almost always include a cat, or two, or eleven. The afterword includes an author's note about both father and daughter and sensible instructions for "Writing an Extraordinary Biography." A time line and sources for all quotations are on the back endpapers. This Cybils Award winner was an Orbis Pictus recommended book.

NOBLEMAN, MARC TYLER

Boys of Steel: The Creators of Superman

Illustrated by Ross MacDonald
New York: Alfred A. Knopf, 2008
ISBN: 978-0-375-83802-6 | **AGES 7–10**

Jerry Siegel and Joe Shuster, bespectacled, short, unathletic, and shy fans of science fiction and superhero stories, collaborated in the 1930s to produce the most successful cartoon superhero of all time—Superman. The author concentrates on their early friendship and twin passions for writing and drawing that resulted in the creation of the Superman character just after they finished high school. Opening with the two standing tall and casting a single caped shadow, the retro-style illustrations work beautifully with the text to make a package that is both biography and a kind of literary history. Cartoon allusions abound; there are thought and speech bubbles, and one double-page spread is told in a series of frames. Rays of light emanate from the image of the two settling on Superman's image, the S on his costume for "super" and "Siegel" and "Shuster." An afterword describes how DC Comics took the profits and even their names off Superman products for a while, and their battles to regain credit. A bibliography and a note that quotations come from interviews with the two men show the factual grounding for this story of a fantastic creation. An ALSC and CBC/NCSS Notable and CBC/IRA Children's Choice.

ART AND ARTISTS

BASS, HESTER

The Secret World of Walter Anderson

Illustrated by E. B. Lewis and Walter Inglis Anderson
Cambridge, MA: Candlewick Press, 2009
ISBN: 978-0-763-63583-1 | **AGES 7–12**

"The most famous American artist you've never heard of" lived in a cottage on the Mississippi coastline but spent most of his life painting fish, animals, birds, and plants on deserted Horn Island, twelve miles offshore, living without proper shelter or running water but in tune with the natural world. A long-time admirer of his work, Bass has created an interesting combination of picture book, with Lewis's glorious double-page illustrations, and an eight-page "author's note" biography illustrated with Anderson's own art. The picture book focuses on the painter's times on the island in the 1950s and '60s. Lewis's watercolors show Anderson preparing for his trip to the island in the predawn hours, eating from a can in the shade of his upturned rowboat, and his astonishingly painted locked and private room. The more detailed biography goes further into Anderson's troubled life, mental illness and separation from his family, the preservation of his work, and the devastation by Hurricane Katrina in 2005. It includes a photograph of that secret room. A selected bibliography includes works illustrated by Anderson for children and compendiums of his art as well as the author's references. This won the Orbis Pictus Award and was a CBC/NCSS Notable.

BERNIER-GRAND, CARMEN T.

Diego: Bigger Than Life

Illustrated by David Diaz
New York: Marshall Cavendish, 2009
ISBN: 978-0-761-45383-3 | **AGES 9–14**

In this companion to *Frida: ¡Viva la vida! Long Live Life!* (Marshall Cavendish, 2007), thirty-four free-verse poems chronicle the life of Diego Rivera, Mexican painter of frescos, lover of Frida Kahlo, and storyteller, revolutionary in his principles and in his art. Diaz seems the perfect choice to illustrate these first-person glimpses of Rivera's life. He matches his technique to Bernier-Grand's description of the muralist's art: "As naturally as I breathe, / I painted in grand scale the colors of Mexico— / clearer, richer, more full of light than colors in Europe." The one-eyed figures in these digital and mixed-media images pose sideways; colors and shapes combine, morph, and shade into others; patterned backgrounds recall traditional art forms. The frames are irregular; sometimes details escape. There are four of Rivera's images, just enough to send readers looking for more. Appropriately for its readers, this biography focuses more on Rivera's work than his lifestyle or political views, but they are not ignored. The end matter includes a glossary, chronology, sources, and extensive notes. This received Pura Belpré honors for both illustration and text. Pair with the bilingual *My Papa Diego and Me* (Children's Book Press, 2009), by Guadalupe Rivera Martin, an Américas Award honorable mention, which includes thirteen reproductions of Rivera's paintings.

BRYAN, ASHLEY, AND BILL MCGUINNESS

Ashley Bryan: Words to My Life's Song

Illustrated by Ashley Bryan with photographs by Bill McGuinness
New York: Atheneum Books for Young Readers, 2009
ISBN: 978-1-416-90541-7 | **AGES 8 AND UP**

Both autobiography and guided tour of Bryan's beloved Little Cranberry Island, this is an exuberant portrayal of the life and work of a prolific artist, storyteller, and poetry singer. Bryan's cheerful narration begins with his Depression-era childhood in the Bronx, going on to tell of World War II army service, art education, and varied experiences leading up to his first children's book contract and successful career. The beautiful design makes use of a variety of typefaces and media. The typography invites readers to approach the text in various ways. There's a straightforward narrative of the Wilder Award winner's long and creative life, with examples of his illustrations, family photos, the puppets and sea-glass panels that decorate his home, and pictures of him at work and with neighboring children. And then there's the daylong tour of his island home with gorgeous photographs of the Maine scenery. A montage of covers demonstrates the range of his work. This structure, with its wealth of images and ideas, represents and celebrates this multifaceted artist's life appropriately. An ALSC, NCTE, and IRA Global Notable and Teachers' Choice, this also won the Golden Kite Award and Parents' Choice Gold Award.

HILL, LABAN CARRICK

Dave the Potter

Illustrated by Bryan Collier
New York: Little, Brown, 2010
ISBN: 978-0-316-10731-0 | **AGES 5–9**

In the mid-nineteenth century a slave called Dave made beautiful large pots out of Carolina clay, shaping them with wheel and coil "like a magician pulling a rabbit out of a hat," and signing some with a poem. Hill's poetic text and Collier's paintings follow the making of such a pot step-by-step: gathering and mixing the clay, pulling the pot up from the mound on his wheel, finishing with coils and finally glaze. Stunning watercolor and collage illustrations focus on the potter at work, but in the background are scenes that remind the reader of the slave's world: a sailing ship on the open ocean, people working in fields, the big house, and Dave's fenced-in space. One page opens out to show a pot rising on the wheel; in another, Collier cuts his images into facets showing both the pot's growth and its fragility. The text is set on strips of color that seem to block out parts of the illustration, as so much of his story is lost. The back matter provides more information, eight poems, author's and illustrator's notes, a bibliography, and some websites to explore. This ALSC Notable and Orbis Pictus recommended book is a splendid reminder that art may flourish anywhere.

KNAPP, RUTHIE

Who Stole Mona Lisa?

Illustrated by Jill McElmurry
New York: Bloomsbury Children's Books, 2010
ISBN: 978-1-599-90058-2 | **AGES 5–9**

Mona Lisa, da Vinci's favorite painting, describes posing for the artist, her many royal owners, her admiring audience in the Louvre, and the horrible experience of being stolen. In this delightfully self-centered first-person narrative, Mona Lisa explains, "I was famous for being famous," and so she is. An author's note states that 80 percent of the Louvre's visitors come just to see her. As the story opens, a crowd of these visitors listen to a guide's explanation but soon Mona Lisa takes over, telling her story herself. McElmurry's gouache paintings are full of humorous detail, crowd scenes, and sequences in which costumes and even the expression in the paintings change. One double-page spread has a map of Paris featuring tiny insets in which French policemen look high and low for the painting. In another, a wildly assorted parade of people from all over the world line up to bring flowers and pay homage to the place where the painting was. Her story ends happily with her back on the wall and celebratory fireworks over the museum. The author also adds facts about the abduction and about da Vinci's sfumato technique. This is a very appealing way to introduce a work of art to young readers.

LANDMANN, BIMBA

I Am Marc Chagall: Text Loosely Inspired by _My Life_ by Marc Chagall

Illustrated by Bimba Landmann
Grand Rapids, MI: Eerdmans Books for Young Readers, 2006
ISBN: 978-0-802-85305-9 | **AGES 7–12**

The first-person text of this account of the Russian/Jewish poet/painter's life flows in curves on the page as it retells major events chronologically. But it is the remarkable illustrations, surreal collages, and models recalling the themes of his art that make this oversized book memorable. Mostly full-bleed double-page spreads, these are photographs of the Italian illustrator's work, three-dimensional constructions, some in shadow boxes, using corrugated cardboard for house walls and roofs, small figures (Chagall's head has wiry, curly gray hair), assorted objects and paint. They depict scenes of his life, from his Russian village childhood; through art school; to Paris, Russia after the revolution, and finally New York. The motifs and even the colors allude to Chagall's work. There are flying cows, violins, buildings, and impressive night skies—reminders of the fantastical nature of his art, the combination of realism and imagination. A photograph of the artist at the beginning and time line at the end enclose this dramatic Italian import, which suggests Chagall's art so intriguingly that readers will surely want to see some of the real thing. This was a CBC/NCSS Notable and won a Sydney Taylor honor.

RAY, DEBORAH KOGAN

Wanda Gág: The Girl Who Lived to Draw

Illustrated by Deborah Kogan Ray
New York: Viking, 2008
ISBN: 978-0-670-06292-8 | **AGES 7–10**

Wanda Gág's personal life was a fairy tale. The German American child quit school to raise and educate her siblings after her father died but held fast to her dream of becoming an artist. Grown up, she left Minnesota to come east, had a successful artistic career, and created a revolution in picture books for children by using double-page spreads for the classic *Millions of Cats*. This charmingly illustrated biography has considerable appeal. Each page begins with a quotation from Gág's diaries and papers. Ray's text tells her story chronologically with just enough detail to bring it to life. On the opposite page, sometimes spreading across the fold, are supporting, white-framed illustrations done in watercolor and colored pencils using shades of yellows, reds, and browns. They give a strong sense of Gág's roots, the art surrounding her at home, the colorful traditional community near her grandmother's farm, and her early twentieth century world. Gág's own cat drawings appear faintly on the endpapers and as decoration on the endnotes. Acknowledgments and bibliography document the author's research, and the tone demonstrates her admiration for this influential artist, still beloved by readers of children's books. This was both an ALSC and CBC/NCSS Notable.

RODRÍGUEZ, RACHEL

Through Georgia's Eyes

Illustrated by Julie Paschkis
New York: Henry Holt, 2006
ISBN: 978-0-805-07740-7 | **AGES 5–10**

This appealing, small book introduces the artist Georgia O'Keefe, summarizing her life and emphasizing her love of light and color and curving shapes. Its simple text and subtly shaded illustrations convey a surprisingly accurate impression of O'Keeffe's work without including any actual examples. A simple, present-tense text refers to the artist only by her first name, and offers few specific details about her life. "For a time, Georgia lives in the city." But young readers or listeners will come away with a strong sense of her work—her choice of flowers and bones as subjects, the large scale of her paintings of small things, her use of blues and reds, and her love for the southwestern landscape. The author points out that O'Keeffe's career as an artist was unusual for her times. In an illustrator's note Paschkis explains that she "wanted to quote specific paintings and photographs" without copying them, so she used paper painted with acrylics in gradations of color to make the gorgeous collages that accompany this chronological account. An afterword offers more about O'Keefe's life for older readers, and a bibliography is included along with author's and illustrator's notes behind the title page. This was a CBC/NCSS Notable.

SHEA, PEGI DEITZ

Patience Wright: America's First Sculptor and Revolutionary Spy

Illustrated by Bethanne Andersen
New York: Henry Holt, 2007
ISBN: 978-0-805-06770-5 | **AGES 7–12**

After she was widowed, New Jersey–born Quaker sculptor Patience Wright took her wax sculpture business to England in 1772, just before the American Revolution. There she made models of important people, chatting with them as they posed, and learning secrets she wrote on messages she hid inside hollow busts she sent back for sale in America. She revealed political decisions, described shipments of men and arms, and identified officials in the colonies who were taking bribes. This intriguing, little-known story is told in a straightforward, admiring fashion. The relatively lengthy text, more suitable for older readers and listeners, is set on gouache-and-pastel paintings, double-page spreads showing the artist at work, and including the kinds of details of costumes and hairdos that make waxwork figures believable. They convey the time and place particularly well. Readers will recognize King George III and Ben Franklin. Not surprisingly, this biography of a strong, independent woman and her sister, also a widow, who made business and artistic careers long before this was customary, made the Amelia Bloomer list and was a CBC/NCSS Notable. Dawn Fitzgerald's *Vinnie and Abraham* (Charlesbridge, 2007) describes another lady sculptor with a role in American history.

STONE, TANYA LEE

Sandy's Circus: A Story about Alexander Calder

Illustrated by Boris Kulikov
New York: Viking, 2008
ISBN: 978-0-670-06268-3 | **AGES 6–9**

What child can resist a circus? This irresistible biography tells how Alexander (Sandy) Calder played with wood and wire, making objects from the time he was a child. After art school and a stint sketching the Ringling Brothers Circus, he made a circus of his own with moveable parts, traveling and performing with it everywhere. At the end readers learn that Calder also invented the idea of the mobile, and that his new moveable art was successful. An afterword explains the author's enthusiasm and includes a photograph of the artist performing his circus and a list of sources. Kulikov's multimedia collages often spread across both pages, zooming in to focus on the artist's face and hands at work and out to show the child Calder at home and the adult in Paris and New York where a muse with an artist's palette (and, later, his circus-filled suitcases) flies over his head. Intrigued young readers can easily find photographs and even a video of the circus in action with a simple Internet search. This focus on a single work of art is an ideal way to introduce this noted sculptor to a new generation. A CBC/NCSS Notable.

MUSIC AND MUSICIANS

ALCORN, STEPHEN

Odetta: The Queen of Folk

Illustrated by Stephen Alcorn
New York: Scholastic Press, 2010
ISBN: 978-0-439-92818-2 | **AGES 7–10**

Born into a Jim Crow world in Birmingham, Alabama, in 1930, Odetta grew up to become a folk music star, strumming her guitar, singing of black history, justice, and equal rights, and selling out integrated concert halls. This tribute, stemming from Alcorn's personal admiration, introduces the African American child who longed to make music, and follows her to Los Angeles and then out into the musical world where she became a star and inspiration for later performers. The admiring text, a free-verse poem by Samantha Thornhill, has the cadences of praise song. Alcorn's casein paintings, double-page spreads with swooping lines and extensive use of angels, birds, clouds, and rainbows, are allusive and suggestive. A water fountain gushes the words "whites only," smoke from a train engine forms Jim Crow's head, and from the sky his pointing finger shoots thunderbolts at Odetta's family, seated on the "wrong train car." Later, freed to make music in California, a bird escapes from the cage of her throat. An endnote by Alcorn describes Odetta's career and legacy in more detail and includes a photograph of the two together. For today's readers, who will know Odetta only through her music, a discography is included. This won a Parents' Choice Gold Award.

CHRISTENSEN, BONNIE

Django

Illustrated by Bonnie Christensen
New York: Flash Point/Roaring Brook Press, 2009
ISBN: 978-1-596-43422-6 | **AGES 7–10**

From his Romani boyhood, Django Reinhardt loved music, playing first the violin and then a banjo-guitar. His determination to keep playing brought him back to a successful jazz career after a fire badly damaged his hand. Christensen opens this triumphant story in free verse reflecting the boy's early nomadic life. When Django goes to Paris to make music professionally, the lines become more orderly, settling into an epic-like trochaic tetrameter beat. But it's the oil and oil pastel illustrations that make this biography sing. Even without text, this story is clear. The first dark spread shows a Roma encampment, the baby silhouetted in the moonlit wagon. A joyful childhood scene shows "Little Django; trout tickler" knee-deep in the river, waving a fish he's caught. Always, some portion of the scene escapes the frame, just as Django's music broke boundaries. There is a striking double-page spread of Django's wagon burning—a calamity so terrible it is shown full-bleed. Gray hospital scenes follow as Django contemplates his bandaged hands. Gradually colors lighten as he relearns to play with the fingers that still work; a final spread shows him onstage again. This won a Schneider Family Book Award for its portrayal of the disability experience and made the CBC/NCSS Notable list.

HOPKINSON, DEBORAH

Home on the Range: John A. Lomax and His Cowboy Songs

Illustrated by S. D. Schindler
New York: G. P. Putnam's Sons, 2009
ISBN: 978-0-399-23996-0 | AGES 7–10

John Henry Lomax grew up singing. On his Texas farm in the middle of the nineteenth century, he could hear cowboys nearby on the Chisholm Trail. He began collecting folk songs, a passion that stayed with him through his university education and became his life's work. The author describes her lively, informative narrative as historical fiction, based on Lomax's autobiography and some other sources cited in her back matter; others catalog it with other musicians' lives. Folksy imagined dialog seems appropriate to the time and place. Bits and pieces of familiar and not-so-well-known cowboy song lyrics appear throughout, including the titular "Home on the Range." Hopkinson's chronological third-person narrative is accompanied by line-and-watercolor illustrations showing quirky, identifiable characters and the beauty of the scenery. Some are vignettes; others spread across two pages. The earth tones of the southwestern landscape predominate. The author ends her story with John's first successful song-gathering expedition. An afterword for older readers expands this nicely focused biography of an ethnomusicologist and talks of the role of the Archive of Folk Culture at the Library of Congress. This CBC/NCSS Notable was also a CCBC Choice.

MYERS, WALTER DEAN

Jazz

Illustrated by Christopher Myers
New York: Holiday House, 2006
ISBN: 978-0-823-41545-8 | AGES 8–14

This series of poems describing the sounds, forms, and some of the personnel of jazz music has been illustrated with evocative full-page, full-bleed paintings of musicians and some dancers. The poetry itself is syncopated and allusive, beautifully presented using two different fonts in a way that helps the reader's understanding. More suggestive than descriptive, it roughly follows the development of the musical genre. Opening and closing with poems that define jazz generally, Myers also honors some specific players and styles, and presents a New Orleans funeral procession, recording sessions, and a final improvisation with three voices. What makes this collection work as an informational book is the front and back matter: a two-page introduction to the musical genre surveying its history, a helpful glossary of jazz terms with clear, extensive definitions, and a time line. Christopher Myers's paintings, done with acrylic with an overlay of black ink on acetate, show figures stretched out like the jazz melodies and improvisations. His perspective is skewed; his lines curve. Deep reds, blues, and purples predominate. They match their subjects perfectly. This made the ALSC, CBC/NCSS, and IRA Global Notable lists, received a CSK honor for its illustration, and Golden Kite and Lee Bennett Hopkins Awards for its poetry, among other awards.

PARKER, ROBERT ANDREW

Piano Starts Here: The Young Art Tatum

Illustrated by Robert Andrew Parker
New York: Schwartz & Wade Books, 2008
ISBN: 978-0-375-83965-8 | **AGES 5–9**

Tatum is the imagined narrator in this biography of the noted jazz pianist, which opens with a description of his childhood love for the instrument. To the boy in Toledo with weak eyes, sounds and smells were what mattered; the piano became his home. By 10, he was playing in the church and school. By 16, he played in bars and on the radio. Parker's illustrations, ink sketches with watercolor wash, both accompany and expand the text. Precise details are lost, just as they would be through Tatum's poor eyesight. But he is specific about the nature of Tatum's playing, his ability to vary sounds and weave songs together, and his signature use of Dvorak's "Humoresque." The endpapers show Tatum in performance. A note in the end summarizes the musician's career. There is no discography or suggestions for further reading, a missed opportunity. Parker provides a bibliography of sources but no attribution for the musician's specific memories; however, his informed imagination rings true. This Cybils finalist and CCBC Choice won the Schneider Family Book Award for its artistic expression of the disability experience and was also on the ALSC and CBC/NCSS Notable lists.

WEATHERFORD, CAROLE BOSTON

Before John Was a Jazz Giant: A Song of John Coltrane

Illustrated by Sean Qualls
New York: Henry Holt, 2008
ISBN: 978-0-805-07994-4 | **AGES 5–9**

Growing up in North Carolina in the 1930s, legendary jazz saxophonist John Coltrane listened to the sounds around him. This deceptively slight story is a poem of eight stanzas describing what he heard—from the ukulele, Grandpa's sermons, birds at sunrise, and sobs at funerals to a crank phonograph, steam engines, tap dancing, and radio big bands. Each stanza begins, "Before John was a jazz giant"; the last concludes, "He was all ears." Laid out with no more than four lines on a double-page full-bleed spread, even the text has motion. Using acrylics, collage, and pencil, Qualls provides allusive illustrations in cool jazz colors and plenty of smoky blues. The rhythmic text conveys a remarkable amount of information, supplemented by an author's note that describes Coltrane's career and importance in the jazz world. There are suggested lists for listening and further reading, clearly aimed at young readers. Behind the dust cover, a set of printed boards shows the boy in front and the adult musician on the back. This received a CSK honor for illustration and Golden Kite Award for its picture book text; it was on both the ALSC and CBC/NCSS Notable lists.

THEATER AND PERFORMERS: ACTORS, DANCERS, AND ENTERTAINERS

ANCONA, GEORGE

¡Olé Flamenco!

Illustrated by George Ancona
New York: Lee & Low Books, 2010
ISBN: 978-1-600-60361-7 | **AGES 7–12**

This introduction to the traditional Roma music and dance style called flamenco highlights the experiences of Janira Cordova, the youngest member of Flamenco's Next Generation, a dance group in Santa Fe, New Mexico. New and archival photographs, taken in New Mexico and in Spain, and even a Doré etching work together to convey the flavor of this unique form and survey its history and tradition. Readers see Janira practicing steps and her brother Nicholas learning the flamenco guitar. These illustrations show traditional hand and arm gestures, facial expressions, accompanying clapping styles that keep the beat, costumes, singers, and instruments: the guitar, the cajón, and castanets. The text, often set as extensive photo captions, uses appropriate Spanish vocabulary, defined in context and in a glossary. Janira practices with her troupe, dances with her family, and, finally, performs in her own long dress with its ruffled skirt for the annual Spanish Market in Santa Fe. This ALSC Notable also includes a map illustrating the Roma migration from India across Northern Africa and Europe and a source list.

COREY, SHANA

Mermaid Queen: The Spectacular True Story of Annette Kellerman, Who Swam Her Way to Fame, Fortune, and Swimsuit History!

Illustrated by Edwin Fotheringham
New York: Scholastic Press, 2008
ISBN: 978-0-439-69835-1 | **AGES 5–9**

Born in Australia in 1903, Kellerman grew up to invent a new style of swimming called water ballet. She went to England to compete and to the States to perform; she created more sensible bathing suits for women. The intriguing design of this picture book biography complements its subject, featuring swirls of color and curves, even in the text, which uses a curly font for emphasis. The text appears directly on the double page spread, artfully fitted into the digitally created illustrations. Dialogue bubbles offer commentary. The story is told in a breathless manner, but the message is clear. With hard work and perseverance, Kellerman made waves, demonstrating that women could be athletic, healthy, and comfortable in themselves. The author's note in the afterword emphasizes her determination and her physical and social challenges in a world just beginning to consider new ways for women. The final double-page spread, showing the change in women's bathing suits over time, makes the point visually. An extensive author's note summarizes the rest of her career. Acknowledgments list the author's sources and include citations for each quotation. A Cybils finalist, this made the Amelia Bloomer list.

GREENBERG, JAN, AND SANDRA JORDAN

Ballet for Martha: Making Appalachian Spring

Illustrated by Brian Floca
New York: Roaring Brook Press, 2010
ISBN: 978-1-596-43338-0 | **AGES 7–10**

A splendid collaboration between two experienced writers about art and a noted illustrator honors the collaboration between Martha Graham, dancer and choreographer, Aaron Copland, composer, and Isamu Noguchi, artist and set designer that produced the modern ballet *Appalachian Spring*. The result is a remarkable evocation of the dance as well as the work behind it. The present-tense narration adds immediacy, but the authors take their time introducing Graham and her unusual style, Copland writing his music, and Noguchi making models of his set. The story is told in short lines, set in paragraphs around or on the illustrations. The square format offers plenty of room for ink-and-watercolor illustrations ranging from sketches to full pages and double-page spreads with generous white space reflecting the spare production. One spread shows the Library of Congress where the premiere took place in Washington, DC, in 1941; others show the dancers on stage. The "Curtain Call" at the end describes the lives of the three artists. The authors include extensive notes and sources and a photograph from the original production. An ALSC Notable and Orbis Pictus Award winner, this beautiful tribute is a welcome way to introduce a dance giant and a beloved piece of music.

KRULL, KATHLEEN, AND PAUL BREWER

Fartiste

Illustrated by Boris Kulikov
New York: Simon & Schuster Books for Young Readers, 2008
ISBN: 978-1-416-92828-7 | **AGES 7–10**

The cover tag line says it all: "An explosively funny, mostly true story." Joseph Pujol's unusual talent—making varied sounds and actual music through his butt—brought him fame and fortune in late nineteenth-century Paris. Joyfully told in rhyming couplets, this is a real kid-pleaser. Kulikov's bright cheerful paintings, done with watercolors, gouache, and ink, emphasize backsides. Usually filling the double-page spreads, they show French soldiers, Moulin Rouge dancers, and audiences from Pujol's own ten children to staid Parisians and nobility "Raising their brows, wanting to deem him obscene." Krull's text presents his life chronologically, from the 8-year-old's discovery of his unusual talent, through army service, marriage, beginnings of his performance career, and triumph in Paris. A long epilogue explains the facts behind Pujol's amazing story, and a few more details about his long life. Sources, including films, are provided on the back endpaper. This would be a treat to read aloud if you could keep a straight face. Given the questionable subject matter, it is not surprising that this title did not turn up on award lists, but you can be sure that any 8-year-old looking for a biography would be thrilled to discover this unusual entertainer.

MCCARTHY, MEGHAN

Aliens Are Coming! The True Account of the 1938 War of the Worlds Radio Broadcast

Illustrated by Meghan McCarthy
New York: Alfred A. Knopf, 2006
ISBN: 978-0-375-83518-6 | **AGES 7–12**

On the eve of Halloween, in 1938, a radio broadcast of a dramatization of H. G. Wells's famous novel terrified listeners across the country who were sure it reported an actual Martian landing in Grover's Mill, New Jersey. McCarthy plays up the science fiction in this story, beginning with endpapers with whizzing rockets and flying saucers. On the title page a goggle-eyed green alien gestures with a tentacle toward earth. She provides the necessary background with an opening explanation that 1930s Americans turned to radio, not TV, for news and entertainment. The narrative summarizes the events and includes excerpts from the play, all set in short segments on the double-page illustrations. McCarthy's chosen palette of grays for real life, and muted reds for the drama, makes it easier for her young readers to see the difference between facts and fancy than it was for the radio audience. (In an informative afterword, the author tells us that listeners missed four different announcements that this was only a play.) The author-illustrator has also included her bibliography and a link to a website with photographs and activities. This Cybils finalist and CBC Children's Choice was also an ALSC Notable.

THOMPSON, LAUREN

Ballerina Dreams: A True Story

Illustrated by James Estrin
New York: Feiwel and Friends, 2007
ISBN: 978-0-312-37029-9 | **AGES 5–9**

Five little girls with muscle disorders, members of a special ballet class, work hard all year toward a recital for friends and family. The determination and joy in the faces of these children, ages 3–7, are evidence of what this class and this experience has meant to them. The focus is on the children, not their adult helpers who discreetly provide support. Excitedly they dress in leotards and tutus and practice their pliés. For the performance, they put on stage makeup and tiaras; they change costumes between scenes as they dance the Sugar Plum Fairy from the *Nutcracker* or swans from *Swan*

Lake. These pictures have the look of snapshots, capturing the girls' spirit. Laid out against a grid of straight lines on a pink background, they show how these youngsters both look and feel like ballerina princesses. Captions serve as text, identifying the girls and describing their hard work and their excitement. An afterword introduces the ballerinas, their teacher Joann Ferrara, their volunteer teen helpers, and the program that serves as a supplement to the girls' physical therapy. There is also an explanation of cerebral palsy. This inspiring photo essay was an ALSC, CBC/NCSS, and IRA Global Notable.

WINTER, JONAH

The Fabulous Feud of Gilbert and Sullivan

Illustrated by Richard Egielski
New York: Arthur A. Levine Books, 2009
ISBN: 978-0-439-93050-5 | **AGES 5–9**

In Victorian England Mr. Gilbert and Mr. Sullivan created a series of splendidly successful, if silly, operas for the stage world of Topsy-Turvydom, but their collaboration almost ended when Mr. Sullivan developed greater aspirations. Fortunately for all musical theater fans, Mr. Gilbert saw a Japanese street fair and was inspired to write *The Mikado*, restoring harmony. Egielski's cartoonlike illustrations appear to be staged, using changing scenery and even spotlights. A personified sun watches the action. The usual front-page order has been reversed to show first the left-hand page and dedication against an illustration of a medley of Gilbert and Sullivan operettas with familiar characters, including a policeman and pirate. Then the title page appears, the opening curtain for a Mikado production—something, as the text says, "completely different." From street scenes to interior views, sharply outlined figures stand out like characters on a stage filled with lavish Victorian decoration. One double-page spread shows Gilbert's model theater with its wooden characters; the next, the Mikado scene fully staged with lavishly costumed players. These illustrations flesh out Winter's crisp account, a Parents' Choice Silver Honor book. An author's note sums up the story, offering further detail and a website for readers who want more.

YOO, PAULA

Shining Star: The Anna May Wong Story

Illustrated by Lin Wang
New York: Lee & Low Books, 2009
ISBN: 978-1-600-60259-7 | **AGES 8–11**

Working in her family's Los Angeles laundry in the early twentieth century, Anna May Wong dreamed of becoming a movie star. She worked to develop acting skills and took the demeaning roles open to her as an Asian American, until, after a trip to China in the 1930s, she determined to portray only positive characters. The story of this almost forgotten actress is interestingly and sympathetically told. The difficulties facing an actress of color at the time are made clear. One example is moviemakers' requirement of no kissing between races on-screen. This lost her the lead in *The Good Earth* because a white man had already been cast in the male role. It seems likely that at least some of the conversations and descriptions of Wong's feelings are imagined, but they ring true. Watercolor and acrylic paintings, a bit static and old-fashioned in their style, support the historical story. The opening double-page spread showing the young girl tied to a track in the face of an approaching steam engine will draw readers in. An author's note sums up her career; a bibliography of the author's sources and a very short list of movies are included. This won the Carter G. Woodson Award.

SPORTS AND ATHLETES

ANCONA, GEORGE

Capoeira: Game! Dance! Martial Art!

Illustrated with photographs by George Ancona
New York: Lee & Low Books, 2007
ISBN: 978-1-584-30268-1 | **AGES 7–11**

This inviting photo essay describes the Brazilian dance game and martial art called capoeira through the experiences of students at Mandinga Academy in Oakland, California, as well as practitioners in northeastern Brazil. This fascinating activity incorporates the graceful movements of dance and acrobatics to outwit and trick an opponent. Ancona introduces the students and some of the basic moves. He shows the instructor teaching traditional songs and using instruments including the *berimbau*, *atabaque, agogô*, and *réco-réco*, and the whole group in a circle, each taking turns to face an opponent who might not be of the same age or ability. He also explains its origin in the traditions of Brazilian slaves, imported from Africa and disguising their fights with music. The book includes a map and photographs of capoeira being practiced formally and informally in Brazil today. Appropriate Portuguese terms are used throughout, defined in context and in a glossary and pronunciation guide at the end. The author's sources and some suggested websites complete the package. This Américas Award commended title was also a CCBC Choice.

BOWEN, FRED

No Easy Way: The Story of Ted Williams and the Last .400 Season

Illustrated by Charles S. Pyle
New York: Dutton Children's Books, 2010
ISBN: 978-0-525-47877-5 | **AGES 5–9**

Ted Williams was determined to be the greatest baseball hitter who ever lived, practicing endlessly to meet that goal. When it came to the last two games of the 1941 series he had a choice: sit out the doubleheader and preserve his .400 average, or play? From the uplifting story, to the Norman Rockwell–style illustrations, to the baseball card page design with its red and gold frames, this book is a tribute to a great athlete and a simpler time. Bowen, who writes sports stories and a regular newspaper column for young readers, describes Williams's feat in ways young readers can understand. His tone is conversational, but there is mounting suspense. Pyle's paintings show Williams's determination; he leaves the frame completely with his final record-breaking hit. Sources and acknowledgments on the left-hand page support the facts of the story, but it is the combination of straightforward storytelling and period images that make this an ideal baseball book. On the back cover, under a running line of his 1941 statistics, Williams signs a ball for some admiring young fans; today's fans should be similarly thrilled.

BROWN, MONICA

Pelé: King of Soccer / Pelé: El rey del fútbol

Illustrated by Rudy Gutierrez
Translated by Fernando Gayesky
New York: Rayo, 2009
ISBN: 978-0-061-22779-0 | **AGES 4–9**

Pelé, number 10, scores a hat trick and his thousandth goal in this exuberant introduction to the Brazilian soccer player who began playing with his father and friends, shoeless and without a real ball, and became world famous. Brown's simple text, in Spanish and English, outlines the athlete's story in the breathless tone of a sportscaster. Gutierrez's energetic full-bleed, double-page gouache paintings add to the excitement. Swirls and swooshes of design and color fill the pages, dramatically capturing the constant motion of the game. When, at 15, Pelé joins a professional team and the coach decides to fatten him up, a splendid array of Brazilian foods illustrates the joy of finally getting enough to eat. Figures are elongated or distorted, but Pelé's face is clearly recognizable—as are the faces of the notables he met in later life, including John F. Kennedy Jr., Martin Luther King Jr., and the Beatles. A short author's note at the end summarizes Pelé's career, but there are no suggestions for further reading or sources. The author has made a specialty of biographies of Latino figures. For young soccer players, this will be a delight and an exciting companion to Cline-Ransome's *Young Pelé: Soccer's First Star* (Schwartz & Wade Books, 2007).

CROWE, ELLIE

Surfer of the Century: The Life of Duke Kahanamoku

Illustrated by Richard Waldrep
New York: Lee & Low Books, 2007
ISBN: 978-1-584-30276-6 | **AGES 7–12**

Though he often faced discrimination, Honolulu beach boy Duke Kahanamoku broke swimming records and won Olympic gold medals. He introduced surfing to Australia and promoted the sport on both U.S. coasts throughout his life. A heart-stopping illustration of a gigantic blue wave towering over a tiny surfing figure illustrates the description of Kahanamoku's riding a thirty-foot wave nearly two miles in 1917 that opens this biography. Backtracking to Kahanamoku's childhood, Crowe then chronicles the life of an athlete "remembered for his kindness and modesty, good sportsmanship, and love of life." He describes Kahanamoku learning to swim and surf at a very young age, his invention of the flutter kick and various surfing tricks, his use of surfboard as rescue equipment, and his triumphs at home and later on the mainland and around the world. The text is relatively difficult for a picture book, but filled with the spirit of *aloha*—love and hospitality—and enhanced by striking, slightly stylized gouache paintings on opposing pages. A time line of highlights of his life and world map showing places named complete the package. The author's sources are listed. This Carter G. Woodson honor book won an APALA Award for its illustrations.

LEWIN, TED

At Gleason's Gym

Illustrated by Ted Lewin
New Milford, CT: Roaring Brook Press, 2007
ISBN: 978-1-596-43231-4 | **AGES 7–10**

This busy, noisy Brooklyn, New York gym, four famous rings of boxing and wrestling action, is a familiar place to 9-year-old Sugar Boy Younan, training for the National Silver Gloves championship. Here he practices with his father, works with trainers, and watches others. The excitement of the place, all movement and sound, spills over onto the pages of this sensually appealing book. The spare, expressive text and energetic illustrations together communicate the feeling of being there. "The noise and smell of sweat hit you in the face like a roundhouse right." Lewin's narrative makes readers a part of the action. Boys and girls alike train here, world champions, wrestlers, even kickboxers from Thailand. "It's everybody's gym"—and it's a busy place. Dramatic paintings in vibrant watercolors include onomatopoetic sound words. One spread is filled with pencil sketches of a father practicing with his 5-year-old daughter. Another shows Sugar Boy dancing, jabbing, punching a rubber dummy. Then, suddenly, there's a quiet moment. Another double-page spread shows the gym almost empty, before the momentum again picks up and Sugar Boy spars with a boy his own age. "THIS IS FUN!" he yells. Readers will agree. Concluding this ALSC Notable, a short glossary defines sports-specific words.

LEWIN, TED

Stable

Illustrated by Ted Lewin
New York: Roaring Brook Press, 2010
ISBN: 978-1-596-43467-7 | **AGES 5–9**

Hanging on in Brooklyn, New York, from a time when horse-drawn vehicles were the norm, one stable remains, providing pony rides and ponies for parties, riding lessons and trail rides in Prospect Park, as well as a horse-drawn carriage for special occasions. Sepia-toned images open the book, depicting a time "when horses did just about everything." There are horses on the beach, pulling other horses in veterinary wagons, and racing to fight fires. Though horses have disappeared from the streets, they can still be found in Kensington Stables, the last of its kind in the area. Lewin's now-colorful watercolors and gentle, simple narrative take readers inside to see the animals, the owner, the farrier, and the families who come for lessons and rides. He shows children riding across a Brooklyn street and in the barn, ponies being loaded into a modern van, and the fancy carriage off for a spin in the park. The book ends with thirty-seven individual, named portraits of Kensington Stables' horses. The target audience for this book appears on the cover, where a helmeted young girl reaches up to pat a horse leaning over the stall door looking directly at the reader. For any horse-happy child, this will be a special treat.

MCCARTHY, MEGHAN

Seabiscuit: The Wonder Horse

Illustrated by Meghan McCarthy
New York: Simon & Schuster Books for Young Readers, 2008
ISBN: 978-1-416-93360-1 | **AGES 4–8**

In the hard times of 1930s, people went to the racetracks to escape. They rooted for a funny-looking underdog horse like themselves, an angry, wild horse no one had wanted but whose owner, trainer, and jockey had gentled and trained so well he was allowed to compete against the sleek, fast War Admiral. In front of a packed crowd and with forty million Americans—including President Roosevelt—listening on the radio, Seabiscuit won that race, although his regular jockey had been hospitalized. To illustrate this heartwarming story, McCarthy adds a smiling horse to her customary cast of bubble-eyed people. The Depression is summed up in the somber tones of an opening double-page spread showing a long breadline. These acrylic paintings lighten up when Seabiscuit appears. The story of his training is shown as a black-and-white photo album introducing the characters and describing the gentling process. The final race scenes are appropriately colorful and exciting. A lengthy author's note continues the story of the horse, his jockey Red Pollard, and the happy ending that allowed the two to race together again. A bibliography is appended. This appealing read-aloud introduction to the sport of kings was a CCBC Choice.

MCCARTHY, MEGHAN

The Story of Charles Atlas, Strong Man

Illustrated by Meghan McCarthy
New York: Alfred A. Knopf, 2007
ISBN: 978-0-375-82940-6 | **AGES 5–9**

Determined to find a way to respond to bullies who attacked him, Italian immigrant Angelo Siciliano devised a resistance training method for bodybuilding that earned him the name Charles Atlas and the title of "The World's Most Perfectly Developed Man." McCarthy's pop-eyed figures portray this pioneering fitness crusader, as well as the bullies who kicked sand in his face. Text and speech bubbles appear directly on the full-bleed acrylic illustrations, ranging from double-page spreads to comic-book blocks and faux black-and-white photographs. They combine to tell the story of the immigrant boy who became a weight lifter, model for statues, World War II military trainer, and worldwide inspiration. She points out that his program included healthy eating and sleeping habits as well. The author's note explains that no one really knows if he was the folk hero he claimed to be. His story grew and changed over the years, but he certainly did live a wholesome life. The author includes instructions for four fitness exercises developed by physical therapists for her young readers. The humorous presentation should draw in young readers who may stay for the wholesome dessert. This was a *Booklist* Editor's Choice.

RIPKEN, CAL

The Longest Season: The Story of the Orioles' 1988 Losing Streak

Illustrated by Ron Mazellan
New York: Philomel Books, 2007
ISBN: 978-0-399-24492-6 | **AGES 7–10**

A former major league baseball player, Cal Ripken Jr. recalls the 1988 season when the Baltimore Orioles lost twenty-one games before winning their first, a season when he learned how much you can learn from losing. Shortstop Ripken is most famous for the fact that he played day in and day out in a record 2,632 consecutive games. But the Hall-of-Famer's first-person narrative focuses on a different, less talked-about aspect of baseball: losing. Chapter by chapter, loss by loss, from 0–1 to 0–21, the relatively simple text chronicles the Orioles' slump. Full-page mixed-media paintings, many on double-page spreads, show Ripken and his teammates (including his brother and his father, who started off the year as coach) in action and in postures of dejection. Knowledgeable fans will recognize various baseball stadiums including the old and new in Baltimore. Ripken admits his frustration, his errors, his anger and embarrassment, and his need to keep emotions in check. "But still, we go out there every game and give it our best." For young athletes everywhere who need to hear messages about losing as well as winning, this CBC/NCSS Notable is a an excellent choice.

STAUFFACHER, SUE

Nothing but Trouble: The Story of Althea Gibson

Illustrated by Greg Couch
New York: Alfred A. Knopf, 2007
ISBN: 978-0-375-83408-0 | **AGES 5–9**

The first African American ever to enter and win at Wimbledon, Althea Gibson changed the sport of tennis in the late 1950s. But she always gave credit to the man who started her on her way. The tallest, wildest tomboy in Harlem was said to be nothing but trouble, but Buddy Walker, a play leader who saw promise in her athletic ability, gave her a racket, helped her get into a tennis club, dress appropriately, and tame her temper enough to become the tennis champion of the world. The author tells Gibson's story succinctly, in a conversational style with lively language appropriate to the time and place. Some imagined dialog adds to the immediacy. Short segments of text are set on double-page spreads, earth-toned paintings created with acrylics and digital imaging. The artist echoes the temper-taming theme; in every picture Althea is surrounded by strokes of red, yellow, and green paint. While she never quite loses that aura, the colors fade as she gains control. While the narrative concentrates on this challenge, an afterword explains about the racism she also faced. This inspiring biography, a CBC/NCSS Notable and CCBC Choice, would be a delight to read aloud.

TAVARES, MATT

Henry Aaron's Dream

Illustrated by Matt Tavares
Somerville, MA: Candlewick Press, 2010
ISBN: 978-0-763-63224-3 | **AGES 7–10**

Growing up in Mobile, Alabama, Henry Aaron knew baseball was a white boy's game but still dreamed of being a major league player. In spite of prejudice and discrimination, he accomplished his goal. Tavares's opening images set the stage: we see boys playing baseball through a chain link fence bearing a sign, "whites only," and, from the back of a pickup truck, a black boy watches others playing high on a hill. As a young child, Henry used only a stick and bottle caps; later, he used a real bat, but held it wrong. Not until he was playing professionally, for the Negro Leagues, did he learn to bat traditionally. The brown tones of Tavares's watercolors emphasize Aaron's "colored" world, until he breaks into the integrated world of major-league baseball. Even then, players were housed and fed separately. But Hank Aaron stands tall. This story ends with a Braves exhibition game in Aaron's hometown, where he beats a throw by his hero Frank Robinson to second base. A concluding author's note and statistics demonstrate his future success: the major league's best-hitter award is named for the man who broke Babe Ruth's all-time home run record. This Cybils finalist was an NCTE Notable.

WINTER, JONAH

You Never Heard of Sandy Koufax?!

Illustrated by André Carrilho
New York: Schwartz & Wade Books, 2009
ISBN: 978-0-375-83738-8 | **AGES 7–10**

Sandy Koufax shocked the baseball world in 1965 when he refused to pitch in the first World Series game when it fell on a Jewish High Holy Day. Winter's unnamed narrator, speaking in irrepressible Brooklynese, expresses surprise that the reader has never heard of the fabulous left-handed pitcher who became suddenly famous in 1961, and retired just as suddenly six years later. From the lenticular cover to boxscore statistics and the dramatic, caricatured illustrations, this is a visual treat. In grays, browns, Dodger blues, and even gold, Carrilho's digitally manipulated pencil-drawing illustrations zoom out to show the field and in to show the pitcher's face and details of his technique. Even the cover moves. Winter describes, but does not repeat, the name-calling and other anti-Semitic acts; his focus is Koufax's astonishing talent, and his tone is conversational. This works well as a read-aloud for younger children; middle grade fans will pore over the statistics. Paring away to the essence of one player's life, Winter and Carrilho demonstrate the appeal of baseball and one of its stars. A teacher's guide on the publisher's website offers suggestions for classroom activities. This ALSC and CBC/NCSS Notable made *Booklist*'s Top of the List.

WISE, BILL

Louis Sockalexis: Native American Baseball Pioneer

Illustrated by Bill Farnsworth
New York: Lee & Low Books, 2007
ISBN: 978-1-584-30269-8 | **AGES 7–10**

From the Penobscot Indian Reservation in Maine, Louis Sockalexis came to the Cleveland Spiders as the first Native American ever to play professional baseball. In 1897, in his first game against the New York Giants, watched by his formerly disapproving father, he hit a towering home run. That hit is the climax and end of this picture book story. An afterword explains that this talented athlete's career was cut short by injury and alcoholism, but the Cleveland team became the Indians because of his connection. The author follows the facts of this little-known story and provides sources, but imagines some of Louis's feelings to add dramatic tension. Oil paintings, in sepia tones and hazy greens, give a sense of the historical nature of the story. From insets and vignettes to full-bleed pictures extending across the gutter and all the way across double-page spreads, they focus on individuals (Louis, his father, hostile fans) and back off to give a sense of the field and the game. For reading aloud or reading alone, this is another reminder of the difficulties of integrating our national game. This won Carter G. Woodson and IRA Children's Book awards and was an IRA Global Notable.

7

The World of Faith
and Festivals

HOLIDAYS ARE THE WAY many children first come to understand different religious faiths, so this combination seems natural. Here are stories from particular traditions, examples of children and their families practicing different religions, and two biographies of religious figures. Writing about religion is not easy. This section includes numerous titles from the National Geographic series Holidays Around the World, certainly the best available resource for children on the world's most significant religions today. These books describe different faiths from the point of view of insiders but with a clear understanding of what outsiders might need and want to know.

AJMERA, MAYA, MAGDA NAKASSIS, AND CYNTHIA PON

Faith

Illustrated with photographs
Watertown, MA: Charlesbridge, 2009
ISBN: 978-1-580-89177-6 | **AGES 5–10**

This attractive photo essay displays the varieties of ways young people from thirty-seven different countries around the world practice their religions. Their activities include praying, chanting and singing, reading holy books, listening and learning from others, ritual cleansing, visiting holy places, celebrating holidays, marking important events, wearing special clothes, fasting or eating distinctive foods, and caring for and helping others. Familiar religions appear in unfamiliar settings: a child in the island nation Mauritius shows off her first communion dress; incense

FACING PAGE ART FROM

Faith by Maya Ajmera,
Magda Nakassis, and Cynthia Pon

Developed by the Global Fund for Children.
Photograph by Alison Wright. Used with permission
by Charlesbridge Publishing, Inc.

and a crucifix are part of a purifying ceremony in Bolivia; blond Muslim children in the United Kingdom break their daily Ramadan fast. Lesser-known and indigenous faiths are included as well: a Russian boy honors the spirit of a seal; an Apache girl dances at a sunrise ceremony. The selection of images is wide ranging, but the underlying message is inclusive, stressing similarities rather than differences. These crisply reproduced photographs, varying in size, are set against a solid background with a simple text and identifying captions. A few pages at the end elaborate on the elements of faith included, a map identifies the countries mentioned, and there is a glossary of potentially unfamiliar words. This Global Fund for Children Book was a Cybils finalist and CBC/NCSS and IRA Global Notable.

BAUM, MAXIE

I Have a Little Dreidel

Illustrated by Julie Paschkis
New York: Scholastic, 2006
ISBN: 978-0-439-64997-1 | **AGES 4–7**

This expanded version of the traditional Hanukkah game song, with the familiar chorus interspersed with verses that describe a festive Hanukkah meal, is ideal for showing and singing with a group. The artwork is bold, and the verses, running underneath on a decorated strip, are printed in large, readable type. These new verses describe the extended family's arrival, assembling and cooking latkes, lighting the candles in a menorah, the special meal, and, finally, the dreidel game. Paschkis uses leafy motifs and open hands to decorate the blue-and-white border carrying the text. Above, in double-page spreads, she illustrates the family visit with bold colors and clear outlines. Her folk art style complements the traditional song, but she has also included amusing details for the careful viewer. A small boy feeds the dog from the table, but later he pulls her tail. The baby throws food on the floor. Music, directions for playing the dreidel game, and a recipe for the traditional potato pancakes called latkes are included. In this extended Jewish family, only Grandpa wears a yarmulke, but all join in the traditional celebration. Useful to introduce the holiday to any audience, this was named a notable book for younger readers by the Association of Jewish Librarians.

COMPESTINE, YING CHANG

D Is for Dragon Dance

Illustrated by Yongsheng Xuan
New York: Holiday House, 2006
ISBN: 978-0-823-41887-9 | **AGES 4–7**

From acrobats to the zodiac, the alphabet serves as organizing principle for information about Chinese New Year traditions in this festive title. Cheerful full-bleed illustrations, done in watercolor, acrylic, and latex paints, show a boy and girl preparing for the fifteen-day holiday, usually accompanied by a cavorting cat and mouse. Many spread across both pages. Their textured background is made of Chinese characters, some showing phrases and others single words. Author and illustrator combine to make this more than a collection of disparate facts. In the entry about calligraphy, the author comments: "Don't get the ink on your new clothes!" referring to the new clothing and haircut children traditionally get for the holiday. The cat turns into a paper cut as Grandma decorates the house. The details are remarkably realistic. The family celebrating together in their compound has twenty-first century acquisitions—a bicycle, a television, satellite antenna, and electric fan—but still a sink with a single faucet, an old-fashioned stove, bedding rolled on the bed, and a string of corn drying outside. There is plenty to ponder here, though readers may need some help to put it all together. This was a Society of International School Librarians honor book.

ELYA, SUSAN MIDDLETON, AND MERRY BANKS

N Is for Navidad

Illustrated by Joe Cepeda
San Francisco: Chronicle Books, 2007
ISBN: 978-0-811-85205-0 | **AGES 4–8**

A Mexican family celebrates the Christmas season, from Las Posadas to Three Kings Day, in a rhyming bilingual book organized by the Spanish alphabet. "H is for *hogar*. / Las Posadas begin. / At each house they say / 'No room at the inn.'" A glossary translates, provides pronunciation, and explains all the Spanish words used, but their meaning is usually clear from the illustrations. Cepeda's lively paintings, done with bright colors in oil and acrylic, show the family decorating and preparing food for the nightly parties preceding Christmas, families and friends on the street during Las Posadas (which begin December 16), preparation of the crèche, the church and the priest, extended family Christmas and New Year's Eve meals, and finally the joy of presents on January 6. In spite of angular lines and odd perspectives, the illustrations are realistic enough to show small details and capture the flavor of that happy time of year. The words presented include traditional foods and decorations as well as some standard words that are appropriate to discussing the season: *excelente*, *iglesia*, *ojos*, and *sonrisa*. This Americás Award commended title is a wonderful introduction to Latino holiday customs as well as the Spanish language.

FARMER, JACQUELINE

O Christmas Tree: Its History and Holiday Traditions

Illustrated by Joanne Friar
Watertown, MA: Charlesbridge, 2010
ISBN: 978-1-580-89238-4 | **AGES 6–10**

From palm branches used by ancient Egyptians to celebrate the winter solstice to today's farm-raised and artificial trees, this informative book traces the development of the custom of decorating Christmas trees and describes the industrialized process that produces these trees today. Relatively lengthy for a picture book, the straightforward text is suitable for older readers; the detailed gouache illustrations will carry them along.

The opening double-page spread shows a traditional scene: the diverse population of a small town celebrates on a snowy green, with music, colored lights on bare tree branches, and a huge decorated evergreen. The rest of the book explains how such customs arose. Readers will see a medieval miracle play, with a fir tree hung with red apples. The author recounts two legends of origin of tree decoration in the sixteenth century, and describes how Christmas was banned as pagan in Massachusetts. She includes White House decoration themes, the development of different forms of tree lighting, the varieties of trees planted today, and even the insects that threaten them. For those curious about the trees we have in our homes each year, this should be a satisfying read, with further resources included.

HEILIGMAN, DEBORAH

Celebrate Easter with Colored Eggs, Flowers, and Prayer

Illustrated with photographs
Washington, DC: National Geographic, 2007
ISBN: 978-1-426-30020-2 | **AGES 5–9**

Photographs from around the world show Christians celebrating Easter in March or April, rejoicing in the Resurrection of Jesus Christ and the return of spring. Heiligman summarizes the Easter story, explains Lent, the six-week preparation for the holiday, and touches on a wide variety of Easter weekend activities. Photographs show pre-Lenten carnival celebrations, bonfires, celebratory masses, and church services, including one at St. Peter's Square in the Vatican and another at the Lincoln Memorial in Washington, DC. Eggs are decorated, searched for, and rolled. There are parades and fancy finery, chocolate candy, and jelly beans. While the effect of the book is joyous, the author doesn't neglect the solemnity of the season, showing penitential processions and prayer services. As is usual in this series, several pages at the end provide further information: fast facts, instructions for a holiday craft—here, Easter eggs with messages—text of two traditional hymns, a cookie recipe, print and web resources for further information, a glossary, world map, and essay from a religious leader, the Reverend George Handzo. A similar title is the author's *Celebrate Christmas with Carols, Presents, and Peace* (National Geographic, 2007).

HEILIGMAN, DEBORAH

Celebrate Rosh Hashanah and Yom Kippur

Illustrated with photographs
Washington, DC: National Geographic, 2007
ISBN: 978-1-426-30076-9 | **AGES 5–9**

Honey, prayers, and blowing the shofar unite Jews around the world in their observance of the High Holy Days. Like others in this series, this title explains the meaning of the holiday but concentrates on the things that people do. Struggling readers will be helped by the enlarged topic sentence on each double-page spread. Illustrated with clearly identified photographs of people in countries around the world, this emphasizes the diversity of the Jewish peoples and the similarities in their celebrations. Men dance in Zimbabwe, father and daughters light candles in California, crowds pray at the Wailing Wall in Jerusalem, and a Portuguese Rabbi demonstrates the shofar. Readers who look carefully at the pictures will smile to see that the Moroccans who bring out Torah scrolls all have prayer shawls, but one young man also wears a baseball cap. The back matter includes fast facts, a prayer, explanations of the Torah and shofar, a recipe for honey cake, suggestions for further exploration, a glossary, and a map. An afterward by Rabbi Shira Stern explains these holidays further and connects them with Sukkot and Simkhat Torah. Like the author's *Celebrate Hanukkah* (National Geographic, 2006) and *Celebrate Passover* (National Geographic, 2007), this was an AJL Notable.

HEILIGMAN, DEBORAH, AND VASUDHA NARAYANAN

Celebrate Diwali

Illustrated with photographs
Washington, DC: National Geographic, 2006
ISBN: 978-0-792-25922-0 | **AGES 5–9**

Colorful photographs illustrate this simple explanation of traditional ways of Diwali, a fall festival of Hindu, Sikh, and Jain faiths, in north and south India and around the world. Sweets, lights, and fireworks are customary. The clear, well-reproduced photographs also show costumes and face painting, flowers, wall and floor designs, ritual baths, noisemaking, and family visits. Child readers can certainly agree: "Diwali is the happiest festival." Pictures range in perspective, size, and placement on the page. Each double-page spread has a line of simple text in large type, and then a few paragraphs developing the topic. The author makes clear that traditions may vary, the stories told at the time may differ, and even the name changes. (It's Deepavali in south India.) But the focus is the same, celebrating the victory of good over evil and light over darkness. Back matter includes further facts, glossary, simple recipe, game, book and web resources, and a map. Two satellite photographs of night lights demonstrate the importance of this festival in India, and an essay by an Indian American provides more information for adult readers. This CBC/NCSS Notable was republished in paperback in 2008 with a slightly longer title.

HEILIGMAN, DEBORAH, AND ELIZABETH H. PLECK

Celebrate Thanksgiving

Illustrated with photographs
Washington, DC: National Geographic, 2006
ISBN: 978-0-792-25928-2 | **AGES 5–9**

In the United States today, Thanksgiving is celebrated the fourth Thursday in November with turkey, family, and counting blessings, but the holiday has a long history. Heiligman's evenhanded presentation of that history dispels some impressions about "the first Thanksgiving." The first U.S. Thanksgiving was actually in Virginia, not Massachusetts, though the one in Plymouth Colony was the first to involve a feast. Only a few years after the Wampanoag Indians came to the Pilgrim's harvest festival, relations between the Europeans and the Native Americans turned sour and hostile, and many of the Wampanoag were killed. Even today, some Indians mourn while others use the occasion to give thanks. Clear, bright, and beautifully reproduced photographs show Americans of many races and cultures traveling, cooking traditional meals involving turkey and our own ethnic and regional foods, saying a blessing, sharing with others, watching parades and football. The two-level text makes it useful as a read-aloud as well. Like others in this series, the book ends with further facts, a time line, a recipe, a glossary, a map, and an essay for adult readers. This useful title was a CBC/NCSS Notable and was republished in paperback in 2008.

HEILIGMAN, DEBORAH, AND NEGUIN YAVARI

Celebrate Ramadan and Eid al-Fitr

Illustrated with photographs
Washington, DC: National Geographic, 2009
ISBN: 978-0-792-25926-8 | **AGES 5–9**

Muslims observe the holy month of Ramadan with praying, fasting, and charity and celebrate its end with the three-day festival of Eid al-Fitr. The layout of this book resembles others in the publisher's holiday series. Each page has a subject phrase in large type, a paragraph of explanation, and captions identifying the photograph or photographs showing Muslims in various parts of the world observing this holy time. A map at the end shows the countries represented which stretch around the world. Prayer and reflection, traditional meals, and daily activities (even karate practice) are all part of the Ramadan experience; Eid includes dancing, fancy foods, and festive clothing. The inclusive text is written in first-person plural. The holiday's connection to the lunar calendar, and the cycle of day and night is emphasized with a striking photo of a crescent moon rising and another of sunset seen from a hillside in Yemen. The back matter includes further facts about Islam, including its Five Pillars; a recipe for "Fatima's Fingers," a baked cheese-and-egg-filled crepe; suggestions for further reading and browsing; a glossary; and an essay for adults. This CBC/NCSS Notable was also republished in paperback in 2009.

HODGES, MARGARET

Moses

Illustrated by Barry Moser
Orlando: Harcourt, 2007
ISBN: 978-0-152-00946-5 | **AGES 6–10**

This dignified retelling of the story of the infant hidden in the river by his mother and raised by the pharaoh's daughter who grew up to lead the Hebrews out from slavery and bring them the Ten Commandments stays reasonably faithful to the Biblical version; Hodges emphasizes details that will appeal to young readers: the boat, the burning bush, plagues, and crossing the Red Sea. She makes the connection with Passover clear. This slim, large-scale picture book is very traditional in its design, using an old-fashioned typeface. Moser's watercolor illustrations are framed in thin red-brown and deep yellow lines and set, each with a caption, on the cream-colored pages opposing the text. His figures are heroic in proportion, and often shown close-up. The illustration of a man wiping lamb's blood over his doorway is particularly striking, as is the one of frightened Hebrews on the shores of the Red Sea disappearing into the blue-black rocks as they hide from the oncoming Egyptian chariots. Ancient and modern Hebrew numbers are contrasted in the illustration and listing of the Ten Commandments that completes this story, the last of Hodges dramatic adaptations of traditional material. This was one of *Booklist*'s Top 10 religion books for youth.

KRENSKY, STEPHEN
Hanukkah at Valley Forge
Illustrated by Greg Harlin
New York: Dutton Children's Books, 2006
ISBN: 978-0-525-47738-9 | **AGES 8–11**

On a snowy night in Valley Forge, curious about a soldier's candle, General George Washington stops to hear the story behind the celebration of Hanukkah. Their somewhat stilted conversations and other details are imagined, but the intent of this attractive book is clearly informational. It's based on an incident said to have happened in December 1778. Presenting the holiday in the context of U.S. history, Krensky uses quotations from Washington's writings to draw parallels between the Americans' fight for freedom and that of the Maccabees. They work. "We too have a cruel enemy who leaves us only with the choice of brave resistance or abject submission," Washington says. Harlin's paintings, in tones of gold, green, and brown, are set in deckle-edged white frames, with white text alongside. When the action is happening at night in Pennsylvania, the background is dusky blue; when it moves to ancient Israel the pages are deep gold. This Sydney Taylor Award winner offers excellent historical background for the holiday that, for many American children, is their first introduction to Judaism, as well as a nice blending of these two histories for those who do celebrate Hanukkah. An author's note describes historical allusions to the incident but doesn't include specific documentation.

MORA, PAT
Book Fiesta! Celebrate Children's Day/Book Day / Celebremos El día de dos niños/El día de los libros
Illustrated by Rafael López
New York: Rayo, 2009
ISBN: 978-0-061-28877-7 | **AGES 4–7**

In Spanish and English, children celebrate Children's Day/Book Day by reading outdoors from morning until night in a variety of languages and increasingly imaginative settings. López fills each double-page spread with lively children—and sometimes animals—reading many different kinds of books. While the text is Spanish and English and the predominant cultural setting is Hispanic, there are allusions to other cultures, including a girl with a dragon kite and an Asian tower as well as a library with a lion. These acrylic paintings feature bright colors, gently rounded lines, stylized figures, and a smiling sun. The cheerful, straightforward text is presented in short lines like a song. The whole is a celebration of the world that opens up to children in books. Fittingly, this was written by the woman who first thought to combine a celebration of books with the traditional Mexican Day of the Child. An afterword tells about El Día del Niño on April 30 and how books have been and can be added to that celebration. This made both the ALSC and NCTE Notable lists.

ROTNER, SHELLEY, AND SHEILA M. KELLY

Many Ways: How Families Practice Their Beliefs and Religions

Illustrated with photographs by Shelley Rotner
Minneapolis: Millbrook Press, 2006
ISBN: 978-0-761-31945-0 | **AGES 4–8**

Photographs and a simple text show children and their families praying, worshiping, and celebrating six different religions: Buddhism, Christianity, Islam, Judaism, Hinduism, and Sikhism. The authors point out that children do many similar things. Though they and their families may have different ways of showing their faith, these have common elements as well. Clear, simply presented photographs show styles and places of worship, holy books, symbols, music played or sung to call to prayer or to celebrate and give thanks, special occasions and foods. There is no more than a line of text per page or double-page spread. The authors conclude: "All their great teachers have taught the same lesson: Love and care for one another and for our beautiful earth." Page by page, an afterword identifies the religions portrayed and identifies what's happening in Rotner's photographs, but without much explanation. No dates or places are given. A Spanish language edition of this CBC/NCSS Notable is also available, *De muchas maneras: Cómo las familias practican sus creencias y religiones.* This is part of the publisher's Shelley Rotner's Early Childhood Library, one of *Booklist*'s Top 10 Early Literacy series.

WINTER, JONAH

The Secret World of Hildegard

Illustrated by Jeanette Winter
New York: Arthur A. Levine, 2007
ISBN: 978-0-439-50739-4 | **AGES 6–10**

From a child who kept her visions secret to scientist, musician, and writer, Hildegard von Bingen was the most important woman of her time, 900 years ago. Through illustrations consciously reflecting the style of a medieval book of hours and a relatively simple text written in allusive language and incorporating some of her own words, this son-and-mother team make the life of an influential mystic accessible to young twenty-first-century readers. The sickly child who saw bright, colorful visions in her gray world is sent away to be educated in a monastery, becomes mistress of the nunnery, an author whose book was acknowledged by the pope, a musician, and a powerful preacher. The gentle, almost primitive illustrations in acrylic and pen incorporate a variety of religious imagery, using a palette of muted colors. Substantial white space surrounds the text and the image on the facing page. Recalling Hildegard's self-description as "a feather on the breath of God," a feather or a small bird appears in almost every picture. A short biography in text, an additional quotation, and a bibliography in the end add substance to this title, which made the Amelia Bloomer list.

8

Our World in History

HIS SECTION INCLUDES A few descriptions of monuments and well-known places of the past, and a number of stories of historical events. But even when the titles emphasize particular events, this is mostly a selection of picture book biographies. This is appropriate. It's through stories of people that most of us come to understand and appreciate other times and places. Even for children who haven't yet gained a sense of history, these are good stories. Some describe famous people, names adults will recognize. But there are also new stories here, stories of people whose lives will be illuminating even for adults who share books with children.

PLACES THROUGH TIME

DEMAREST, CHRIS

Arlington: The Story of Our Nation's Cemetery

Illustrated by Chris Demarest
New York: Roaring Brook Press, 2010
ISBN: 978-1-596-43517-9 | **AGES 6–10**

Arlington National Cemetery, across the Potomac River from nation's capital, once the home of George Washington's stepgrandson, has been a burial place for men and women who have served this country since the Civil War. This straightforward description was written and illustrated by a man who served as an official artist for the U.S. Coast Guard. He provides a short history, a glimpse into traditions such as the riderless horse,

FACING PAGE ART FROM

Pharaoh's Boat by David Weitzman

the pre–Memorial Day "flags in," and the changing of the guard at the Tomb of the Unknown Soldier, as well as names of some better-known people buried there. The relatively substantial text includes details that will interest young readers, especially those with some awareness of history. Its respectful tone suits the subject. Demarest's boxed watercolor illustrations, extending across the gutter, provide a realistic picture of the place, giving a sense of the dignity of its green expanse. He adds to the aura of time passing by showing changing seasons and the growth of an oak tree. A time line includes further information about the slaves who once worked there, and an author's note describes his own connections to the story, adding acknowledgments, recommended reading, and websites. A graceful treatment of an unusual subject.

FOSTER, MARK
Whale Port: A History of Tuckanucket
Illustrated by Gerald Foster
Boston: Houghton Mifflin, 2007
ISBN: 978-0-618-54722-7 | **AGES 8–13**

Settled in 1683, the imagined but representative small colony of Tuckanucket in New England grew, prospered, and withered with the fortunes of the whaling industry, only to revive again with tourism and whale watching today. This is both a believable story of a coastal port and a description of all aspects of whaling as it was carried out in New England between 1690 and 1919. Intricate, unframed colored-pencil-and-ink illustrations carry much of the information. A careful reader of pictures can follow the fortunes of various parts of the whole: the Wampanoag village that is, today, a casino; the oil and candleworks factory, now a museum; the trading schooner wrecked in the early 1700s, now an archaeological site. A fairly extensive text relates the history of the settlement; a second level of text explains details from the illustration. A back page includes a short index, a list of sources, a map of whaling areas, and a bit of further information about whaling ports. This will appeal particularly to those readers who have enjoyed earlier titles by David Macaulay and Bonnie and Arthur Geisert. Teachers may be interested in the reading guide prepared by the Massachusetts Center for the Book.

HARTLAND, JESSIE
How the Sphinx Got to the Museum
Illustrated by Jessie Hartland
Maplewood, NJ: Blue Apple Books, 2010
ISBN: 978-1-609-05032-0 | **AGES 6–10**

A cumulative explanation of how a granite sphinx, built thousands of years ago for the pharaoh Hatshepsut and buried by her successor, was discovered, retrieved, shipped to New York, restored, and added to the collection of the Metropolitan Museum of Art. This lively account of how a museum acquires an art object and the many steps to its display opens with a class museum visit. Rough, childlike sketches of objects adorn the end papers and the title page; painted double-page spreads carry the actual story. The titles of the people involved (from pharaoh and sculptor to artist and photographer) are given a recognizable shape, color, and font; as they reappear in collage on the pages they can be "read" through a variety of clues. Intriguingly, the author varies her verbs. "Smashed and cracked by the stepson" becomes "busted up," "destroyed," "crushed and buried," "left to be forgotten," "shattered to bits," "demolished," "wrecked," and "broken" in succeeding repetitions. The end matter includes more about the discovery, what's precisely known about that female pharaoh, additional facts and figures, and places to visit to see more granite sphinxes and Hatshepsut's restored temple in Luxor. Full of interesting details, this is ideal field trip preparation.

LOW, WILLIAM

Old Penn Station

Illustrated by William Low
New York: Henry Holt, 2007
ISBN: 978-0-805-07925-8 | **AGES 4–9**

In the late nineteenth century, a "palace" was built in New York City as the station for the Pennsylvania Railroad. This magnificent building stood throughout the first half of the twentieth century until its destruction prompted a movement to save old buildings. Low has created a monument of his own, an oversized album of tribute to the historic landmark. The full-bleed, often double-page spreads use a variety of vantage points, showing construction workers up close, details of the statuary, the magnificent façade, and, perhaps most impressively, from high above the crowd, the concourse filled with travelers at the end of World War II. They emphasize the play of light and dark on his subject. His spare text includes plenty of detail in telling of its construction and destruction, but it is the art that makes this book stand out. Begun as a master's thesis, it utilizes a combination of oil paintings and a digital painting program simulating the brush strokes of painting in oils, creating a similar texture. A reading group guide, available on the Web from the publisher, describes the process and also points up the research behind this lovingly created picture book. This was a CBC/NCSS Notable and a CBC/IRA Children's Choice.

OSBORNE, MARY POPE

Pompeii: Lost and Found

Illustrated with frescoes by Bonnie Christensen
New York: Alfred A. Knopf, 2006
ISBN: 978-0-375-82889-8 | **AGES 7–10**

Discoveries in this city, frozen in time by the eruption of Mount Vesuvius in the first century, allow us to imagine what life was like for the Romans who lived there. Osborne's text introduces the catastrophe and describes what has been learned from the ruins, wall paintings, everyday objects, and plaster casts of bodies buried in the ash. Christensen's frescoes are a perfect match. Their slightly blurred effect and faded tones suggest the antiquity of the finds and the interpretive work of archaeologists.

Often they spread across the gutter, with a rectangle of text and an image of a found item on the right. Some are framed double-page spreads. All combine to give a clear sense of how these Romans lived. There are families dining, children playing marbles, shoppers in a market, gladiators in the ring, actors on stage, and even modestly toga-clad gentlemen in the baths. The final two spreads offer before-and-after scenes: a street of villas, shops, and an arch in A.D. 79, and the same street with a few tourists today. An afterword includes a note on the making of frescoes, answers to a picture quiz on found items, and acknowledgments. A CBC/NCSS Notable.

PLATT, RICHARD

Through Time: London

Illustrated by Manuela Cappon
New York: Kingfisher, 2009
ISBN: 978-0-753-46255-3 | **AGES 8–12**

From Neolithic camp in 3500 BCE to today's economic center preparing for the 2012 Summer Olympic Games, London has been a place where people settle and mix, fight and prosper. This large-format book uses detailed pictures, cutaways, and a symbolic map along with blocks of text, and facts in small captions to show changes over time. There's the Roman city in 225, Norman London in 1091, the Great Fire in 1666, the Blitz in 1940, and even Carnaby Street and the Beatles in 1963. Bird's-eye illustrations offer details almost too small to distinguish: Viking raiders disembarking from their oared ship; a religious procession during the Plague; a procession of geese across a busy Georgian street. The book opens with maps showing London in the world and in the British Isles, as well as a time line in the text. A visual time line of the period covered by the book serves as illustrated table of contents; glossary and index complete the package. Though some highlighted details seem randomly chosen, they are interesting; overall, text and illustrations combine to provide a substantial amount of information in this CBC/NCSS Notable, one of a series which includes *Pompeii* (Kingfisher, 2007) and *Beijing* (Kingfisher, 2008, also a CBC/NCSS Notable), and *New York* (Kingfisher, 2010).

RAPPAPORT, DOREEN

Lady Liberty: A Biography

Illustrated by Matt Tavares
Cambridge, MA: Candlewick Press, 2008
ISBN: 978-0-763-62530-6 | **AGES 7–10**

Twelve first-person free-verse poems focus on people involved in the planning, design, financing, construction, and appreciation of the Statue of Liberty, erected in New York harbor in 1886. Opening in her own voice, describing her immigrant grandfather, Rappaport goes on to imagine the thoughts of people involved: from Édouard de Laboulaye, who had the idea, to a journalist covering opening day. Appropriately for the topic, this oversized book has large-scale paintings, done in watercolor, ink, and pencil. One lifts up to reveal the completed statue. The poems, with their many narrators, emphasize the many people involved in the project, packing plenty of information into a relatively small amount of text. With the author's and illustrator's notes and the quotations from other admirers of Lady Liberty at the end, they serve as an important reminder of the role of immigration in our nation's history. The end matter also includes a list of dimensions, a time line, selected sources (demonstrating the primary source research that underlies both text and pictures), and suggested further reading and exploration. This splendid celebration made the CBC/NCSS Notable list. It was a CCBC Choice and an IRA Teachers' Choice.

TALBOTT, HUDSON

River of Dreams: The Story of the Hudson River

Illustrated by Hudson Talbott
New York: G. P. Putnam's Sons, 2009
ISBN: 978-0-399-24521-3 | **AGES 8–11**

An idealized cover image of Hudson's *Half Moon* sailing up river, bathed in the sun's rays and watched by Native Americans in the shadows, sets the stage for this account. Opening and closing with his own connection to this "river of dreams," Talbott chronicles its history, from its glacial beginnings and first Native American inhabitants, through the Dutch, the English who became Americans, and the immigrants who followed. Besides the history, he touches on ships, canals, ice harvesting, literature, and art. Noting its unintended but inevitable degradation, he finishes up with the environmental movement, the Scenic Hudson Decision, and return of native animals. A wavy river runs through the pages, often carrying a time line and always carrying the reader along. The text is set traditionally, but around it are a multitude of details; large-scale illustrations, including some double-page spreads emphasizing the expanse of the river; vignettes; and inset maps. The paintings, done in watercolors, colored pencil, and ink, demonstrate "the breathtaking grandeur" that the Hudson River School celebrated and the sewer the Hudson became before the rise of the environmental movement. There are suggestions for further reading and websites. This stellar tribute was an ALSC and CBC/NCSS Notable.

WEITZMAN, DAVID

Pharaoh's Boat

Illustrated by David Weitzman
Boston: Houghton Mifflin Harcourt, 2009
ISBN: 978-0-547-05341-7 | **AGES 8–12**

A wooden boat, built by hand with ancient tools and methods to guide deceased Egyptian pharaoh Cheops through the underworld after his death 4,600 years ago, was rediscovered in 1954 and meticulously restored and reassembled for viewers today. Weitzman is equally meticulous in his description of this archeological achievement. He provides background, explaining Egyptian religious beliefs as well as craftsmen's techniques of the time before turning to the modern discovery and reconstruction under the supervision of Hag Ahmed Youssef Moustafa. His detailed illustrations, done in earth tones with colored pencil and pen and ink on matte film, stretch across two pages, and give the effect of Egyptian paintings. They show the construction and reconstruction step-by-step. Each part of the intricately constructed ship is identified. Workmen of the past are shown sideways; the modern, three-dimensional style of portraying people appears in the reconstruction section. A gatefold shows the finished product. The endpapers offer different and elaborate scenes of ancient Egyptian life. Through the description of this unique discovery, Weitzman manages to introduce middle grade readers to a fascinating ancient culture. An acknowledgment section, set on a map of the Nile (not named), provides his sources. This ALSC and CBC/NCSS Notable also won an Africana Award.

EVENTS

BROWN, DON

All Stations! Distress! April 15, 1912: The Day the *Titanic* Sank

Illustrated by Don Brown
New York: Flash Point/Roaring Brook Press, 2008
ISBN: 978-1-596-43222-2 | **AGES 7–10**

The translation of the Morse code signal used before the adoption of the better-known SOS serves as title for this straightforward account of how, on its maiden voyage across the Atlantic in 1912, the "unsinkable" *Titanic* struck an iceberg and sank, taking with it more than 1,500 passengers and crew. Designed for young readers, this retelling is unusually gentle. Brown is careful to mention the too few and unfilled lifeboats, the presence of the president of the shipbuilding company and the absence of women and children from steerage among the rescued, as well as the ship that did not come to their aid—but in tones more of puzzlement than blame. From the extensive information available, he chooses details that will appeal to his readers and stick in their minds. His watercolor-and-ink illustrations are realistic but not horrifying. The boat gradually settles on its nose and sinks into the blue night. Washed in browns and grays, swift sketches of the passengers and crew mark the progress of the event with specific incidents. A bibliography supports his research but the quotations are unsourced. This ALSC Notable is an appealing introduction to a storied subject.

FARRIS, CHRISTINE KING

March On! The Day My Brother Martin Changed the World

Illustrated by London Ladd
New York: Scholastic Press, 2008
ISBN: 978-0-545-03537-8 | **AGES 7–10**

Martin Luther King, Jr.'s sister offers a personal recollection of the historic March on Washington for Jobs and Freedom in 1963, led by her brother and attended by thousands. Beginning with a childhood memory of parents who encouraged them to do good but not to be "chesty" about it, she moves quickly to her subject, describing the people who came to Washington and her brother's work on his speech the night before. Ladd's dramatic paintings highlight important points. Varying in shape and size but often extending across the gutter, into the text, and even filling a double-page spread, they show civil rights leaders, the sea of people stretching from the Lincoln Memorial back to the Washington Monument, opposition placards, Mahalia Jackson singing, and King delivering his dream speech. Important lines of text are boldfaced: "Black people held hands with white people." "The sea of marchers parted for Martin and his friends." In an afterword, the author names other leaders, provides more background, and explains that she and her parents watched the march on television as did many others that day. This stirring introduction to a pivotal event in U.S. history was an IRA Teachers' Choice and a Cybils finalist.

HOPKINSON, DEBORAH

Sweet Land of Liberty

Illustrated by Leonard Jenkins
Atlanta: Peachtree, 2007
ISBN: 978-1-561-45395-5 | **AGES 7–10**

This interesting take on the story of Marian Anderson's performance at the Lincoln Memorial in 1939 focuses on a different player in the drama. Oscar Chapman, the governmental official whose organizing efforts made it possible, grew up poor in a part of Virginia where Civil War feelings were still strong. He was once expelled from school for hanging up a picture of Abraham Lincoln. When Anderson was refused permission to sing at Constitution Hall, Chapman was the man who got President Roosevelt involved, and he also invited important federal officials: "Oscar Chapman was a man who liked to keep stirring things up." Hopkinson makes the point that childhood experiences can have a profound effect on adult lives, telling this story simply and effectively. Though some dialogue appears to have been invented, she otherwise sticks to the facts. Her author's note describes her research and adds information about others involved in the event. Jenkins's mixed-media illustrations use a dark palette. They include crayon scribbles, odd angles, and sharp edges, suggesting the turbulent times. The major players are recognizable, and the author's note includes some photographs. This CBC/NCSS Notable and IRA Teachers' Choice would make an excellent read-aloud.

JUDGE, LITA

One Thousand Tracings: Healing the Wounds of World War II

Illustrated by Lita Judge
New York: Hyperion Books for Children, 2007
ISBN: 978-1-423-10008-9 | **AGES 6–10**

After World War II, the narrator's family sent a package to a needy German friend, the beginning of a project that sent thousands of packages including shoes, clothes, coats, and canned food to European survivors, described here in fourteen poems. This gentle postwar story is based on an actual fact; the campaign by ornithologists to help their European colleagues was one American relief effort. It was not without hardship for the donors, either. The narrator's mother gives up her winter coat; a neighbor cans and sells green beans to pay postage. Nostalgic watercolor paintings combine with collage illustrations made up of letters and postcards, photographs, lists, notes, and actual foot tracings found in the author's grandmother's attic. Photographs also show realia from the late 1940s, including cans of food and a homemade rag doll. Interestingly, the Germans are never referred to as the "enemy," and there is some sense of parallel wartime experiences, as first the narrator and then one of the children they correspond with wait for their fathers to come home. This extraordinary story made the ASLC, NCTE, and IRA Global Notable lists, won the IRA Children's Book Award, and was a Jane Addams honor book.

JULES, JACQUELINE

Unite or Die: How Thirteen States Became a Nation

Illustrated by Jef Czekaj
Watertown, MA: Charlesbridge, 2009
ISBN: 978-1-580-89189-9 | **AGES 7–10**

The Constitutional Convention of 1786–87 becomes the subject of a school play illustrated in this child-friendly treatment of a pivotal event in American history. Beginning with an overview of governmental problems arising after the Treaty of Paris, spare text summarizes events in a straightforward fashion. Humorous illustrations bring the story to life. Colorful cartoons depict a multiracial cast of characters, each personally identifiable and in costumes representing their states' current shapes. A variety of props and painted backdrops support each scene. Details of the staging make the history easier to understand and remember. Three costumed branches of government march down a red-carpeted aisle like models; big and small states line up against a height chart backdrop to demonstrate the problem of the Virginia Plan; Rhode Island, refusing to participate, is the smallest in the cast, reappearing only in the end with the discussion of the adoption of the Bill of Rights. An afterword describes the flexibility of the Constitution that was adopted and includes a map. Endnotes, still written for the elementary school reader, answer questions that may have been raised by specific pages. The bibliography conflates the author's sources and other children's titles. The publisher offers a script online.

PINKNEY, ANDREA DAVIS

Sit-In

Illustrated by Brian Pinkney
New York: Little, Brown, 2010
ISBN: 978-0-316-07016-4 | **AGES 6–10**

"A doughnut and coffee, with cream on the side, is not about food—it's about pride." In 1960, at a Woolworth's lunch counter where they'd been refused service, four

African American college students refused to leave, beginning a series of sit-ins that spread across the country and helped desegregate public accommodations. In a picture book format ideal for reading aloud, the Pinkneys make clear the relentless force of peaceful protest. Short, punchy sentences, full of imagery and ideas that connect from page to page, lead the reader to the inexorable conclusion of integration shown in a triumphant foldout page. A larger block of type on each spread highlights the main point. Watercolor-and-ink illustrations in a palette rich with yellows, oranges, and tans add to the triumphant tone. The lines of the lunch counter, straight at first, begin to bend and cross and swirl across the country, culminating in the loop-the-loop of the world-changing Civil Rights Act of 1964. An extensive but still accessible civil rights time line and an afterword about the Greensboro students and the philosophy of nonviolence, plus suggestions for further reading and browsing, complete this Cybils finalist. The Pinkneys' earlier *Boycott Blues: How Rosa Parks Inspired a Nation* (Greenwillow Books, 2008) was an IRA Teachers' Choice and a CBC/NCSS Notable.

RUELLE, KAREN GRAY, AND DEBORAH DURLAND DESAIX

The Grand Mosque of Paris: A Story of How Muslims Saved Jews during the Holocaust

Illustrated by Karen Gray Ruelle and Deborah Durland DeSaix
New York: Holiday House, 2008
ISBN: 978-0-823-42159-6 | **AGES 8–12**

When the Nazis came to Paris in 1940, they brought their campaign against Jews, eventually deporting them to death camps. Some unknown number were sheltered and saved by Muslims working and living in the Grand Mosque of Paris. This picture book for older children describes this little-known rescue, emphasizing the slippery nature of its history. There are few specific details, a few people known to have been given new, Muslim identities, stories of people sheltered for a short time, and people said to have been smuggled through the labyrinth of underground tunnels to boats. Most stories are based on a French documentary film from 1990. The illustrations, painted in oil, are stunning. Muted in color, and often showing people's backs, they support and enhance the mystery of this wartime activity. Details of the mosque's tile work are beautifully re-created. An afterword describes the authors' research; a glossary and extensive bibliography of resources in French and English promote further research. This splendid addition to any Holocaust collection was an ALSC and CBC/NCSS Notable and Orbis Pictus recommended book. An educator's guide is available on the publisher's website.

PEOPLE

BOGACKI, TOMEK

The Champion of Children: The Story of Janusz Korczak

Illustrated by Tomek Bogacki
New York: Farrar Straus Giroux, 2009
ISBN: 978-0-374-34136-7 | **AGES 7–12**

Raised in comfort in Russian-occupied Warsaw, Korczak, a Polish doctor, became a champion of underprivileged children, opening and running orphanages that were models of progressive treatment for the early twentieth century. The serious, thoughtful tone of this biography reflects what must have been this extraordinary man's personality. The author/illustrator describes childhood experiences that may have aroused his compassion. He contrasts the boy's harsh schooling with the self-government he allowed the children in the orphanage and their unusual opportunities. Acrylic paintings show the dreamy boy at play, Warsaw street scenes, hungry children, and the cheerful surroundings of the orphanage. Appealing little sketches accompany the list of orphanage policies. Shadowed at first, the colors lighten for orphanage scenes, but return to gray with the German invasion and occupation. Korczak and the children of his Jewish orphanage were forced to move to the ghetto, where he continued to attempt to nourish them physically and spiritually. The gentle narrative continues right to the end as the doctor quietly leads his children to the train to the Treblinka extermination camp, where he died. An author's note includes a map and a narrative description of his sources. This sobering, inspiring story was a CBC/NCSS and AJL Notable.

CAPALDI, GINA

A Boy Named Beckoning: The True Story of Dr. Carlos Montezuma, Native American Hero

Illustrated by Gina Capaldi
Minneapolis: Carolrhoda Books, 2008
ISBN: 978-0-822-57644-0 | **AGES 7–10**

Carlos Montezuma was a Yavapai boy named Wassaja when he was captured in 1871 and taken into slavery by rival tribesmen. They sold him to an Italian American photographer who raised him mostly in Chicago. There he did well in school, ultimately becoming a medical doctor and a crusader for Native American rights. The author has adapted a long letter about his life Montezuma sent to the Smithsonian in 1905, weaving in words from his other writings to tell his story chronologically. A few paragraphs on each double-page spread describe a single experience. Each spread includes a captioned photograph from the times, often taken by Montezuma's adoptive father, and a painting extending across the gutter and under the first-person narrative. The sepia photos and acrylic paintings, done in desert browns and reds, combine to bring his story and his world alive. (One, a map of Arizona showing river labels that don't correspond to those of today, may concern readers who know the area.) The author's extensive research is described in an endnote and bibliography. This unusual biography was a CBC/NCSS Notable and Orbis Pictus recommended book and received a Carter G. Woodson honor.

DEMI

Tutankhamun

Illustrated by Demi

Tarrytown, NY: Marshall Cavendish Children, 2009

ISBN: 978-0-761-45558-5 | **AGES 7–10**

This gloriously illuminated biography of the boy-king Tutankhamun describes his background, upbringing, and the two religions he managed to reconcile in his brief reign. The text is clear but the illustrations are the attraction here. With Chinese and Egyptian inks and liberal use of a shining gold for highlights and even some backgrounds, the artist has reproduced the style and content of ancient Egyptian imagery. Each picture is semi-enclosed in a border and set on what appears to be linen. Most pages include another small image: boats, animals, people, and religious symbols. There are intriguing details of Tutankhamun's boyhood, hunting ostrich and lions and watching acrobats, dancers, and musicians. Demi portrays the rivalry between his two guardians, Ay and Horemheb; his apparently happy marriage to a half-sister; his early death and swift, secret burial; and, finally, the discovery of his tomb more than 3,200 years later. At the end, she includes a family tree and a map. Her research is cited in a note opposite the title page. The religious differences and historical details may be a bit abstract for the intended audience, but the glamour of this boy-king's life will surely attract young readers of this CBC/NCSS Notable. Demi's other biographies, such as *Marco Polo* (Marshall Cavendish, 2008), may also appeal.

DRAY, PHILIP

Yours for Justice, Ida B. Wells: The Daring Life of a Crusading Journalist

Illustrated by Stephen Alcorn

Atlanta: Peachtree, 2008

ISBN: 978-1-561-45417-4 | **AGES 7–10**

Ida B. Wells was an effective writer and crusader for social justice who launched a national crusade through her articles on lynching. Born into slavery and orphaned early, Lizzie Wells supported her siblings by teaching school before she turned to journalism. The lynching of a friend in 1892 spurred her campaign; threats from white men and the destruction of her Memphis newspaper office sent her north to work for a New York paper and gain a national voice. Historian Dray ably tells her story, choosing details meaningful for young readers such as her early court fight against segregation on trains. Alcorn's dramatic illustrations, with their elongated faces and swooping curves, swirl across the gutter of the double-page spreads to express and extend the ideas of the text. These giclée inkjet prints, hand-tinted with watercolors, invite readers into her story. Both text and pictures are sophisticated, appropriate for older elementary school readers; the back matter is particularly helpful. An afterword offers more about Wells's life, including her support for women's suffrage, a time line, more about lynching, and a bibliography including suggested reading, but no page numbers or index. This made the NCTE Notable and Amelia Bloomer lists.

GLASER, LINDA
Emma's Poem: The Voice of the Statue of Liberty

Illustrated by Claire A. Nivola
Boston: Houghton Mifflin Books for Children, 2010
ISBN: 978-0-547-17184-5 | **AGES 5–9**

Unlike other women of her comfortable class in the 1880s, writer Emma Lazarus cared about immigrants and worked to help them. For a campaign to fund the Statue of Liberty pedestal, she wrote a poem whose last lines were eventually placed on a plaque at the entrance and learned by schoolchildren across the country. Simply told in short lines, this celebration of that poem is illustrated with watercolor and gouache paintings showing late nineteenth century New York in tiny, wonderful detail. Chandeliers gleam through windows of brownstones. Shelves of books, walls decked with paintings, and rooms full of partygoers give a sense of the time and contrast with the immigrants shown trudging through streets, waiting at dockside, aboard ship, and—once, at a distance—fleeing fires in their European homes. The Statue of Liberty is secondary to this narrative, shown under construction toward the end and finally, triumphantly, in the distance and up close, welcoming another generation of immigrants. The author acknowledges sources and the help of subject experts and provides the URL where children's voices sing the well-known words: "Give Me Your Tired, Your Poor." This Sydney Taylor honor book also made the Amelia Bloomer list.

GREENWOOD, MARK
The Donkey of Gallipoli: A True Story of Courage in World War I

Illustrated by Frané Lessac
Cambridge, MA: Candlewick Press, 2008
ISBN: 978-0-763-63913-6 | **AGES 7–10**

Jack Kirkpatrick, a stretcher bearer in the Australian army, used donkeys like those he'd used in his childhood to carry out the wounded at the battle of Gallipoli in Turkey. He and his donkeys rescued more than 300 men, including a former childhood friend. This World War I story is told simply but effectively. Accompanying folk art paintings, done in gouache, are full of fascinating detail. They begin with scenes from his early years in northeastern England. A page of vignettes summarize his Australian activities. The narrative focus is his army experience. On one double-page spread, soldiers practice in the shadow of the pyramids and play with a kangaroo mascot they'd brought; on another, Jack sets off for the last time while his comrades wake and prepare for their day. Indian gunners, Australian soldiers, and medics stand together in a field of crosses after his death. Endnotes add further information and include a quotation from Turkish General Atatürk; the author also lists his sources. This Australian import, by a husband-and-wife team, celebrates the heroism of Australian soldiers in that war, but also reflects its grim toll and futility. A CBC/NCSS Notable and USBBY Outstanding International Book.

HOPKINSON, DEBORAH

Abe Lincoln Crosses a Creek: A Tall, Thin Tale (Introducing His Forgotten Frontier Friend)
Illustrated by John Hendrix
New York: Schwartz & Wade Books, 2008
ISBN: 978-0-375-83768-5 | **AGES 5–9**

When Abe Lincoln was a child in Kentucky, his best friend Austin Gollaher once pulled him out of a rushing creek and saved his life. Little more is known about this historical event, but Hopkinson and Hendrix use it not only to introduce Lincoln's boyhood but also to demonstrate the craft of writing and illustrating biography. The storyteller's voice is apparent from the beginning: "Now here's an old tale of two boys who got themselves into more trouble than bear cubs in a candy store." The illustrator's hand paints the Kentucky valley where the boys lived in 1816, and later sketches alternative story lines in pencil. Both boys walk across the creek on a fallen tree, but Lincoln falls in. Or did they crawl across? The story is told and shown both ways. And how did Austin rescue him? No one knows. "That's the thing about history—if you weren't there you can't know for sure." An author's note at the beginning documents the sources for her few facts. This appealing and humorous tale is an ideal read-aloud and springboard for a discussion of reading and writing history. An ALSC Notable.

KAY, VERLA

Rough, Tough Charley
Illustrated by Adam Gustavson
Berkeley: Tricycle Press, 2007
ISBN: 978-1-582-46184-7 | **AGES 6–10**

Rhyming couplets set as quatrains tell the story of Charley Parkhurst, a nineteenth-century stagecoach driver who knew horses, shot a bandit, lost an eye to a horse's kick, and voted when woman couldn't, keeping her true sex a secret from all—including the reader—until her death. The short lines suggest Charley's taciturn nature as well as the speech patterns of her time and place: "Charley, orphan, / Runs from town. / Hides in stable, / Hunkers down." Some dialogue is imagined early on when the orphan is discovered, and later as ladies gossip about Charley's habits, and finally as the deathbed doctor makes an announcement. An afterword of facts about Charley's life is nicely set on a silhouette map of the United States, showing where these events took place on the east and west coasts. Realistic oil paintings in a muted palette convey a sense of the time. Set on a yellow background at the beginning and end, they spread across the gutter; in the middle, where the stagecoach action is, they fill two pages. This story of a woman who demonstrated early in our history that women could do exactly what men can do made the CBC/NCSS Notable and Amelia Bloomer lists.

KERLEY, BARBARA

What to Do about Alice? How Alice Roosevelt Broke the Rules, Charmed the World, and Drove Her Father Teddy Crazy!

Illustrated by Edwin Fotheringham
New York: Scholastic Press, 2008
ISBN: 978-0-439-92231-9 | **AGES 5–8**

Although he had done many dangerous things, U.S. president Theodore Roosevelt never could tame his first-born daughter, Alice, who "ate up the world" doing just what she wanted all her life. This exuberant biography celebrates the antics of an unusually energetic and willful child who grew up to be that kind of adult. Even the text runs riot, in a controlled way, with varied sizes, fonts, and placement on the page and highlights in all caps. Jumping on the couch, riding a bicycle no-handed, sliding down the White House steps on trays, and leaping fully clothed into a swimming pool—Alice's behavior is unpredictable. Fotheringham's digital media illustrations—in peach, maroon, grayed greens, and Alice blue—feature near-caricatures of the main characters and extend the text. Always moving, always different, there is energy in every page. The end matter (unfortunately on endpapers partially obscured by the book jacket) includes an author's note with further information and sources for the direct quotations, even an acknowledgment to the fact checker. Young readers will be delighted by the humor, proof that history need not be boring. This made both ALSC and CBC/NCSS Notable lists.

LEVINE, ELLEN

Henry's Freedom Box

Illustrated by Kadir Nelson
New York: Scholastic Press, 2007
ISBN: 978-0-439-77733-9 | **AGES 5–9**

After his wife and children were sold away, Henry, a Virginia slave, determined to run away. He had himself nailed into a box and traveled as mail for twenty-seven hours from Richmond to Philadelphia, where he was unpacked into freedom. The skinny small boy with a big head and hands on the cover will draw young readers into this astonishing story. Five double-page spreads give the essential background: Henry grew up in the big house with his mother, was sold away, married and had children, and saw them sold away, too. The rest of the narrative focuses on the feat that made him famous. He is packed into a dark wooden crate, tumbled around in his journey, and finally unpacked into light and freedom. Nelson's pencil, watercolor, and oil paintings use a box motif throughout. From the darkness of his slave days, the pages become filled with light, first when steamboat employees turn him back upright, and finally when his box is opened. Lightly fictionalized, the story nevertheless presents the facts, further explained by an author's note at the end. Her bibliography includes his autobiography. This book won a Caldecott honor and appeared on a variety of lists, including CBC/NCSS Notable, ALSC Notable, IRA Global Notable, and IRA Teachers' Choice.

LOVE, D. ANNE

Of Numbers and Stars: The Story of Hypatia

Illustrated by Pam Paparone
New York: Holiday House, 2006
ISBN: 978-0-823-41621-9 | **AGES 5–9**

In the fourth century CE an enlightened father in Alexandria, Egypt, educated his daughter Hypatia, who grew up to be a famous mathematician, teacher, and philosopher and "a symbol of learned women for centuries to come." Paparone's acrylic illustrations include both Greek and Egyptian motifs and add information to the text. For example, opposite the page describing her nature studies are drawings of seeds and trees from the natural world she might have known, and on the page describing her studies of philosophy are images of thinkers whose ideas she might have encountered. This narrative tells more about her education (including fishing, rowing, and horseback riding as well as studying math and history) than her actual accomplishments. In spite of the title, the reader will get little idea of Hypatia's own work in mathematics or astronomy—and may get a distorted idea from illustrations showing Arabic numerals, and a sky with two big dippers. Some emotion and even dialogue are imagined. Still, this is a useful biography of an unusually intellectually influential woman from long ago. A map, helpful endnotes, and a bibliography complete the package, which was a CBC/NCSS Notable and CCBC Choice and made the Amelia Bloomer list.

NELSON, VAUNDA MICHEAUX

Bad News for Outlaws: The Remarkable Life of Bass Reeves, Deputy U.S. Marshall

Illustrated by R. Gregory Christie
Minneapolis: Carolrhoda Books, 2009
ISBN: 978-0-822-56764-6 | **AGES 7–10**

Born a slave, Bass Reeves, a head taller than most men, a crack shot, master of disguise, and "honest as the day is long," became a U.S. marshal in the Oklahoma Indian Territory, serving for thirty-two years until Oklahoma became a state. Nelson tells the story of this frontier lawman chronologically in double-page spreads, each with only a paragraph or two of text. What distinguishes her telling is the picturesque language: "Bass was as right as rain from the boot heels up." Examples of Reeves's tricks and disguises provide humor as well. The text is set in boxes on sepia-toned pages, suggestive of old paper, or with a background of Christie's oil paintings with their characteristic heavy brush strokes and angular lines. The exemplary end matter includes a glossary of "Western Words," a time line, suggestions for further reading, and ancillary material, as well as a selected bibliography. Solid information presented in an entertaining matter, this Carter G. Woodson honor book highlights an important and relatively unfamiliar figure in both frontier and African American history. This was a CBC/NCSS, ALSC, and IRA Global Notable, won the CSK author award, and received a Golden Kite honor for its illustrations.

PINKNEY, ANDREA DAVIS

Sojourner Truth's Step-Stomp Stride

Illustrated by Brian Pinkney
New York: Disney/Jump at the Sun Books, 2009
ISBN: 978-0-786-80767-3 | **AGES 5–9**

Born into slavery, Sojourner Truth escaped to freedom and spent the rest of her life speaking out about slavery and women's rights. With a storyteller's cadences and a step-stomp stride of her own, the author recounts a life of hardship and determination, stopping to linger on the "Ain't I a Woman?" speech and including some familiar quotations. In a departure from his familiar scratchboard technique, the illustrator uses a skittery dry-brush ink line on watercolored backgrounds of yellow and orange. The images emphasize the strength and sheer imposing size of this famous abolitionist. We see her carrying a pile of logs, sold away from her parents, running away and arriving in a Quaker home; later, she wanders the world, "spreading the word about freedom," and dictates her book. Two spreads focus on her face and fists as she pounds the podium: "Nobody ever helps me into carriages." Two pages of end matter include additional information, two photographs, and suggestions for further reading. While some of Truth's feelings may be imagined, the husband-and-wife team effectively captures the spirit of this indomitable woman. This fine read-aloud choice won a Jane Addams honor and made the Amelia Bloomer list.

RAPPAPORT, DOREEN

Abe's Honest Words: The Life of Abraham Lincoln

Illustrated by Kadir Nelson
New York: Hyperion Books for Children, 2008
ISBN: 978-1-423-10408-7 | **AGES 6–10**

Following the successful format of *Martin's Big Words* (2001), the author summarizes the life of the sixteenth president, interspersing quotations from Lincoln's writings that illustrate his eloquence and simplicity. The spare, almost poetic narrative emphasizes his humble origins, his love for books and words, and his abhorrence of slavery. In the opening image a small boy with a fishing rod is dwarfed by the wilderness behind him. But after that, Nelson's powerful paintings, stretching three-quarters of the way across each double-page spread, look up at Lincoln, almost from ground level, making him appear the larger-than-life figure he is in history. These realistic, color-saturated illustrations show others as well: slaves chained together in New Orleans, a crowd listening to the young campaigner, African American soldiers, and white lawmakers. The back matter includes a time line of important dates, suggestions for further reading and web research, and the full text of the Gettysburg Address. Although the author includes a bibliography, she doesn't actually provide sources for these quotations. They are familiar enough that a simple Google search will lead curious readers to the original. Both an IRA Teachers' Choice and a CCBC Choice, this is a splendid introduction to an American icon.

RAPPAPORT, DOREEN

Eleanor, Quiet No More

Illustrated by Gary Kelley

New York: Disney/Hyperion Books, 2009

ISBN: 978-0-786-85141-6 | **AGES 5–9**

"Do something every day that scares you." Eleanor Roosevelt's advice opens this remarkable biography of this remarkable woman who became First Lady of the World. The outsize format reflects her outsized reputation at a time when "presidents' wives were supposed to be silent partners," as the author explains in a short afterword. Large-type quotations combine with spare text presented in well-spaced short lines, inviting young readers to the story of the shy, unappreciated child who learned to speak for herself, encouraged her husband Franklin's political career, and spent her adult life speaking out for others, defending the weak and fighting for freedoms. Unframed illustrations, painted in muted colors, concentrate on people and places, with close-ups of Eleanor as she grows up, her husband, and her intrusive mother-in-law as well as their homes. We also see working children, soldiers in hospital and in the field, a family in need, Marian Anderson at the Lincoln memorial, and interned Japanese Americans—reminders of issues she concerned herself with. No specific sources are provided for the quotations, but the author has appended a list of selected research sources, appropriate further reading and websites, and a chronology. This made the Bloomer list and was a CCBC Choice and Orbis Pictus recommended book.

RAY, DEBORAH KOGAN

Down the Colorado: John Wesley Powell, the One-Armed Explorer

Illustrated by Deborah Kogan Ray

New York: Frances Foster Books/Farrar Straus Giroux, 2007

ISBN: 978-037-4318-383 | **AGES 7–10**

In spite of losing an arm in the Civil War, Powell continued his lifetime passion to explore the natural world, most notably leading an expedition down the Colorado River, the first ever recorded to pass through the Grand Canyon. This picture-book biography is notable for its well-crafted story. After a brief introduction covering his childhood and Civil War service, Ray concentrates on the titular expedition, emphasizing its danger and difficulty. The suspense of this episode is heightened by the use of double-page spreads where the reader sees small boats and churning rapids and, worse, Powell clinging to the rock face high above the river. Ray's dramatic paintings, done with watercolor, gouache, and colored pencil, make liberal use of shades of brown and red; their colors blend into the yellowed paper of the text pages. Organized chronologically and topically, the text is lengthy for a picture book, but suitable for middle grade readers. It concludes with a map and time line of Powell's journey down the Colorado and a chapter summarizing his later achievements. The end matter includes a chronology of the explorer's life, an author's note, and her bibliography. This made the ALSC and CBC/NCSS Notable lists.

ROCKWELL, ANNE F.

Big George: How a Shy Boy Became President Washington

Illustrated by Matt Phelan
Orlando: Harcourt, 2009
ISBN: 978-0-152-16583-3 | **AGES 5–9**

A tall, shy boy, raised by a much older half-brother, George Washington worked to conquer his shyness and his temper, went to war first for and later against the British king, and became the first president of the United States. This excellent biography avoids the most common platitudes and presents Washington as a real human being. Rockwell mentions his early readings, the sad time when the brother he admired died, his disagreements with General Braddock about strategy, and his enjoyment of farming. The second half of the book describes Washington as a hands-on commander of the colonists' army, worrying about his soldiers during the difficult winter at Valley Forge and victorious at Yorktown. She concludes with his election. None of this was easy. Phelan's pencil-and-gouache illustrations portray a man who often scowls—young George on the cover, then later, as a young British soldier, a commander crossing the Delaware, and a leader who doesn't want a crown. Where British red-coated soldiers appear, they stand out against Phelan's palette of yellows, browns, and grays. An afterword talks about the issue of slavery; sources and suggestions for further research are included. This was an IRA Teachers' Choice.

STONE, TANYA LEE

Elizabeth Leads the Way: Elizabeth Cady Stanton and the Right to Vote

Illustrated by Rebecca Gibbon
New York: Henry Holt, 2008
ISBN: 978-0-805-07903-6 | **AGES 5–9**

In a time when women couldn't even own property, Elizabeth Cady grew up determined to change things. She started the movement to change unfair laws and give women voting rights in the mid-nineteenth century. Stone draws young readers and listeners right in with an opening question. Setting the historical stage, she challenges readers to think about a time when things were different, when women's voices didn't matter, and their votes didn't count. She describes two formative childhood experiences in Stanton's life, followed by her education, marriage, housekeeping, and meetings with other like-minded women that culminated in the historic Seneca Falls convocation in 1848. A short author's note continues the story through the adoption of the nineteenth amendment, and there is a bibliography. The short lines of text, set as if they were poetry, appear inviting and accessible. Gibbon's quirky gouache-and-color-pencil illustrations use a folk art style appropriate to the historical subject. The body language and facial expressions of the people clearly convey their reactions to her radical ideas. More than biography, this is also a well-thought-out introduction to the concept of women's suffrage which made the Amelia Bloomer, ALSC, and CBC/NCSS Notable lists.

THOMAS, PEGGY

Farmer George Plants a Nation

Illustrated by Layne Johnson
Honesdale, PA: Calkins Creek/Boyds Mills Press, 2008
ISBN: 978-1-590-78460-0 | **AGES 8–12**

For longer than he was commander in chief of the Revolutionary Army and the first president of the United States, George Washington was a serious farmer who researched, experimented with fertilizers and crops, and set an example for others in the new agrarian country. Illustrations—painted in oils on canvas whose texture shows—reflect one of Washington's revolutionary farming ideas: he stopped growing soil-depleting tobacco as a cash crop, and instead grew flax and created a cloth-making industry at his Mount Vernon plantation. The author describes some of Washington's inventions, including a plow that also planted. Smiling slaves in some illustrations may seem unrealistic, but in keeping with the positive portrayal of Washington's world. In an afterword the author writes about the man's conflicted feelings about slavery. The relatively lengthy text, set on double-page spreads, is accompanied by occasional quotations in a more formal font from Washington's own journals. Endpapers show a map of Mount Vernon at the time. The back matter also includes a time line and suggestions for further exploration, including a field trip to the restored estate. The author's bibliography is extensive, and the artist also describes his research for this CBC/NSTA Outstanding Science Trade Book and Cybils finalist.

WEATHERFORD, CAROLE BOSTON

Moses: When Harriet Tubman Led Her People to Freedom

Illustrated by Kadir Nelson
New York: Hyperion Books for Children, 2006
ISBN: 978-0-786-85175-1 | **AGES 5–9**

Hearing the voice of God, Harriet Tubman runs away from the plantation where she works as a slave, hiding in the woods, under a blanket in a farmer's wagon, and for seven days in a potato hole, before finally finding freedom in Philadelphia. But God continues to call her. After learning the routes of the Underground Railroad, she returns south, over and over again, to lead others north. Frankly a work of imagination, this goes well beyond the usual definition of informational as providing "documentable, factual material." But it works well as an introduction to this driven and very religious woman's life and is cataloged as history. Kadir Nelson's atmospheric paintings add depth to the story. The gloomy darkness of her travels gives way to a sunlit expanse when she arrives in Philadelphia. At the end, Tubman is bathed in a cloud of glory. These illustrations received a Caldecott honor and CSK award. In faith communities where God is believed to guide individual choices, Weatherford's poetic narrative will be inspirational, but she provides no documentation for Tubman's visions. The book was listed on the ALSC, CBC/NCSS, and IRA Global Notable, and IRA Teachers' Choices lists.

9

Our World Today

INALLY, HERE ARE STORIES of places and people today. "Around the
World" includes both general descriptions and particular stories that bring
a culture to life through the experience of an individual, perhaps real and
perhaps a composite or imagined character. Some describe lands and cultures
far away from the United States; others are closer to home. The biographies in "People"
are true stories of individuals known to have made a difference. These are mostly people
who have been personally active socially and politically in ways that have affected
others in their country and around the world.

AROUND THE WORLD

ALARCÓN, FRANCISCO X.

Animal Poems of the Iguazú

Illustrated by Maya Christina Gonzalez
San Francisco: Children's Book Press, 2008
ISBN: 978-0-892-39225-4 | **AGES 5–12**

Twenty-six bilingual poems, ranging from a few lines to a full page, celebrate wonders
of Iguazú National Park, a dazzling waterfall in the rainforest located at the borders of
Argentina, Brazil, and Paraguay. Toucans, caimans,
coatis, jaguars, monkeys, and more speak in their
own voices, first in Spanish and then in an English
translation by the Chicano author, conveying "the
green voice / of the rainforest." There is some
gentle humor: the hummingbird poem plays with
its Spanish name, "picaflor"; both monkeys and

FACING PAGE ART FROM

Planting the Trees of Kenya:
The Story of Wangari Maathai
by Claire A. Nivola

giant ants comment on the tourists. Two poems describe relevant Guaraní myths. The artist painted and cut paper for illustrations that reflect the poet's description: "in this paradise / of plants and animals / . . . every day / offers more colors / than the rainbow." Chock full of curving shapes and variations in color, the art conveys the abundance of the region. The poetry, sometimes shaped, becomes a part of the scene. Gently, at the end, Alarcón encourages readers to "protect all of us / for the Earth's fate / for your own sake." This stunning celebration won an Américas Award honorable mention and was a Cybils finalist.

BAASANSUREN, BOLORMAA

My Little Round House

Illustrated by Bolormaa Baasansuren
Adapted by Helen Mixter
Toronto, ON: Groundwood Books, 2009
ISBN: 978-0-888-99934-4 | **AGES 5–9**

A Mongolian infant describes his first year of life, his family, their portable *ger* (yurt), travel to their winter home, a spring festival, the lambs that share their quarters, and the family's return to their summer home. Although the narrator is imagined, the intent and effect of this book are informational, offering an intriguing glimpse into an unfamiliar culture. In gouache, with rich, dark colors, the Mongolian author-illustrator has painted pictures full of details of nomadic life. On full-bleed, full-page and double-page spreads, the pictures extend the circular image of the title and yearly journey, from the baby's round face to his traveling basket, the hole in the roof of his little round house, and a variety of round tools and equipment, including a fireplace. There's no effort to explain these details: foods, clothing, various vessels, saddles, even outdoor tools are there for the reader to puzzle out. Extra images such as pieces of the *ger* under construction appear with the text on white pages opposing the pictures. Pair with the Lewin's *Horse Song* (below) to introduce this Asian culture, or use this to add variety to a unit on families. Originally published in Japan in 2006, this was a USBBY Outstanding International Book.

BARDHAN-QUALLEN, SUDIPTA

Flying Eagle

Illustrated by Deborah Kogan Ray
Watertown, MA: Charlesbridge, 2009
ISBN: 978-1-570-91671-7 | **AGES 7–10**

At sunset, a tawny eagle soars over the Serengeti Plain seeking food for its chick. Even the red-orange cover seems to warn readers: this is not your usual nature book. The fiery sunset background darkens to deep blue as night comes, the light dims, and the color in Ray's watercolor-and-colored-pencil illustrations is almost all in the surroundings. The animals pictured can be fearsome: hippos and crocodiles with "toothy smiles," "spitting cobras," "roaring lions," even a human poacher. Others—the zebras, dik-diks, and a small hare—are frightened. Written in couplets with a throbbing, trochaic beat and shortened end lines, this description of the Serengeti ecosystem is impressive. But the moment when the eagle finally catches and kills a "frantic" weaver bird is jarring. Certainly not a bedtime story (though it takes place in the evening), this stark depiction of the world of predator and prey may not be appropriate for a very young audience at any time of day; parents, teachers, and librarians will want to be sure that readers and listeners have been prepared. An afterword gives more information about tawny eagles, Tanzania's Serengeti National Park, and its night life. The bibliography of this CBC/NSTA Outstanding Science Trade Book includes both books and websites.

CRANDELL, RACHEL

Hands of the Rainforest: The Emberá People of Panama

Illustrated with photographs by Rachel Crandell
New York: Henry Holt, 2009
ISBN: 978-0-805-07990-6 | **AGES 5–8**

Pounding rice, spearing fish, collecting roof thatch, the hands of the Emberá people in Panama are seldom still. The simple text and clear images of this photo essay provide a glimpse into a little-known indigenous culture. Resettled in villages along the Sambú River, the Emberá still live far from the modern world. These small pictures, often two or three to a page, give the effect of an album, emphasizing that the author writes from her personal experiences. She knows these people; they have names. We see young children in school, showing off their pets, making music with homemade instruments, and washing in the river. A man harvests plantains, which his wife cooks over a fire. A woman weaves a decorative basket; a girl carries another using a band on her head. Adults and children share the work. The green background and leaf silhouettes on these pages remind the reader of the jungle world. Unfamiliar words are italicized and defined in a glossary. The opening map and author's note provide background for the older reader, but even nonreaders can enjoy this window into an unfamiliar world, a CBC/NCSS Notable like its predecessor, *Hands of the Maya* (Henry Holt, 2002).

CUNNANE, KELLY

For You Are a Kenyan Child

Illustrated by Ana Juan
New York: Atheneum Books for Young Readers, 2006
ISBN: 978-0-689-86194-9 | **AGES 4–8**

A Kenyan boy assigned the task of watching his grandfather's cattle wanders off to find a pancake, chase a monkey, visit the village chief, drink some sweet milk, and play with friends before remembering his responsibilities. The simple text—which won an Ezra Jack Keats new writer award—reads aloud well. It is supported and extended by full-page acrylic and crayon illustrations, with bright colors and rounded, sometimes elongated shapes. These pictures extend beyond their page to connect with the text and add further imagery. The wide-eyed boy takes in all he sees, a vivid representation of Kenyan village life from rooster crow to bedtime. Swahili words and phrases are sprinkled throughout the text, their meaning clear in context. Each visit begins "'Hodi!' Anybody home? 'Karibu!' Welcome!" Translations and a pronunciation guide are in the opening note. This narrative arc is imagined and the boy a product of the author's mind, a composite character rather than one based on a real person, but the informational intent and experience are clear. This was an IRA Global Notable and Teachers' Choice.

DEEDY, CARMEN AGRA, IN COLLABORATION WITH WILSON KIMELI NAIYOMAH

14 Cows for America

Illustrated by Thomas Gonzalez
Atlanta: Peachtree, 2009
ISBN: 978-1-561-45490-7 | **AGES 4–7**

A Maasai student who had been visiting in New York when the twin towers fell returned to his home in Kenya to relate what he saw. His people responded by donating fourteen cows, symbols of life, to be kept sacred there and never slaughtered. That student collaborated in writing this story and contributes an afterword. The text is simple, though formal; stunning illustrations bring it to life. Bright acrylic paintings, with airbrush and pen-and-ink embellishments, glow with the reds of Maasai clothing and brilliant sunsets recalling the fires in New York. They show the Maasai up close and in small groups, including young warriors "in full tribal splendor" dancing in welcome to the American ambassador who accepts the cows on behalf of his country. On almost every double-page spread, a pair of vertical lines recalls the towers. This excellent read-aloud will surely provoke discussion as an example of cultural differences and the universal human wish to respond in times of tragedy. A website adds additional information. This Parents' Choice Gold Award winner and Cybils finalist was a CBC/ NCSS and IRA Global Notable, and an IRA Teachers' Choice. It is now available in Spanish, as well.

FLOOD, BO

The Navajo Year, Walk through Many Seasons

Illustrated by Billy Whitethorne
Flagstaff: Salina Bookshelf, 2006
ISBN: 978-1-893-35406-7 | **AGES 7–10**

Coyote watches twelve months and thirteen moons pass, the Navajo cycle of seasons, each with its appropriate weather and activities. Each month in this beautiful book is described in a free-verse poem, told in a storyteller's rhythms. Poems include the name of the month in the Navajo language. "Atsá Biyáázh brings the hatching of young eagles." "Hurry! Ya' iishjáásh Tosh is for the planting of late crops!" The print is relatively small; the images have priority here. Watercolors on double-page spreads emphasize the many different shades of color in the scenery and include a wealth of detail. There are hidden images in the lines of the pictures, even cutaways. Farmers, cowboys, and families with children wear modern clothing, except for those engaged in dancing. The coyote is a little cartoonlike but appealing. The second edition of this title includes a pronunciation guide for Navajo words, provided by a native speaker. It is complicated, but will help adults read the text correctly. The author teaches at the Diné College; the Navajo illustrator contributed suggestions and changes to the text as well. This unique title made both the CBC/NCSS Notable and Children's Choices lists.

HOLLYER, BEATRICE

Our World of Water: Children and Water around the World

Illustrated with photographs
New York: Henry Holt, 2009
ISBN: 978-0-805-08941-7 | **AGES 6–10**

Six children from around the world tell how they get and use water every day and on a special occasion in this well-designed photo essay published in association with Oxfam. An opening map introduces each child and their home: the mountains of Peru, the seaside in Mauritania, suburban Southern California, low-lying Bangladesh, dry southern Ethiopia, and mountainous Tajikistan near the Afghanistan border. Descriptive explanations from the author alternate with quotations from the young people. Each six-page section is illustrated with clear, beautifully reproduced photographs, two or three to a page, bringing the child reader into the subject's world. The effect is a photo album of the family of man, celebrating the variety of children's lives around the world. The uncertain nature of the supply, the effects of global warming, and the need to avoid waste are mentioned explicitly. But the children are cheerful, and their lives and holidays interesting. The end matter includes "What to Know about Water," a glossary, and a few facts about each country. This CBC/NSTA Outstanding Science Trade Book and CBC/NCSS Notable will be especially welcomed in elementary classrooms, sharing a shelf with earlier titles in the series: *Wake Up, World!* (Henry Holt, 1999) and *Let's Eat!* (Henry Holt, 2004).

KERLEY, BARBARA

One World, One Day

Illustrated with photographs
Washington, DC: National Geographic, 2009
ISBN: 978-1-426-30460-6 | **AGES 5–9**

Photographs from twenty-nine different countries demonstrate that from morning to night, children have remarkably similar days: "At dawn . . . kids around the world get up, wash up, and celebrate a new day. Porridge. Pancakes. Churros. Toast. Hot sweet tea with plenty of milk. Lots of things taste good for breakfast." This beautiful photo essay shows children bathing, eating, going to school, and, after school, work and play, homework, chores, dinner, evening family times, quiet times, and sleeping and dreaming. The combination of the general and particular works exceptionally well to convey the message that kids around the world have much in common. The simple text by a former Peace Corps volunteer is brought to life with clear, interestingly composed, and artfully arranged photographs. An afterword for the older reader includes explanations for each shot—setting it in place and telling something of its circumstances. In rural China a girl crosses a river on a zip line to get to school; in Madagascar a boy herds zebu; in New York a child and dog nap on the floor. A map also serves as an index demonstrating the truly multicultural nature of the selections. This varied, intriguing, effective collection was a CBC/NCSS Notable and an IRA Teachers' Choice.

LEWIN, TED, AND BETSY LEWIN

Horse Song: The Naadam of Mongolia

Illustrated by Ted and Betsy Lewin
New York: Lee & Low Books, 2008
ISBN: 978-1-584-30277-3 | **AGES 7–12**

Intrigued by the idea of the Naadam, these experienced world travelers journey to Mongolia to watch a traditional summer horse racing festival where small boys like 9-year-old Tamir race half-wild horses from their families' herds. The lively present-tense narrative brings the reader into that colorful culture. They include countless particulars: sights, smells, tastes, and sounds, and relevant Mongolian words (defined in context and in a pronouncing glossary). Three days of roadless travel gets them to the horse training camp, where they watch trainers and Tamir's family at work and eat traditional foods. They marvel at the chaos of race day. (Ignoring the starting line, the horses gallop off to the finish, fourteen miles away.) Ted's full-page or double-page watercolor paintings emphasize the breadth of the scenery and the colorfully clad riders and their horses; Betsy's pen-and-ink sketches, also watercolored, show fascinating details. Tamir is a composite character, but the story is based on events of the authors' 2004 trip. The back matter includes "ger facts" and further information about the country and customs. This ALSC Notable will appeal to both horse lovers and armchair travelers who may also enjoy visiting India with *Balarama: A Royal Elephant* (Lee & Low Books, 2009).

MILLER, DEBBIE S.

Big Alaska

Illustrated by Jon Van Zyle
New York: Walker, 2006
ISBN: 978-0-802-78069-0 | **AGES 7–10**

Following the flight of a bald eagle, this collection of Alaskan superlatives introduces the largest of the United States. From Admiralty Island, with the world's greatest concentration of nesting bald eagles; through the Matanuska River Valley, where the world's heaviest vegetables have grown; over the Yukon River, with the world's biggest gold rush; north to the Arctic National Wildlife Refuge; and back south to the Chilkat Bald Eagle Preserve, the eagle journeys 3,100 miles. Striking acrylic paintings on double-page spreads focus on the vast landscape and some of its inhabitants, including humpback whales, Kodiak bears, walruses, and an occasional human. On the endpapers, a map shows the eagle's stopping places and the route of the Iditarod Trail. The introduction includes a silhouette map of the forty-eight states with Alaska superimposed, showing its enormous size. The back matter adds additional statistics and information including websites for further investigation of each of the sixteen special places described. Young readers who love world records will find this an intriguing approach to geography. They will surely point out that Prince William Sound has been overtaken as the site of the worst oil spill in the United States, but the more attractive records described in this CBC/NSTA Outstanding Science Trade Book still stand.

MILWAY, KATIE SMITH

One Hen: How One Small Loan Made a Big Difference

Illustrated by Eugenie Fernandes
Toronto, ON: Kids Can, 2008
ISBN: 978-1-664-53028-1 | **AGES 7–10**

When his mother borrows a small amount of money from her Ghanaian village neighbors, Kojo buys a small brown hen with a few coins and with hard work parlays that into an education, a farm, and a thriving community. The narrative works on two levels. For listeners, there's a rhythmic "This is the hen . . . ," "These are the eggs . . . ," "This is the town that grows . . ." line on acrylic paintings showing Kojo's changing world. These paintings, full of real and surreal details of daily life, stretch across the gutter, leaving a side column for the more detailed but still accessible text describing how Kojo's single brown hen grew into a small flock, which supported his schooling, which led to buying a farm and building a community around his flourishing chicken business. Loosely based on the true story of a real Ghanaian businessman whose life is described in an afterword, this is frankly a demonstration of the working of microfinance, an unusual topic for a picture book. The back matter includes further examples of lives changed through small loans. This Children's Africana Award winner made USBBY's Outstanding International Book list and was a CBC/IRA Children's Choice and IRA Global Notable.

ONYEFULU, IFEOMA

Ikenna Goes to Nigeria

Illustrated with photographs by Ifeoma Onyefulu
London: Frances Lincoln Children's Books, 2007
ISBN: 978-1-845-07585-9 | **AGES 7–12**

Photographs document Ikenna's trip to various parts of Nigeria where the London resident visited family, celebrated his birthday, watched the Osun festival, and played football with cousins when they weren't in school. Through her son's eyes and in her son's voice, writer/photographer Onyefulu describes their trip. This appealing record of a family visit shows a modern African world—tall buildings, modern houses, and a swimming pool near Lagos—as well as rural sights like highway billboards, the painted front of a hair salon, and a roadside shop. Ikenna visits cities beyond Lagos: Onitsha, Oshogbo, and the capital, Abuja, as well as Nkwelle, a village where a great-uncle lives. A cousin gives him a truck he made out of cardboard and glue; an aunt cooks a special rice dish. These photos show his extended family and their houses, as well as street and festival scenes. They offer both a view of today's Nigeria and a reminder that visiting relatives is pretty much the same the world over. The back matter includes a glossary, an index, and a recipe for *jellof* rice; on the cover and endpapers are additional snapshots. Like Onyefulu's *Here Comes Our Bride!* (Frances Lincoln Children's Books, 2005), this won the Children's Africana Award.

RUMFORD, JAMES

Silent Music

Illustrated by James Rumford
New York: Roaring Brook Press, 2008
ISBN: 978-1-596-43276-5 | Ages 6–10

An imagined boy, Ali from Baghdad, explains his love for calligraphy in this introduction to the beauty of the flowing Arabic script. Establishing his credentials as an ordinary boy through his love for soccer, Ali quickly turns to an explanation of the "trail of dots and loops" that forms the sentences in Arabic writing. He emphasizes the need for practice and the illustrations also show his attempts. He tells the story of Yakut, a thirteenth-century calligrapher who created beautiful script in the midst of war. The author-illustrator shows readers the Arab words, the easy "harb" for war, the more difficult "salām" for peace. The message is clear. Rumford's mixed-media and computer-enhanced illustrations are filled with examples of calligraphy and geometric Arabic design elements. Desert golds and oranges predominate in the background—except on one frightening dark night of bombing in 2003. An author's note adds information about the script, Yakut, and the use of calligraphy to make beautiful editions of the Koran. As in several other titles in this section, the character is imagined, but the intent of this book is clearly as informational as was Rumford's Sibert honor–winning *Sequoyah* (Houghton Mifflin, 2004). This won Charlotte Zolotow and Jane Addams honors and appeared on the NCTE, ALSC, and IRA Global Notable lists.

TINGLE, TIM

Saltypie: A Choctaw Journey from Darkness into Light

Illustrated by Karen Clarkson
El Paso, TX: Cinco Puntos Press, 2010
ISBN: 978-1-933-69367-5 | **AGES 5–9**

Tingle reaches back into his childhood to tell about his Choctaw grandmother who called injuries and disappointments "saltypie" and who, after years of blindness, received an eye transplant and could see again. This true story is told in a leisurely, literary fashion. When the young Tom is stung by a bee, his grandmother explains the origin of the family phrase: something his father said as a child when, shortly after they had moved to Texas, a thrown stone hit her in the eye. Vignettes reveal details of her daily life. During her eye operation the entire family gathers to tell stories while they wait. Clarkson's paintings, double-page spreads, focus on the individuals at first, then back off to show the gathered family toward the end. Ghostly ancestors surround their circle. One moving all-blue image shows the grandmother as a sad young child left alone at her Indian boarding school during the Christmas holidays; in another, silhouettes of people holding hands recall the Trail of Tears. In an afterword, Tingle explains his goal: to present modern-day Indians in today's world. Tingle's grandmother's story appeared first in a collection for older readers; this picture book version, an ALSC Notable, is an excellent cultural introduction.

PEOPLE

ANNINO, JAN GODOWN

She Sang Promise: The Story of Betty Mae Jumper, Seminole Tribal Leader

Illustrated by Lisa Desimini
Washington, DC: National Geographic, 2010
ISBN: 978-1-426-30592-4 | **AGES 7–10**

Born in the Everglades in a traditional Seminole community in 1923, Betty Mae Tiger was threatened by tribal leaders because of her white father. She grew up on a more accepting reservation after her family escaped. Seeking education, she left Florida, but returned to serve her people and was eventually elected tribal leader herself. Short poetic stanzas tell the story of a woman whose achievements were remarkable for her times and her male-dominated culture. Annino notes the importance of her mission faith, blended with traditional beliefs of her medicine woman forebears and her thirst for education. As a young wife, Jumper wrestled alligators; later, she helped set up a tribal council and start a newspaper; today, she shares stories of her past. A ribbon of embroidery tops each column of text on a bland fabric background contrasting with the glowing colors of Desimini's lively, naive paintings. Details of Seminole life are visible in each picture; the glossary serves as an index to pictures and text. The back matter of this Amelia Bloomer selection includes an afterword from Jumper's son, chronology, additional biographical facts, author's note, selected bibliography, and websites for further information.

GRIMES, NIKKI

Barack Obama: Son of Promise, Child of Hope

Illustrated by Bryan Collier
New York: Simon & Schuster Books for Young Readers, 2008
ISBN: 978-1-416-97144-3 | **AGES 4–9**

A mother tells her young son about the man they see on television, a boy with divorced parents who lived in Hawaii with his grandparents and later in the Philippines, worked for social change in Chicago, traveled to Africa to find his roots, and dreamed of bringing hope to all Americans. This frankly admiring biography, written before the election, is probably the best of the many for young readers about the nation's forty-fourth president. The frame story allows the tone to be both instructive and loving; the narrative is accompanied by the son's questions and his mother's answers, set off at the bottom of the page so they don't interrupt the story's flow. Basing her inspiring free-verse text on Obama's own biography, Grimes summarizes the main points of his life, including his doubts and uncertainties and the hope his religious faith provided. Quotations are not specifically sourced. Collier's watercolor and collage illustrations show realistic people against often abstract backgrounds. Faces and hands are important. On the title page, Obama's portrait leaps from its frame, and on the cover, the small boy is shown against a background of the rays of the rising sun, overlaid with that same portrait. A CBC/NCSS Notable.

MORTENSON, GREG, AND SUSAN L. ROTH

Listen to the Wind: The Story of Dr. Greg and *Three Cups of Tea*

Illustrated by Susan L. Roth
New York: Dial Books for Young Readers, 2009
ISBN: 978-0-803-73058-8 | **AGES 5–10**

The children of Korphe describe how their village took care of "Dr. Greg," a lost mountain climber, and how he returned the favor by bringing building materials, helping the townspeople build a needed bridge and then a school, and seeing to it that they had books and supplies. Mortenson's story, told first in an adult best seller, has been retold for young readers in a variety of ways. Roth worked with him for this picture book for the very youngest readers and listeners. Her collage illustrations, made of rough-textured papers and woven fabrics, incorporate traditional designs and include considerable detail. The text runs on strips within the page, on a background that is often a pale, textured blue-gray paper suggesting the mountains that surround this village. The end matter includes a scrapbook of photographs, some of which make clear just how forbidding these mountains are. Two maps pinpoint the location of Pakistan in the world and Korphe in Pakistan. There is even a bibliography—unusual in a book for this age level. The story is heartwarming in any version, but this ALSC and CBC/NCSS Notable and IRA Teachers' Choice is particularly engaging.

NAPOLI, DONNA JO

Mama Miti: Wangari Maathai and the Trees of Kenya

Illustrated by Kadir Nelson
New York: Simon & Schuster Books for Young Readers, 2010
ISBN: 978-1-416-93505-6 | **AGES 5–9**

Born into a traditional world that respects trees, Wangari grew up to care for them herself. As an elder consulted by women with a variety of problems, she suggested planting trees to meet their needs. This version of the work of Nobel Peace Prize winner Wangari Maathai uses an oral storytelling pattern, with a repeated refrain, "*Thayu nyumba*—Peace, my people." Her work and her spirit seem larger than life. Only her first name is used, and the narrative, though placing her story in Kenya, offers little background; more explanation comes in an afterword. Nelson's extraordinary illustrations, done on gessoed board in an iconic style, reflect the tone of the text. In an illustrator's note he explains his decision to use printed fabrics as well as his customary oil paints. A glossary defines Kikuyu words, and an author's note describes her sources. This admiring biography is a gorgeous additional title but might not be the best for introducing this extraordinary woman. Johnson's *Seeds of Change* (Lee & Low Books, 2010)—another beautifully illustrated title, but for slightly older readers—tells more about her education. Both books made the Amelia Bloomer list.

NIVOLA, CLAIRE A.

Planting the Trees of Kenya: The Story of Wangari Maathai

Illustrated by Claire A. Nivola

New York: Farrar Straus Giroux, 2008

ISBN: 978-0-374-39918-4 | **AGES 5–10**

When Wangari Maathai returned from college in the United States, she found the once-forested Kenyan landscape denuded, so she organized women to develop tree nurseries and plant them. To illustrate this chronological narrative, Nivola uses tiny lines and dots of watercolor, making the landscape come alive. Kenyan women in their traditional clothing gather to hear Maathai explain her plan and show them how to collect seeds, plant them, and nurture the seedlings that become the new trees. Kenyan children in school uniforms receive seedlings, too. A map of Kenya appears on the wall as Maathai encourages soldiers to carry seedlings as well as guns. The connection between cutting down trees and erosion is made clear for young readers. A long author's note describes the career of this founder of Kenya's Green Belt Movement in more detail. The author cites sources, including Maathai's own memoir. This won the Jane Addams Award and a Parents' Choice Gold Award and was a CBC/NSTA Selectors' Choice. It was also an ALSC and IRA Global Notable, an IRA Teachers' Choice, Cybils finalist, and Africana honor book. Pair with Winter's *Wangari's Trees of Peace* (Harcourt, 2008), another Selectors' Choice, or the titles mentioned above to see different approaches to this inspiring story.

VAN WYK, CHRIS

Long Walk to Freedom

Illustrated by Paddy Bouma

New York: Roaring Brook Press, 2009

ISBN: 978-1-596-43566-7 | **AGES 7–10**

From boyhood in a tribal village through years of protest against South African apartheid, twenty-seven years in jail and the election that made him that country's first elected president, Mandela tells the story of his own long walk. This adaptation of Mandela's autobiography preserves the first-person voice of the original but adapts the story appropriately for young readers and listeners. The text is straightforward and chronological. Watercolor-and-ink paintings, varying in size and placement on the page, show a variety of South African settings including the rolling hills of his boyhood, boarding school, the tiny houses of the segregated township where he lived outside Johannesburg, the aftermath of the Sharpsville protest, and long lines waiting to vote in 1994. There are pictures of Mandela as a child, of his children, and of the children of South Africa, as well as of the Mandela the adult as lawyer and protester, jail inmate, loving grandfather, and president of his country. The yellow, green, red, and black of the South African flag are echoed in a band of decoration above and below the text as well as on the cover—a nice touch. An opening map and closing time line and glossary add to the information value of this uplifting story, a CBC/NCSS Notable.

WINTER, JEANETTE

Biblioburro: A True Story from Colombia

Illustrated by Jeanette Winter
New York: Beach Lane Books, 2010
ISBN: 978-1-416-99778-8 | **AGES 5–9**

When Luis runs out of space for the books he loves to collect, he opens a traveling library, using his burros to carry books to children in rural areas who delight in borrowing them and hearing the stories Luis tells. This charming, small story is based on the work of Luis Soriana, who now serves over 300 people in northern Colombia, traveling on weekends with his burros, Alfa and Beto. A simply written narrative describes the library's beginnings and follows Luis on a journey to a village called El Tormento. Along the way one burro balks and a bandit threatens but is satisfied with a book. Winter's vibrant acrylic paintings, shapes on a white background, include stylized images of butterflies, birds, plants, and trees of the area. Pen-and-ink speech balloons are used sparingly. One double-page spread shows Luis reading the story of the three little pigs to a group wearing pig masks; cartoon balloons reveal the familiar tale without ever giving its name. In spite of the small trim, the clear shapes and bright pastel colors of the illustrations make this suitable for reading aloud; the book is inviting for small hands to hold as well.

WINTER, JONAH

Sonia Sotomayor: A Judge Grows in the Bronx / La juez que creció en el Bronx

Illustrated by Edel Rodriguez
Translated by Argentina Palacios Ziegler
New York: Atheneum Books for Young Readers, 2009

ISBN: 978-1-442-40303-1 | **AGES 5–9**

From her childhood in the South Bronx, supported by her Puerto Rican mother's love and hard work, Sonia grew up to be determined and exceptionally successful in her chosen career as a judge. Winter's bilingual text emphasizes the ways Sotomayor exemplifies the American Dream. Surrounded by Puerto Rican friends and extended family in her housing project home, the bookish, diabetic child who loves Nancy Drew works so hard in school she makes it to Princeton. Although sometimes uncomfortable in that new, privileged world, she graduates at the top of her college class. Addressing readers directly, Winter skips over the details of most of her career (developed further in an author's note) and ends with her history-making confirmation as the nation's first Latin American Supreme Court justice. Rodriguez has used pastels, acrylic, spray paint and oil-based ink for vignettes, full-bleed, and even double-page spreads focusing on the subject but also illustrating her "Nuyorican" world. Title page and endpapers extend Winter's metaphor of the unexpected moonflower blossom. This inspirational story, related by a versatile writer of biographies for children, made the Amelia Bloomer list and was an Americás Award commended title.

Appendix

A List of Awards and Best-of-the-Year Book Lists Mentioned in the Annotations

This list includes sponsoring organizations, scope, and websites with further information.

AAAS/Subaru SB&F Prize for Excellence in Science Books and Best Books List
Sponsored by the American Association for the Advancement of Science (AAAS), Subaru, and Science Books and Films Online (SB&F), the prize goes each year to exemplary science books in four categories: children's, middle grades, young adult, and hands-on. Both author and illustrator receive an award in the children's category.
http://sbfonline.com/SubaruAward/aboutSubaruAward.htm

Africana Award
The Outreach Council of the African Studies Association annually honors authors and illustrators of outstanding children's books about Africa published or distributed in the United States. The Africana Awards are given in two categories, young children and older children; the age range is 4–18.
www.africaaccessreview.org/aar/nomination_process_2009.html

· ·

Links to all American Library Association awards and book lists can be found at
www.ala.org/ala/awardsgrants/index.cfm

ALA Amelia Bloomer List
The Amelia Bloomer Book List is an annual annotated bibliography of "well-written and well-illustrated books with significant feminist content."[1] It is selected from books published for readers from birth to age 18 by a committee of the Feminist Task Force of the Social Responsibilities Round Table, a section of the American Library Association.

ALA CSK Awards and Honor Books
EMIERT, ALA's Ethnic and Multicultural Information Exchange Round Table, now oversees the Coretta Scott King (CSK) Award, which annually recognizes outstanding

books for young adults and children by African American authors and illustrators that reflect the African American experience.

ALA Schneider Family Book Award and Honor Books
The Schneider Family Book Award, sponsored by the American Library Association as a whole, honors an author or illustrator for a book that "embodies an artistic expression of the disability experience for child and adolescent audiences."[2]

ALA/ALSC Caldecott Award and Honor Books
The Caldecott is awarded annually by the Association of Library Service for Children to the artist of the most distinguished picture book published in the United States. As with other ALSC Awards, the recipient must be a citizen or resident of the United States.

ALA/ALSC Geisel Award and Honor Books
The Theodor Seuss Geisel Award is given annually to the author(s) and illustrator(s) of the most distinguished beginning reader books published in the United States.

ALA/ALSC Notable Books
Members of ALSC's Notable Children's Books Committee are charged with the daunting task of selecting for a list of the very best of the best books for children from 0 to 14. Books that have received other ALSC awards and honors are automatically included on this list.

ALA/ALSC Pura Belpré Award and Honor Books
The Pura Belpré Award is presented to a Latino/Latina writer and illustrator whose work best portrays, affirms, and celebrates the Latino cultural experience in an outstanding work of literature for children and youth.

ALA/ALSC Sibert Award and Honor Books
The Robert F. Sibert Informational Book Medal is given annually to the author(s) and illustrator(s) of the most distinguished informational book published in English in the preceding year.

Americás Book Award and Commended Titles
The Americás Book Award for Children is sponsored by the national Consortium of Latin American Studies Programs and focuses across the Americas. The award jury looks at books published in English and Spanish that portray Latin America, the Caribbean, or Latinos in the United States.
www4.uwm.edu/clacs/aa/index.cfm

APALA Awards
The Asian Pacific American Librarians Association (APALA), an affiliate of the American Library Association, looks at books about Asian-Pacific Americans and their heritage. These books do not have to be written or illustrated by an Asian American,

but they do have to be published in the United States, and they must have been written originally in English.

www.apalaweb.org/awards/literature-awards/

Association for Jewish Libraries Notable Book List and Sydney Taylor Award and Honor Books

The Jewish experience is the focus of the Sydney Taylor Award, presented by the Association of Jewish Libraries (AJL), which also produces a yearly list of Notable Books for Children and Teens with Jewish Content.

www.jewishlibraries.org/ajlweb/awards/stba/STBA_SubmissionInstructions.htm

Bergh Award

The American Society for the Prevention of Cruelty to Animals sponsored the Henry Bergh Children's Book Award, which particularly honored books for children (ages 0–12) about animal treatment. The award was given in three categories: companion animals, humane heroes, and environment and ecology.[3] The last award was given in 2009, and the program has been discontinued.

Boston Globe–Horn Book Award and Honor

The Boston *Globe* and *The Horn Book* jointly sponsor annual book awards in Picture Book, Fiction, Poetry, and Nonfiction categories. The books must be published in the United States.

http://archive.hbook.com/bghb/

Carter G. Woodson Award

The National Council for the Social Studies sponsors a set of book awards, the Carter G. Woodson Award. These awards were designed to encourage writing about ethnic minorities and relations between different ethnicities; one is given for books written for elementary school readers (grades K–6).

www.socialstudies.org/awards/woodson

CBC/IRA Children's Choices

In conjunction with the Children's Book Council (CBC, a publishers' trade association), the International Reading Association (IRA) publishes an annotated list of Children's Choices in *The Reading Teacher*, one hundred books selected from a list of over 500 submitted by publishers and voted on by thousands of children across the country.

www.reading.org/Resources/Booklists/ChildrensChoices.aspx

CBC/NCSS Notable Trade Books for Young People

Members of the National Council for the Social Studies (NCSS) also collaborate with the Children's Book Council to produce a list of notable trade books for students in grades K–8.

www.socialstudies.org/resources/notable

CBC/NSTA Outstanding Science Trade Books for Students K–12

Members of the National Science Teachers Association (NSTA) also collaborate with the Children's Book Council to produce notable book lists. Those at the top of this list are called Selectors' Choices.

www.nsta.org/publications/ostb/

CCBC Choices and the Zolotow Award

The Cooperative Children's Book Center at the University of Wisconsin in Madison sponsors the Charlotte Zolotow Award for the best picture book text each year. They look only at picture books for young children (0–7), and they include a commended book list. CCBC also offers a lengthy list of "Choices" each year, highly regarded for its combination of broad multicultural scope and attention to quality as well as reader appeal, and freely available on the Web.

www.education.wisc.edu/ccbc/books/zolotow.asp
www.education.wisc.edu/ccbc/books/choices.asp

Cybils

A loose collection of children's literature bloggers sponsor the Cybils Awards. They look for books that combine literary merit (not defined more specifically) and child appeal. Nominations are open to the public. Nonfiction picture books are one of their categories, and any book published in English within the given year frame is eligible.

http://dadtalk.typepad.com/cybils/winners/

Golden Kite Award

The Golden Kite Award is the only major children's book award chosen and presented by a jury of children's book writers and illustrators. Sponsored by the Society of Children's Book Writers and Illustrators, it is given in four categories: fiction, nonfiction, picture book text, and picture book illustration.

www.scbwi.org/Pages.aspx/Golden-Kite-Award

IRA Children's Book Award

The International Reading Association (IRA), an organization of literacy professionals many of whom work directly with children up to age 12, gives an award to a "promising author" for his or her first or second published book.

www.reading.org/Resources/AwardsandGrants/childrens_ira.aspx

IRA Global Notable Books

Children's Literature and Reading (formerly known as the Children's Literature Association), a special interest group of the International Reading Association (IRA), publishes an annual list of books with an international focus. Notable Books for a Global Society are chosen from books published for young people in grades K–12.

www.csulb.edu/org/childrens-lit/proj/nbgs/intro-nbgs.html

IRA Teachers' Choices

Every year the IRA also produces a selected list called "Teachers' Choices" designed to highlight books especially useful in classrooms, books that parents also might want to provide and even read aloud. The selection process involves regional field testing of books submitted by publishers—actual use in classrooms rather than the simple judgment of adult experts.

www.reading.org/Resources/Booklists/TeachersChoices.aspx

Jane Addams Peace Award and Honor Books

The Jane Addams Peace Association searches for books for children ages 2 to 12 that promote world community, gender and racial equality, peace, and social justice. These awards are given jointly by that association and the Women's International League for Peace and Freedom.

www.janeaddamspeace.org/jacba/index_jacba.shtml

John Burroughs List

The John Burroughs Association (affiliated with the Museum of Natural History in New York) has a helpful list of books for young people about natural history to which they add a few titles each year.

http://research.amnh.org/burroughs/young_readers_list.html

Lee Bennett Hopkins Award for Poetry

Poet Lee Bennett Hopkins, the (Pennsylvania) University Libraries, the Pennsylvania Center for the Book, and the Pennsylvania School Librarians Association provide an annual award for the best book of children's poetry published in the United States.

http://pabook.libraries.psu.edu/activities/hopkins/

NCTE Notable Books in the Language Arts

The Children's Literature Assembly of NCTE produces this list of notable books. Their list is limited to thirty books per year, and the books are for students in grades K–8.

www.childrensliteratureassembly.org/notables.html

New York Times Best Illustrated List

Newspapers and professional magazines regularly make year-end best book lists, but one of the best-known is the yearly list of best illustrated children's books published by the *New York Times* at Christmastime every year since 1952.

http://events.nytimes.com/gift-guide/holiday-2010/best-illustrated-childrens-books-2010/list.html

Orbis Pictus Award, Honor, and Recommended Book List

The National Council of Teachers of English (NCTE) sponsors the Orbis Pictus Award, the very first award given specifically for an informational book for young readers. Books are expected to be useful in classroom teaching in grades K–8.

www.ncte.org/awards/orbispictus

Parents' Choice Award

The Parents' Choice Foundation has been evaluating children's media and toys since 1978. Its jurors look for "books with honesty and integrity of characters, illustration of elegance and imagination, . . . storytelling that teaches us lessons from lands and cultures close and far away." Book award levels noted here include classic, gold, and silver medals.

> www.parents-choice.org/aboutawards.cfm

USBBY Outstanding International Book List

The United States Board on Books for Young People (USBBY), an affiliate of IBBY, the International Board on Books for Young People, produces an annual list of around forty outstanding international books—books published or distributed in the United States that originated in another country, were originally or simultaneously published abroad. Their scope is grades K–12.

> www.usbby.org/outstanding_international_books_list.htm

Zolotow Award

See Cooperative Children's Book Center.

NOTES

1. "The Amelia Bloomer Book List," www.ala.org/template.cfm?template=/CFApps/
   awards_info/award_detail_home.cfm&FilePublishTitle=Awards,%20Grants%20and%20
   Scholarships&uid=571079592A8D790A, last accessed April 4, 2012.
2. "Schneider Family Book Award," www.ala.org/template.cfm?template=/CFApps/awards
   _info/award_detail_home.cfm&FilePublishTitle=Awards,%20Grants%20and%20Scholar
   ships&uid=A839B3A9DB37CD78, last accessed April 4, 2012.
3. "ASPCA Announces 2008 Henry Bergh Children's Book Award Winners," http://
   web.archive.org/web/20090620212756/http://www.aspca.org/pressroom/press
   -releases/050109.html, last accessed April 4, 2012.

Title Index

Page numbers in bold indicate annotations. Page numbers in italic indicate illustrations.

14 Cows for America, **158**

A

Abe Lincoln Crosses a Creek: A Tall, Thin Tale (Introducing His Forgotten Frontier Friend), 5, **147**

Abe's Honest Words: The Life of Abraham Lincoln, **150**

Aliens Are Coming! The True Account of the 1938 War of the Worlds Radio Broadcast, **114**

All about Manatees, 63

All in Just One Cookie, **87–88**

All Stations! Distress! April 15, 1912: The Day the Titanic Sank, 15, **140**

An Island Grows, **78–79**

Animal Poems of the Iguazú, **155–156**

Ape, 65

Arlington: The Story of Our Nation's Cemetery, **135–136**

Arroz con leche / Rice Pudding, 86

Ashley Bryan: Words to My Life's Song, **104–105**

At Gleason's Gym, **118**

B

Babies in the Bayou, **41–42**

Bad News for Outlaws: The Remarkable Life of Bass Reeves, Deputy U.S. Marshall, **149**

Balarama: A Royal Elephant, 160

Ballerina Dreams: A True Story, **114–115**

Ballet for Martha: Making Appalachian Spring, **113**

Barack Obama: Son of Promise, Child of Hope, **163–164**

Barnum Brown: Dinosaur Hunter, **76**

Beach, 87

Before John Was a Jazz Giant: A Song of John Coltrane, 15–16, **111–112**

Biblioburro: A True Story from Colombia, 12, **166**

Big Alaska, **160–161**

Big Belching Bog, **44**

Big George: How a Shy Boy Became President Washington, **152**

Blockhead: The Life of Fibonacci, **81**

Bones: Skeletons and How They Work, **49**

Book Fiesta! Celebrate Children's Day/Book Day / Celebremos El día de los niños/El día de los libros, x, **131–132**

Born to Be Giants: How Baby Dinosaurs Grew to Rule the World, **73–74**

Boy, Were We Wrong about Dinosaurs!, 80

Boy, Were We Wrong about the Solar System!, 80

A Boy Named Beckoning: The True Story of Dr. Carlos Montezuma, Native American Hero, **144–145**

The Boy Who Invented TV: The Story of Philo Farnsworth, **94**

Boycott Blues: How Rosa Parks Inspired a Nation, 142

Boys of Steel: The Creators of Superman, **103**

Bug Zoo, **68**

Bug-a-Licious, **87**

Butterflies and Moths, 69

Butterfly Eyes and Other Secrets of the Meadow, 45

The Buzz on Bees: Why Are They Disappearing?,
  70–71

C

Can You Count to a Googol?, 79

Capoeira: Game! Dance! Martial Art!, **116**

Celebrate Christmas with Carols, Presents, and Peace, 128

Celebrate Diwali, 6, **129**

Celebrate Easter with Colored Eggs, Flowers, and
  Prayer, **128**

Celebrate Hanukkah, 129

Celebrate Passover, 129

Celebrate Ramadan and Eid al-Fitr, **130**

Celebrate Rosh Hashanah and Yom Kippur, **128–129**

Celebrate Thanksgiving, 129–130

The Champion of Children: The Story of Janusz
  Korczak, **144**

The Chiru of High Tibet: A True Story, **66–67**

City Hawk, 61

Come See the Earth Turn: The Story of Léon Foucault,
  95–96

Compost Stew: An A to Z Recipe for the Earth, **89–90**

Construction Zone, **92**

Crocodile Safari, **56**

Cycle of Rice, Cycle of Life: A Story of Sustainable
  Farming, 89

D

D Is for Dragon Dance, **126–127**

Dark Emperor and Other Poems of the Night, 45

Darwin: With Glimpses into His Private Journal and
  Letters, 40

Dave the Potter, **105**

The Day-Glo Brothers, **93–94**

Deron Goes to Nursery School, 25

Did a Dinosaur Drink This Water?, 79

Diego: Bigger Than Life, **104**

Dinosaur Mountain: Digging into the Jurassic Age,
  15, **75**

Dinosaurs, 15, **74**

Dinothesaurus: Prehistoric Poems and Paintings, 73

Django, **109–110**

Dogs and Cats, **28**

The Donkey of Gallipoli: A True Story of Courage in
  World War I, **146–147**

Down, Down, Down: A Journey to the Bottom of the
  Sea, **43**

Down the Colorado: John Wesley Powell, the One-
  Armed Explorer, **151**

E

An Egg Is Quiet, 53

Eggs, 53

Eleanor, Quiet No More: The Life of Eleanor
  Roosevelt, **151**

Elephants of Africa, **63–64**

Elizabeth Leads the Way: Elizabeth Cady Stanton
  and the Right to Vote, **152**

Emma's Poem: The Voice of the Statue of Liberty,
  146

Even an Ostrich Needs a Nest: Where Birds Begin, **59**

The Extraordinary Mark Twain (according to Susy),
  102–103

F

The Fabulous Feud of Gilbert and Sullivan,
  115

Fabulous Fishes, **55**

Faith, 124, **125–126**

Families, 24

The Fantastic Undersea Life of Jacques Cousteau, **41**

Farm, 86–87

Farmer George Plants a Nation, **153**

Fartiste, **113–114**

Fire Trucks and Rescue Vehicles, **90–91**

First Dog Fala, **29**

The First Pup: The Real Story of How Bo Got to the
  White House, **29**

Flying Eagle, **156**

For Good Measure: The Ways We Say How Much, How
  Far, How Heavy, How Big, How Old, **82**

For You Are a Kenyan Child, **157–158**

The Frog Scientist, 7

Frogs, 6, 57

G

The Grand Mosque of Paris: A Story of How Muslims
  Saved Jews during the Holocaust, **143**

Grandma Comes to Stay, 24–25

Gregor Mendel: The Friar Who Grew Peas, **38–39**

Growing Patterns: Fibonacci Numbers in Nature,
  80–81

Guess What Is Growing inside This Egg, **50–51**

H

The Handiest Things in the World, **30**
Hands of the Maya, 157
Hands of the Rainforest: The Emberá People of Panama, **157**
Hanukkah at Valley Forge, **131**
Heavy Equipment Up Close, **90**
Hello, Bumblebee Bat, **65–66**
Henry Aaron's Dream, **121**
Henry's Freedom Box, **148**
Hip-Pocket Papa, **57–58**
Hiromi's Hands, **86**
Home on the Range: John A. Lomax and His Cowboy Songs, **110**
Horse Song: The Naadam of Mongolia, **160**
Horses, **67–68**
Hotshots!, 98
How Many Baby Pandas?, **66**
How Many Ways . . . Can You Catch a Fly?, **50**
How the Sphinx Got to the Museum, **136–137**
How to Clean a Hippopotamus: A Look at Unusual Animal Partnerships, 18, **49–50**
Human Body, 22, **29–30**
Hurricane Hunters! Riders on the Storm, **98**

I

I Am Marc Chagall: Text Loosely Inspired by My Life *by Marc Chagall*, **106**
I Feel Better with a Frog in My Throat: History's Strangest Cures, **32**
I Have a Little Dreidel, **126**
Ice Bears, **64**
Ikenna Goes to Nigeria, **161–162**
I'm a Pill Bug, **72–73**
I'm Getting a Checkup, **33**
In the Belly of an Ox: The Unexpected Photographic Adventures of Richard and Cherry Kearton, **39**
In the Trees, Honey Bees, **70**
Insect Detective, **71**
Into the Deep: The Life of Naturalist and Explorer William Beebe, **40–41**
Inventions, **96**
It's a Butterfly's Life, 59

J

Jazz, **110–111**
John Brown, 16

John Muir: America's First Environmentalist, **39–40**
Just One Bite, **51**

K

Kindergarten Day USA and China / Kindergarten Day China and USA, **25–26**
Knut, 65

L

Lady Liberty: A Biography, **138–139**
Let's Eat!, 159
Life in the Boreal Forest, **42–43**
Lightship, **91**
Listen to the Wind: The Story of Dr. Greg and Three Cups of Tea, 15, **164**
Little Kids Big Book of Animals, **48–49**
Little Lions, Bull Baiters, and Hunting Hounds: A History of Dog Breeds, **27**
Living Color, 50
Living Sunlight: How Plants Bring the Earth to Life, 5, **77**
Lizards, **6**, 56
Long Walk to Freedom, **165–166**
The Longest Season: The Story of the Orioles' 1988 Losing Streak, **120**
Looking Closely along the Shore, **44–45**
Looking Closely in the Rain Forest, 45
Looking for Miza, 65
Louis Sockalexis: Native American Baseball Pioneer, **122**

M

The Magic School Bus and the Climate Challenge, 5, **78**
Mama Miti: Wangari Maathai and the Trees of Kenya, 20, **164–165**
A Manatee Morning, 63
Manfish, 41
Many Ways: How Families Practice Their Beliefs and Religions, **132**
Maple Syrup Season, **88–89**
March On! The Day My Brother Martin Changed the World, **140–141**
Marsupials, 69
Marvelous Mattie: How Margaret E. Knight Became an Inventor, **95**
May I Pet Your Dog? The How-to Guide for Kids Meeting Dogs (and Dogs Meeting Kids), **27**

Mayday! Mayday!, 98

Mermaid Queen: The Spectacular True Story of Annette Kellerman, Who Swam Her Way to Fame, Fortune, and Swimsuit History!, 112–113

Monarch and Milkweed, 69–70

Moon Landing, 99

Moonshot: The Flight of Apollo 11, 98

Moses, 130–131

Moses: When Harriet Tubman Led Her People to Freedom, 9, 153

Mosquito Bite, 34

My Bones and Muscles / Huesos y músculos, 31

My Brother Charlie: A Sister's Story of Autism, 25

My Little Round House, 5, 156

My Name Is Celia, 102

My Name Is Gabito: The Life of Gabriel García Márquez, 101–102

My Name Is Gabriela, 102

My Papa Diego and Me, 104

My Senator and Me: A Dog's-Eye View of Washington, D.C., 28

N

N Is for Navidad, 127

Nasreen's Secret School: A True Story from Afghanistan, 26

The Navajo Year, Walk through Many Seasons, 158–159

Neo Leo: The Ageless Ideas of Leonardo da Vinci, 93

No Easy Way: The Story of Ted Williams and the Last .400 Season, 14, 116–117

Not My Boy! A Father, a Son, and One Family's Journey with Autism, 25

Nothing but Trouble: The Story of Althea Gibson, 120–121

Now and Ben: The Modern Inventions of Ben Franklin, 93

O

O Christmas Tree: Its History and Holiday Traditions, 127–128

Odetta: The Queen of Folk, 109

Of Numbers and Stars: The Story of Hypatia, 149

Old Penn Station, 137

Older Than the Stars, 17, 79–80

¡Olé Flamenco!, 112

One Giant Leap, 97

One Hen: How One Small Loan Made a Big Difference, 161

One Thousand Tracings: Healing the Wounds of World War II, 141–142

One World, One Day, 159–160

Our Grandparents: A Global Album, 23–24

Our World of Water: Children and Water around the World, 159

Owen and Mzee, 65

P

Pale Male: Citizen Hawk of New York City, 20, 61

Patience Wright: America's First Sculptor and Revolutionary Spy, 107–108

Pelé: King of Soccer / Pelé El rey del fútbol, 117

Pharaoh's Boat, 134, 139–140

Piano Starts Here: The Young Art Tatum, 111

Pierre the Penguin: A True Story, 60

A Place for Birds, 61–62

Planting the Trees of Kenya: The Story of Wangari Maathai, 20, 154, 165

A Platypus' World, 62

Poetrees, 47

Pompeii: Lost and Found, 137–138

Pop! The Accidental Invention of Bubble Gum, 94–95

Predators, 52

R

Redwoods, 6, 46–47

River of Dreams: The Story of the Hudson River, 139

A River of Words: The Story of William Carlos Williams, 100, 102

Roadwork, 84, 92–93

Rough, Tough Charley, 147

S

Sabertooth, 74–75

Saltypie: A Choctaw Journey from Darkness into Light, 162–163

Sandy's Circus: A Story about Alexander Calder, 108

Sea Horse: The Shyest Fish in the Sea, 54

Seabiscuit: The Wonder Horse, 119

The Secret World of Hildegard, 132–133

The Secret World of Walter Anderson, 103–104

A Seed Is Sleepy, 46

Seeds of Change, 165

Shades of People, 32

Sharks, 55

She Sang Promise: The Story of Betty Mae Jumper, Seminole Tribal Leader, 163

Shining Star: The Anna May Wong Story, 115–116

Silent Music, 5, **162**

Sisters and Brothers: Sibling Relationships in the Animal World, **50**

Sit-In, **142–143**

Skunks, **67**

Sky Boys: How They Built the Empire State Building, **91–92**

Slippery, Slimy Baby Frogs, **58**

Slow Down for Manatees, 5, **62–63**

Sneaky, Spinning Baby Spiders, 58

Sneeze!, **34**

Snowflake Bentley, 78

Soar, Elinor!, **97**

Sojourner Truth's Step-Stomp Stride, **150**

Sonia Sotomayor: A Judge Grows in the Bronx / La juez que creció en el Bronx, **166–167**

Sopa de frijoles: Un poema para cocinar / Bean Soup: A Cooking Poem, **85–86**

Spiders, 6, 36, **69**

Stable, **118**

The Story of Charles Atlas, Strong Man, **119–120**

The Story of Snow: The Science of Winter's Wonder, **77**

Supercroc: Paul Sereno's Dinosaur Eater, **75–76**

Surfer of the Century: The Life of Duke Kahanamoku, **117–118**

Sweet Land of Liberty, 17, 20, **141**

T

Tale of Pale Male, 61

Tarantula Scientist, 7

Through Georgia's Eyes, **107**

Through Time: Beijing, 138

Through Time: London, **138**

Through Time: New York, 138

Through Time: Pompeii, 138

Tough, Toothy Baby Sharks, 58

Tracks of a Panda, 63

Turtle, Turtle, Watch Out!, **58–59**

Turtle Crossing, 57

Tutankhamun, **145**

U

Ubiquitous: Poetry and Science about Nature's Survivors, 9, **52–53**

Under the Snow, **45–46**

Unite or Die: How Thirteen States Became a Nation, 9, **142**

Up, Up, and Away, **71–72**

V

Vinnie and Abraham, 108

Vulture View, **60–61**

W

Wake Up, World!, 159

Wanda Gág: The Girl Who Lived to Draw, **106–107**

Wangari's Trees of Peace, 165

We All Move, **31**

Whale Port: A History of Tuckanucket, 9, **136**

What Bluebirds Do, **59–60**

What in the Wild, 52

What Is Science?, **37–38**

What to Do about Alice? How Alice Roosevelt Broke the Rules, Charmed the World, and Drove Her Father Teddy Crazy!, 6, 15, **148**

What's inside Your Tummy, Mommy?, **30**

What's So Special about Planet Earth?, 79

When the Wolves Returned: Restoring Nature's Balance in Yellowstone, **43–44**

Where Else in the Wild, 52

Where in the Wild? Camouflaged Creatures Concealed—and Revealed: Ear-Tickling Poems, **51–52**

Who Stole Mona Lisa?, **105–106**

Why Are Animals Blue?, **53–54**

Why Do Elephants Need the Sun?, 79

Wild Tracks! A Guide to Nature's Footprints, **38**

Wings, **48**

Wings of Light, 70

Winter Trees, **47–48**

Winter's Tail: How One Little Dolphin Learned to Swim Again, **64–65**

Wolfsnail: A Backyard Predator, **72**

The Wolves Are Back, 15, **42**

Y

You Never Heard of Sandy Koufax?!, **121–122**

Young Pelé: Soccer's First Star, 117

Your Body Battles a Skinned Knee, **33**

Yours for Justice, Ida B. Wells: The Daring Life of a Crusading Journalist, **145–146**

Yum! ¡Mmmm! ¡Qué rico! Americas' Sproutings, 9, **88**

Z

Zero Is the Leaves on the Tree, **81–82**

Author and Illustrator Index

Page numbers in bold indicate annotations. Page numbers in italic indicate illustrations.

A

Abramson, Serlin Andra, **90**
Ajmera, Maya, **23–24**, *124*, **125–126**
Alarcón, Francisco X., **155–156**
Alcorn, Stephen, **109**, **145–146**
Alexandra, Siy, 34, **34**
Allén, Raúl, **95–96**
Allen, Rick, **45**
Ancona, George, **112**, **116**
Andersen, Bethanne, **107–108**
Annino, Jan Godown, **163**
Aoyagi, Nora, **77**
Arbo, Cris, **70**
Argueto, Jorge, **85–86**, 86
Arihara, Shino, **81–82**
Arnold, Caroline, **62**
Arnosky, Jim, 5, **38**, **41–42**, **56**, **62–63**, 63
Aston, Dianna Hutts, **46**, 53
Azarian, Mary, **40**

B

Baasansuren, Bolormaa, 5, **156**
Baker, Nick, **68**
Bang, Molly, 5, **77**
Barasch, Lynne, **86**
Bardhan-Quallen, Sudipta, **156**
Bardoe, Cheryl, **38–39**
Barretta, Gene, **93**, 93

Barton, Chris, **93–94**
Bass, Hester, **103–104**
Baum, Maxie, **126**
Beccia, Carlyn, **32**
Bergum, Constance R., **45–46**
Berne, Jennifer, **41**
Bernier-Grand, Carmen T., **104**
Bishop, Nic, 6, *36,* **56**, 57, 69, **69**
Bogacki, Tomek, **144**
Bond, Higgins, **61–62**
Bond, Rebecca, **39**
Bouma, Paddy, **165–166**
Bowen, Betsy, **44**
Bowen, Fred, 14, **116–117**
Brewer, Paul, **113–114**
Brickman, Robin, **48**
Brown, Don, 15, **140**
Brown, Monica, **101–102**, 102, 117, **117**
Bryan, Ashley, **104–105**
Bryant, Jen, *101,* **102**
Burleigh, Robert, **97**
Bush, Timothy, **87–88**
Butterworth, Christine, **54**

C

Calabresi, Linda, *22,* **29–30**
Calmenson, Stephanie, **27**
Campbell, Richard P., **72**, **80–81**

Campbell, Sarah C., **72**, **80–81**
Capaldi, Gina, **144–145**
Cappon, Manuela, **138**
Carrilho, André, **121–122**
Cassino, Mark, **77**
Cepeda, Joe, **127**
Chin, Jason, 6, **46–47**
Chisholm, Penny, 5, **77**
Christensen, Bonnie, **109–110**, **137–138**
Christie, R. Gregory, **149**
Chrustowski, Rick, **57**
Clarkson, Karen, **162**
Clements, Andrew, **30**
Cobb, Vicki, **33**
Cocovini, Abby, **30**
Cole, Joanna, 5, **78**
Collard, Sneed B., **48**
Collier, Bryan, **105**, **163–164**
Colón, Raúl, **101–102**
Compestine, Ying Chang, **126–127**
Cooper, Elisha, **86–87**, 87
Coppendale, Jean, **90–91**
Corey, Shana, **112–113**
Couch, Greg, **94**, **120–121**
Crandell, Rachel, 157, 157
Crosby, Jeff, **27**
Crowe, Ellie, **117–118**
Cunnane, Kelly, **157–158**
Czekaj, Jef, 9, **142**

D

D'Agnese, Joseph, **81**
Davis, Nancy, 17, **79–80**
Degen, Bruce, 5, **78**
Demarest, Chris L., 98, **98**, **135–136**
Demi, **145**
DeSaix, Deborah Durland, **143**
Desimini, Lisa, **163**
Diaz, David, **104**
DK Publishing Inc., **68**
Dotlich, Rebecca Kai, **37–38**
Dowson, Nick, **63**
Dray, Philip, **145–146**

E

Egielski, Richard, **115**
Elya, Susan Middleton, **127**

Estrin, James, **114–115**
Evans, Leslie, **47–48**
Evans, Shane, **25**

F

Farmer, Jacqueline, **127–128**
Farnsworth, Bill, **122**
Farris, Christine King, **140–141**
Fellows, Stanley, **39–40**
Felstead, Cathie, **78–79**
Fernandes, Eugenie, **161**
Fitzgerald, Dawn, 108
Floca, Brian, **91**, 97, **98**, 113
Flood, Bo, **158–159**
Florian, Douglas, **47**, 73
Foster, Gerald, 9, **136**
Foster, Mark, 9, **136**
Fotheringham, Edwin, 6, 15, **102–103**, **112–113**, 148
Fox, Karen C., 17, **79–80**
Franco, Betsy, **81–82**
Friar, Joanne, **127–128**
Frost, Helen, **69–70**

G

George, Jean Craighead, 15, **42**
Gerber, Carole, **47–48**
Gibbon, Rebecca, **152**
Gibbons, Gail, **63–64**
Glaser, Linda, **146**
Goldish, Meish, 87
Gonzalez, Maya Christina, **155–156**
Gonzalez, Thomas, **158**
Goodman, Susan E., **87–88**
Gore, Leonid, **69–70**
Greenwood, Mark, **146–147**
Grimes, Nikki, **163–164**
Guiberson, Brenda Z., **42–43**, 64
Gustavson, Adam, **147**
Gutierrez, Rudy, 117

H

Harlin, Greg, **131**
Harris, Andrew, **33**
Hartland, Jessie, **136–137**
Hartman, Cassie, **43–44**
Hatkoff, Craig, **64–65**, 65

Hatkoff, Isabella, **64–65,** 65
Hatkoff, Juliana, **64–65,** 65
Hawcock, David, **99**
Heiligman, Deborah, 6, 128, **128, 128–129,** 129, 129, **129–130,** 130
Hendrix, John, 16, **147**
Hill, Laban Carrick, **105**
Hinshaw, Dorothy, **43–44**
Hodges, Margaret, **130–131**
Hollyer, Beatrice, 159, **159**
Hopkinson, Deborah, 17, 20, **91–92,** 110, 141, 147
Hudson, Cheryl Willis, **92**
Hughes, Catherine D., **48–49**

J
Jackson, Shelley Ann, **27**
Jaramillo, Raquell, **30**
Jenkins, Leonard, 17, 20, **141**
Jenkins, Martin, **65**
Jenkins, Steve, 18, **28, 43,** 49, **49–50,** 50, **60–61**
Johnson, Jen Cullerton, 165
Johnson, Layne, **153**
Jordan, Sandra, **113**
Juan, Ana, **157–158**
Judge, Lita, **73–74, 141–142**
Jules, Jacqueline, 9, **142**

K
Kay, Verla, **147**
Kelley, Gary, **151**
Kelly, Irene, 59, **59**
Kelly, Sheila M., **32, 132**
Kennedy, Edward M., **28**
Kerley, Barbara, 6, 15, **102–103,** 148, **159**
Kinkade, Sheila, **23–24**
Kirby, Pamela F., **59**
Knapp, Ruthie, **105–106**
Krensky, Stephen, **131**
Krull, Kathleen, **94,** 113
Kudlinski, Kathleen V., 80, **80**
Kuklin, Susan, **24**
Kulikov, Boris, **108,** 113–**114**
Kunkel, Dennis, 33, **33,** 34, **34**

L
Ladd, London, **140–141**
Landmann, Bimba, **106**

Lasky, Kathryn, **39–40**
Lawrence, John, **54**
Lessac, Frané, **146–147**
Levine, Ellen, **148**
Lewin, Betsy, 160, **160**
Lewin, Ted, **118,** 160, **160**
Lewis, E. B., **103–104**
Lewis, Tami, **97**
Long, John A., 15, **74**
Long, Sylvia, **46**
López, Rafael, *x,* 9, **88, 131–132**
Love, D. Anne, **149**
Lovelock, Brian, *84,* **92–93**
Low, William, **137**
Lumpkin, Susan, **52**
Lunde, Darrin P., **65–66**
Lunis, Natalie, **75–76**

M
MacDonald, Ross, **103**
Markle, Sandra, **57–58,** 58, **58, 66**
Marks, Alan, **57–58**
Martin, Guadalupe Rivera, **104**
Martin, Jacqueline Briggs, **66–67,** 78
Marx, Trish, **25–26**
Marzollo, Jean, **60**
Mason, Adrienne, **67**
Mazellan, Ron, **120**
McCarthy, Meghan, 61, **94–95,** 114, 119, **119–120**
McCully, Emily Arnold, **95**
McElmurry, Jill, **105–106**
McGinty, Alice B., **40**
McGuinness, Bill, **104–105**
McMillan, Beverly, **55**
Milgrim, David, **33**
Miller, Debbie S., **160–161**
Millner, Denene, **25**
Milway, Katie Smith, **161**
Minor, Wendell, 15, 17, **42**
Montgomery, Michael, **29**
Montgomery, Sy, **7**
Mora, Pat, *x,* 9, **88, 131–132**
Mortensen, Lori, **70, 95–96**
Mortenson, Greg, 15, **164**
Moser, Barry, **130–131**
Murphy, Glenn, **96**
Musick, John A., **55**

Myers, Christopher, **110–111**
Myers, Walter Dean, **110–111**

N

Naiyomah, Wilson Kimeli, **158**
Nakassis, Magda, *124*, **125–126**
Napoli, Donna Jo, 20, **164–165**
Narayanan, Vasudha, 6, **129**
Nelson, Jon, **77**
Nelson, Kadir, 5, 9, 20, **148**, **150**, **153**, **164–165**
Nelson, Vaunda Micheaux, **149**
Nivola, Claire A., 20, **146**, *154*, **165**
Nobleman, Marc Tyler, **103**

O

O'Brien, John, **81**
O'Brien, Patrick, **74–75**
Ogle, Nancy Gray, **67**
Onyefulu, Ifeoma, **24–25**, 25, **161–162**
Ormerod, Jan, **27**
Osborne, Mary Pope, **137–138**

P

Page, Robin, 18, **49**, 49, **49–50**, 50
Paparone, Pam, **149**
Parker, Robert Andrew, **111**
Parrish, Margaret, **68**
Paschkis, Julie, **107**, **126**
Patterson, Annie, **58–59**
Peete, Holly Robinson, **25**
Peete, Rodney, **25**
Pérsiani, Tony, **93–94**
Phelan, Matt, **152**
Pinkney, Andrea Davis, 142, **142–143**, **150**
Pinkney, Brian, 142, **142–143**, **150**
Platt, Richard, **99**, 138, **138**
Pleck, Elizabeth H., **129–130**
Pon, Cynthia, **23–24**, *124*, **125–126**
Posada, Mia, **50–51**
Prange, Beckie, 9, **52–53**
Purmell, Ann, **88–89**
Pyle, Charles S., 14, **116–117**

Q

Qualls, Sean, 15–16, **111–112**

R

Ransome, James, **91–92**
Rappaport, Doreen, 5, **138–139**, **150**, **151**

Rau, Dana Meachen, **31**
Ray, Deborah Kogan, 15, **75**, **106–107**, **151**, **156**
Regan, Laura, **60**
Reynolds, Jan, **89**
Ripken, Cal, **120**
Rissman, Rebecca, **31**
Robbins, Ken, **82**
Roca, François, **97**
Rocco, John, **80**
Rockwell, Anne F., **152**
Rodriguez, Edel, **166**
Rodríguez, Rachel, **107**
Rong, Yu, **63**
Root, Phyllis, **44**
Roth, Susan L., 15, **164**
Rotner, Shelley, **32**, **70–71**, **132**
Ruelle, Karen Gray, **143**
Rumford, James, 5, **162**

S

Sayre, April Pulley, **58–59**, **60–61**
Schaefer, Lola M., **51**, **78–79**
Schindler, S. D., **110**
Schulman, Janet, 20, **61**
Schwartz, David M., **51–52**, 52
Schy, Yael, **51–52**, 52
Seidensticker, John, **52**
Senisi, Ellen B., **25–26**
Serafini, Frank, **44–45**, 45
Sereno, Paul C., **75–76**
Shea, Pegi Dietz, **107–108**
Sheldon, David, **40–41**, 76
Siddals, Mary McKenna, **89–90**
Sidman, Joyce, 9, 45, **45**, **52–53**
Simon, Seymour, **67–68**
Singer, Marilyn, **33**, **53**
Small, David, **28**
Smith, Joseph A., **38–39**
So, Meilo, 20, **61**
Sobol, Richard, **92**
Spirin, Gennady, **42–43**
Spirin, Ilya, **64**
Staake, Bob, **29**
Stauffacher, Sue, **120–121**
Steenwyk, Elizabeth Van, **29**
Stewart, Melissa, **45–46**, **53–54**, **61–62**
Stockdale, Susan, **55**
Stone, Tanya Lee, **108**, **152**
Sutton, Sally, *84*, **92–93**

Sweet, Melissa, *100,* **102**
Swinburne, Stephen, 70

T
Takahashi, Kiyoshi, **72–73**
Talbott, Hudson, **139**
Tavares, Matt, **121, 138–139**
Thomas, Peggy, **153**
Thompson, Lauren, **114–115**
Tingle, Tim, **162**
Tokuda, Yukihisa, **72–73**
Turner, Pamela, 6

V
Van Wyk, Chris, **165–166**
Van Zyle, Jon, **160–161**
Vilela, Fernando, 86
Voake, Charlotte, **71**
Voake, Steve, **71**

W
Wadsworth, Ginger, **71–72**
Waldrep, Richard, **117–118**
Wang, Lin, **115–116**
Waring, Geoff, 51

Weatherford, Carole Boston, 9, **15–16, 111–112, 153**
Weber, Jill, **88–89**
Weitzman, David, *134,* **139–140**
Wells, Robert E., 79, **79**
White, Vicky, **65**
Whitethorne, Billy, **158–159**
Wimmer, Mike, **97**
Wingerter, Linda S., **66–67**
Winter, Jeanette, *12,* **26,** 61, **132–133,** 165, **166**
Winter, Jonah, **115, 121–122, 132–133, 166**
Wise, Bill, **122**
Wolff, Ashley, **89–90**
Woodhull, Anne Love, **70–71**
Wynne, Patricia, **65–66, 71–72**

X
Xuan, Yongsheng, **126–127**

Y
Yaccarino, Dan, **41**
Yavari, Neguin, **130**
Yockteng, Rafael, **85–86**
Yoo, Paula, **115–116**
Yoshikawa, Sachiko, **37–38**

Subject Index

Index includes only works that are annotated, not works mentioned within commentary or annotations. Page numbers in bold indicate annotations. Page numbers in italic indicate illustrations.

A

Aaron, Hank, 1934–
  Henry Aaron's Dream, **121**
abolitionists
  Moses: When Harriet Tubman Led Her People to Freedom, 9, **153**
  Sojourner Truth's Step-Stomp Stride, **150**
accuracy in informational books, 16, 18
actors and entertainers, 112–116
  Fartiste, **113–114**
  Mermaid Queen: The Spectacular True Story of Annette Kellerman, Who Swam Her Way to Fame, Fortune, and Swimsuit History!, **112–113**
  Shining Star: The Anna May Wong Story, **115–116**
Afghanistan
  Nasreen's Secret School: A True Story from Afghanistan, **26**
Africa. *See* Ghana; Kenya; Nigeria; South Africa; Tanzania
  14 Cows for America, **158**
  Elephants of Africa, **63–64**
  Flying Eagle, **156**
  For You Are a Kenyan Child, **157–158**
  Grandma Comes to Stay, **24–25**
  Ikenna Goes to Nigeria, **161–162**
  Long Walk to Freedom, **165–166**
  Mama Miti: Wangari Maathai and the Trees of Kenya, 20, **164–165**
  One Hen: How One Small Loan Made a Big Difference, **161**
  Planting the Trees of Kenya: The Story of Wangari Maathai, 20, *154*, **165**
African American abolitionists
  Moses: When Harriet Tubman Led Her People to Freedom, 9, **153**
  Sojourner Truth's Step-Stomp Stride, **150**
African American athletes
  At Gleason's Gym, **118**
  Henry Aaron's Dream, **121**
  Nothing but Trouble: The Story of Althea Gibson, **120–121**
African American authors and artists
  Ashley Bryan: Words to My Life's Song, **104–105**
  Dave the Potter, **105**
African American journalists
  Yours for Justice, Ida B. Wells: The Daring Life of a Crusading Journalist, **145–146**
African American leaders
  Barack Obama: Son of Promise, Child of Hope, **163–164**
  March On! The Day My Brother Martin Changed the World, **140–141**
African American musicians
  Before John Was a Jazz Giant: A Song of John Coltrane, 15–16, **111–112**
  Odetta: The Queen of Folk, **109**
  Piano Starts Here: The Young Art Tatum, **111**
  Sweet Land of Liberty, 17, 20, **141**

African Americans
  Bad News for Outlaws: The Remarkable Life of Bass Reeves, Deputy U.S. Marshall, **149**
  Henry's Freedom Box, **148**
  Sit-In, **142–143**
African Studies Association (ASA). Africana Award, 169
Africana Award, 169
air pilots
  Soar, Elinor!, **97**
Alaska
  Big Alaska, **160–161**
  Life in the Boreal Forest, **42–43**
alphabet books
  Compost Stew: An A to Z Recipe for the Earth, **89–90**
  D Is for Dragon Dance, **126–127**
  N Is for Navidad, **127**
American Association for the Advancement of Science (AAAS)/Subaru SB&F Prize for Excellence in Science Books and Best Books List, 169
American Library Association (ALA) Amelia Bloomer List, 169
American Library Association (ALA) Coretta Scott King Awards and Honor Books, 169–170
American Library Association (ALA) Schneider Family Book Award and Honor Books, 170
American Library Association (ALA)/Association for Library Service to Children (ALSC) Caldecott Award and Honor Books, 170
American Library Association (ALA)/Association for Library Service to Children (ALSC) Geisel Award and Honor Books, 170
American Library Association (ALA)/Association for Library Service to Children (ALSC) Notable Books, 170
American Library Association (ALA)/Association for Library Service to Children (ALSC) Pura Belpré Award and Honor Books, 170
American Library Association (ALA)/Association for Library Service to Children (ALSC) Sibert Award and Honor Books, 170
Americás Book Award and Commended Titles, 170
amphibians and reptiles, 56–59
  Crocodile Safari, **56**
  Hip-Pocket Papa, **57–58**
  Lizards, 6, **56**
  Slippery, Slimy Baby Frogs, **58**
  Turtle, Turtle, Watch Out!, **58–59**
  Turtle Crossing, **57**
Anderson, Marian, 1897–1993
  Sweet Land of Liberty, 17, 20, **141**
Anderson, Walter Inglis, 1903–1965
  The Secret World of Walter Anderson, **103–104**
animal babies
  Babies in the Bayou, **41–42**
  Born to Be Giants: How Baby Dinosaurs Grew to Rule the World, **73–74**
  Eggs, **53**
  Guess What Is Growing inside This Egg, **50–51**
  Sisters and Brothers: Sibling Relationships in the Animal World, **50**
  Tracks of a Panda, **63**
animal communication
  How to Clean a Hippopotamus: A Look at Unusual Animal Partnerships, 18, **49–50**
animals, 48–54
  Animal Poems of the Iguazú, **155–156**
  Just One Bite, **51**
  Life in the Boreal Forest, **42–43**
  Little Kids Big Book of Animals, **48–49**
  Predators, **52**
  Ubiquitous: Poetry and Science about Nature's Survivors, 9, **52–53**
  Where in the Wild? Camouflaged Creatures Concealed–and Revealed: Ear-Tickling Poems, **51–52**
  Why Are Animals Blue?, **53–54**
  Wild Tracks! A Guide to Nature's Footprints, **38**
  Wings, **48**
  See also amphibians and reptiles; birds; fish; insects and spiders; invertebrates; mammals
anthropomorphism, 5, 7, 14, 16
apes
  Ape, **65**
appeals of informational books, 13–14
arctic environments
  Ice Bears, **64**
  Life in the Boreal Forest, **42–43**
Argentina
  Animal Poems of the Iguazú, **155–156**
Arlington Cemetery
  Arlington: The Story of Our Nation's Cemetery, **135–136**

armed services
    Arlington: The Story of Our Nation's Cemetery, **135–136**
    The Donkey of Gallipoli: A True Story of Courage in World War I, **146–147**
art and artists, 103–109
    Ashley Bryan: Words to My Life's Song, **104–105**
    Ballet for Martha: Making Appalachian Spring, **113**
    Boys of Steel: The Creators of Superman, **103**
    Dave the Potter, **105**
    Diego: Bigger than Life, **104**
    I Am Marc Chagall: Text Loosely Inspired by My Life *by Marc Chagall,* **106**
    Patience Wright: America's First Sculptor and Revolutionary Spy, **107–108**
    Sandy's Circus: A Story about Alexander Calder, **108**
    The Secret World of Walter Anderson, **103–104**
    Through Georgia's Eyes, **107**
    Wanda Gág: The Girl Who Lived to Draw, **106–107**
    Who Stole Mona Lisa?, **105–106**
Asia. *See* Afghanistan; China; India; Indonesia; Mongolia; Pakistan; Tibet
    Celebrate Diwali, 6, **129**
    The Chiru of High Tibet: A True Story, **66–67**
    Cycle of Rice, Cycle of Life: A Story of Sustainable Farming, **89**
    Horse Song: The Naadam of Mongolia, **160**
    How Many Baby Pandas?, **66**
    Kindergarten Day USA and China / Kindergarten Day China and USA, **25–26**
    Listen to the Wind: The Story of Dr. Greg and Three Cups of Tea, 15, **164**
    My Little Round House, 5, **156**
    Nasreen's Secret School: A True Story from Afghanistan, **26**
    Tracks of a Panda, **63**
Asian Pacific American Library Association Awards (APALA), 170–171
Association for Jewish Libraries (AJL)
    Notable Book List and Honor Books, 171
    Sydney Taylor Award and Honor Books, 171
athletes, 116–122
    At Gleason's Gym, **118**
    Capoeira: Game! Dance! Martial Art!, **116**
    Mermaid Queen: The Spectacular True Story of Annette Kellerman, Who Swam Her Way to Fame, Fortune, and Swimsuit History!, **112–113**

Nothing but Trouble: The Story of Althea Gibson, **120–121**
    Pelé, King of Soccer / Pelé, El rey del fútbol, **117**
    The Story of Charles Atlas, Strong Man, **119–120**
    Surfer of the Century: The Life of Duke Kahanamoku, **117–118**
    See also baseball
Atlas, Charles, 1893–1972
    The Story of Charles Atlas, Strong Man, **119–120**
Australia
    The Donkey of Gallipoli: A True Story of Courage in World War I, **146–147**
    Hip-Pocket Papa, **57–58**
    Mermaid Queen: The Spectacular True Story of Annette Kellerman, Who Swam Her Way to Fame, Fortune, and Swimsuit History!, **112–113**
    A Platypus' World, **62**
authors and poets, 101–103
    Ashley Bryan: Words to My Life's Song, **104–105**
    Emma's Poem: The Voice of the Statue of Liberty, **146**
    The Extraordinary Mark Twain (according to Susy), **102–103**
    The Fabulous Feud of Gilbert and Sullivan, **115**
    My Name Is Gabito: The Life of Gabriel García Márquez, **101–102**
    A River of Words: The Story of William Carlos Williams, 100, **102**
autism
    My Brother Charlie: A Sister's Story of Autism, **25**
awards, 18–20, 169–174

B

babies
    What's inside Your Tummy, Mommy?, **30**
    See also animal babies
balance in collections, 14
ballet dance. *See* dance
baseball
    Henry Aaron's Dream, **121**
    The Longest Season: The Story of the Orioles' 1988 Losing Streak, **120**
    Louis Sockalexis: Native American Baseball Pioneer, **122**
    No Easy Way: The Story of Ted Williams and the Last .400 Season, 14, **116–117**
    You Never Heard of Sandy Koufax?!, **121–122**

bats
   Hello, Bumblebee Bat, 65–66
Bears
   Ice Bears, 64
   See also pandas
Beebe, William, 1877–1962
   Into the Deep: The Life of Naturalist and Explorer William Beebe, 40–41
bees
   The Buzz on Bees: Why Are They Disappearing?, 70–71
   In the Trees, Honey Bees, 70
Bergh Award, 171
best-of-the year lists, 18–20, 169–174
Bible stories
   Moses, 130–131
Big Bang theory
   Older than the Stars, 17, 79–80
bilingual books
   Animal Poems of the Iguazú, 155–156
   Book Fiesta! Celebrate Children's Day/Book Day / Celebremos El día de los niños/El día de los libros, x, 131–132
   My Bones and Muscles / Huesos y músculos, 31
   My Name Is Gabito: The Life of Gabriel García Márquez, 101–102
   N Is for Navidad, 127
   Pelé, King of Soccer / Pelé, El rey del fútbol, 117
   Sonia Sotomayor: A Judge Grows in the Bronx / La juez que creció en el Bronx, 166–167
   Sopa de frijoles: Un poema para cocinar / Bean Soup: A Cooking Poem, 85–86
biography
   illustrations in, 16
   invented dialogue in, 5, 16
   Abe's Honest Words: The Life of Abraham Lincoln, 150
   Bad News for Outlaws: The Remarkable Life of Bass Reeves, Deputy U.S. Marshall, 149
   Barack Obama: Son of Promise, Child of Hope, 163–164
   Big George: How a Shy Boy Became President Washington, 152
   A Boy Named Beckoning: The True Story of Dr. Carlos Montezuma, Native American Hero, 144–145
   The Champion of Children: The Story of Janusz Korczak, 144
   Down the Colorado: John Wesley Powell, the One-Armed Explorer, 151
   Eleanor, Quiet No More: The Life of Eleanor Roosevelt, 151
   Elizabeth Leads the Way: Elizabeth Cady Stanton and the Right to Vote, 152
   Emma's Poem: The Voice of the Statue of Liberty, 146
   Moses: When Harriet Tubman Led Her People to Freedom, 9, 153
   Rough, Tough Charley, 147
   Saltypie: A Choctaw Journey from Darkness into Light, 162–163
   She Sang Promise: The Story of Betty Mae Jumper, Seminole Tribal Leader, 163
   Soar, Elinor!, 97
   Sojourner Truth's Step-Stomp Stride, 150
   Sonia Sotomayor: A Judge Grows in the Bronx / La juez que creció en el Bronx, 166–167
   Yours for Justice, Ida B. Wells: The Daring Life of a Crusading Journalist, 145–146
biography—artists
   Ashley Bryan: Words to My Life's Song, 104–105
   Boys of Steel: The Creators of Superman, 103
   Dave the Potter, 105
   Diego: Bigger than Life, 104
   I Am Marc Chagall: Text Loosely Inspired by My Life by Marc Chagall, 106
   Patience Wright: America's First Sculptor and Revolutionary Spy, 107–108
   Sandy's Circus: A Story about Alexander Calder, 108
   The Secret World of Walter Anderson, 103–104
   Through Georgia's Eyes, 107
   Wanda Gág: The Girl Who Lived to Draw, 106–107
biography—athletes
   Henry Aaron's Dream, 121
   The Longest Season: The Story of the Orioles' 1988 Losing Streak, 120
   Louis Sockalexis: Native American Baseball Pioneer, 122
   Mermaid Queen: The Spectacular True Story of Annette Kellerman, Who Swam Her Way to Fame, Fortune, and Swimsuit History!, 112–113
   No Easy Way: The Story of Ted Williams and the Last .400 Season, 14, 116–117

Nothing but Trouble: The Story of Althea Gibson, **120–121**

Pelé, King of Soccer / Pelé, El rey del fútbol, **117**

The Story of Charles Atlas, Strong Man, **119–120**

Surfer of the Century: The Life of Duke Kahanamoku, **117–118**

You Never Heard of Sandy Koufax?!, **121–122**

biography—authors and poets

   Boys of Steel: The Creators of Superman, **103**

   The Extraordinary Mark Twain (according to Susy), **102–103**

   My Name Is Gabito: The Life of Gabriel García Márquez, **101–102**

   A River of Words: The Story of William Carlos Williams, **100, 102**

biography—entertainers

   Shining Star: The Anna May Wong Story, **115–116**

biography—explorers

   Down the Colorado: John Wesley Powell, the One-Armed Explorer, **151**

   Into the Deep: The Life of Naturalist and Explorer William Beebe, **40–41**

biography—inventors

   The Boy Who Invented TV: The Story of Philo Farnsworth, **94**

   Marvelous Mattie: How Margaret E. Knight Became an Inventor, **95**

biography—musicians

   Before John Was a Jazz Giant: A Song of John Coltrane, **15–16, 111–112**

   Django, **109–110**

   Home on the Range: John A. Lomax and His Cowboy Songs, **110**

   Odetta: The Queen of Folk, **109**

   Piano Starts Here: The Young Art Tatum, **111**

biography—scientists

   Blockhead: The Life of Fibonacci, **81**

   Come See the Earth Turn: The Story of Léon Foucault, **95–96**

   Gregor Mendel: The Friar Who Grew Peas, **38–39**

   Into the Deep: The Life of Naturalist and Explorer William Beebe, **40–41**

   John Muir: America's First Environmentalist, **39–40**

birds

   Big Alaska, **160–161**

   Even an Ostrich Needs a Nest: Where Birds Begin, **59**

   Flying Eagle, **156**

   In the Belly of an Ox: The Unexpected Photographic Adventures of Richard and Cherry Kearton, **39**

   Pale Male: Citizen Hawk of New York City, **20, 61**

   Pierre the Penguin: A True Story, **60**

   A Place for Birds, **61–62**

   Vulture View, **60–61**

   What Bluebirds Do, **59–60**

bluebirds

   What Bluebirds Do, **59–60**

bodybuilders

   The Story of Charles Atlas, Strong Man, **119–120**

bones

   Bones: Skeletons and How They Work, **49**

books and reading

   Biblioburro: A True Story from Colombia, **12, 166**

   Book Fiesta! Celebrate Children's Day/Book Day / Celebremos El día de los niños/El día de los libros, **x, 131–132**

Boston Globe–Horn Book Award and Honor, **171**

boxing

   At Gleason's Gym, **118**

Brazil

   Animal Poems of the Iguazú, **155–156**

   Capoeira: Game! Dance! Martial Art!, **116**

   Pelé, King of Soccer / Pelé, El rey del fútbol, **117**

brothers and sisters

   My Brother Charlie: A Sister's Story of Autism, **25**

   Sisters and Brothers: Sibling Relationships in the Animal World, **50**

Brown, Barnum, 1873–1963

   Barnum Brown: Dinosaur Hunter, **76**

Brown, Henry Box, b. 1816

   Henry's Freedom Box, **148**

Bryan, Ashley, 1923–

   Ashley Bryan: Words to My Life's Song, **104–105**

bubble gum

   Pop! The Accidental Invention of Bubble Gum, **94–95**

buildings. *See* construction

burros. *See* donkeys and burros

butterflies

   Monarch and Milkweed, **69–70**

C

Calder, Alexander, 1898–1976

   Sandy's Circus: A Story about Alexander Calder, **108**

calligraphy, Arabic
Silent Music, 5, 162
camouflage (biology)
*Where in the Wild? Camouflaged Creatures
Concealed—and Revealed: Ear-Tickling
Poems,* 51–52
Why Are Animals Blue?, 53–54
capoeira (dance)
Capoeira: Game! Dance! Martial Art!, 116
Carter G. Woodson Award, 171
cartoonists
Boys of Steel: The Creators of Superman, 103
cats
Dogs and Cats, 28
Sabertooth, 74–75
cerebral palsied children
Ballerina Dreams: A True Story, 114–115
Chagall, Marc, 1887–1985
I Am Marc Chagall: Text Loosely Inspired by My
Life *by Marc Chagall,* 106
Chapman, Oscar L., 1896–1978
Sweet Land of Liberty, 17, 20, 141
children
One World, One Day, 159–160
*Our World of Water: Children and Water around
the World,* 159
Children's Book Council (CBC)/International
Reading Association (IRA) Children's
Choices, 171
Children's Book Council (CBC)/National Council
for the Social Studies (NCSS) Notable
Trade Books for Young People, 171
Children's Book Council (CBC)/National Science
Teachers Association (NSTA) Outstanding
Science Trade Books for Students K–12,
172
China
How Many Baby Pandas?, 66
*Kindergarten Day USA and China /
Kindergarten Day China and USA,* 25–26
Tracks of a Panda, 63
Chinese American actors and actresses
Shining Star: The Anna May Wong Story,
115–116
Chinese New Year
D Is for Dragon Dance, 126–127
chiru
The Chiru of High Tibet: A True Story, 66–67

Choctaw Indians
*Saltypie: A Choctaw Journey from Darkness into
Light,* 162–163
Christian holidays. *See* Christmas; Easter
Christmas
N Is for Navidad, 127
*O Christmas Tree: Its History and Holiday
Traditions,* 127–128
circus in art
Sandy's Circus: A Story about Alexander Calder, 108
civil rights movement
*March On! The Day My Brother Martin Changed
the World,* 140–141
Sit-In, 142–143
Sweet Land of Liberty, 17, 20, 141
*Yours for Justice, Ida B. Wells: The Daring Life of a
Crusading Journalist,* 145–146
Clemens, Susy, 1872–1896
*The Extraordinary Mark Twain (according to
Susy),* 102–103
climate change
The Magic School Bus and the Climate Challenge,
5, 78
Colombia
Biblioburro: A True Story from Colombia, 12, 166
*My Name Is Gabito: The Life of Gabriel García
Márquez,* 101–102
Colorado River (Colo.-Mexico)
*Down the Colorado: John Wesley Powell, the One-
Armed Explorer,* 151
colors
The Day-Glo Brothers, 93–94
Shades of People, 32
Why Are Animals Blue?, 53–54
Coltrane, John, 1926–1967
*Before John Was a Jazz Giant: A Song of John
Coltrane,* 15–16, 111–112
compost
Compost Stew: An A to Z Recipe for the Earth,
89–90
conservationists. *See* naturalists and
conservationists
construction, 90–93
Construction Zone, 92
Heavy Equipment Up Close, 90
Roadwork, 84, 92–93
*Sky Boys: How They Built the Empire State
Building,* 91–92

cookies
  All in Just One Cookie, **87–88**
cooking. *See* foods and cooking
Cooperative Children's Book Center Choices
  (CCBC) and the Zolotow Award, 172
Copland, Aaron
  Ballet for Martha: Making Appalachian Spring,
  113
cosmology
  Older Than the Stars, 17, **79–80**
counting books
  How Many Baby Pandas?, **66**
Cousteau, Jacques, 1910–1997
  The Fantastic Undersea Life of Jacques Cousteau,
  41
crocodiles
  Crocodile Safari, **56**
  Supercroc: Paul Sereno's Dinosaur Eater, **75–76**
Cybils, 172

D

dance
  Ballerina Dreams: A True Story, **114–115**
  Ballet for Martha: Making Appalachian Spring,
  113
  Capoeira: Game! Dance! Martial Art!, **116**
  ¡Olé Flamenco!, **112**
Darwin, Charles, 1809–1882
  *Darwin: With Glimpses into His Private Journal
  and Letters,* **40**
Dave, fl. 1834–1864
  Dave the Potter, **105**
Diemer, Walter, 1904–1998
  Pop! The Accidental Invention of Bubble Gum,
  94–95
dinosaurs
  Barnum Brown: Dinosaur Hunter, **76**
  *Born to Be Giants: How Baby Dinosaurs Grew to
  Rule the World,* **73–74**
  *Dinosaur Mountain: Digging into the Jurassic
  Age,* 15, **75**
  Dinosaurs, 15, **74**
  Dinothesaurus: Prehistoric Poems and Paintings,
  73
  Supercroc: Paul Sereno's Dinosaur Eater, **75–76**
  See also extinct animals
Divali
  Celebrate Diwali, 6, **129**

dogs
  Dogs and Cats, **28**
  First Dog Fala, **29**
  *Little Lions, Bull Baiters, and Hunting Hounds:
  A History of Dog Breeds,* **27**
  *May I Pet Your Dog? The How-to Guide for Kids
  Meeting Dogs (and Dogs Meeting Kids),* **27**
  *My Senator and Me: A Dog's-Eye View of
  Washington, D.C.,* **28**
dolphins
  *Winter's Tail: How One Little Dolphin Learned to
  Swim Again,* **64–65**
donkeys and burros
  Biblioburro: A True Story from Colombia, 12, **166**
  *The Donkey of Gallipoli: A True Story of Courage
  in World War I,* **146–147**
Douglass, Earl, 1862–1931
  *Dinosaur Mountain: Digging into the Jurassic
  Age,* 15, **75**
durability of picture books, 17

E

eagles and hawks
  Big Alaska, **160–161**
  Flying Eagle, **156**
  Pale Male: Citizen Hawk of New York City, 20, **61**
earth, **77–79**
  *Come See the Earth Turn: The Story of Léon
  Foucault,* **95–96**
  An Island Grows, **78–79**
  *Living Sunlight: How Plants Bring the Earth to
  Life,* 5, **77**
  The Magic School Bus and the Climate Challenge,
  5, **78**
  The Story of Snow: The Science of Winter's Wonder,
  77
  Why Do Elephants Need the Sun?, **79**
Easter
  *Celebrate Easter with Colored Eggs, Flowers, and
  Prayer,* **128**
eggs
  Eggs, **53**
  Guess What Is Growing inside This Egg, **50–51**
Egypt
  How the Sphinx Got to the Museum, **136–137**
  Of Numbers and Stars: The Story of Hypatia, **149**
  Pharaoh's Boat, **134**, **139–140**
  Tutankhamun, **145**

elephants
    Elephants of Africa, **63–64**
Emberá people
    *Hands of the Rainforest: The Emberá people of
        Panama,* **157**
emergency vehicles
    Fire Trucks and Rescue Vehicles, **90–91**
Empire State Building (New York, N.Y.)
    *Sky Boys: How They Built the Empire State
        Building,* **91–92**
endangered species
    Hello, Bumblebee Bat, **65–66**
    How Many Baby Pandas?, **66**
    Redwoods, 6, **46–47**
    Tracks of a Panda, **63**
    *When the Wolves Returned: Restoring Nature's
        Balance in Yellowstone,* **43–44**
    The Wolves Are Back, 15, **42**
environments and ecosystems, 42–46
    Guess What Is Growing inside This Egg, **50–51**
    *How to Clean a Hippopotamus: A Look at
        Unusual Animal Partnerships,* 18, **49–50**
    *Into the Deep: The Life of Naturalist and Explorer
        William Beebe,* **40–41**
    Just One Bite, **51**
    Little Kids Big Book of Animals, **48–49**
    The Magic School Bus and the Climate Challenge,
        5, **78**
    A Place for Birds, **61–62**
    Poetrees, **47**
    Under the Snow, **45–46**
    *When the Wolves Returned: Restoring Nature's
        Balance in Yellowstone,* **43–44**
    The Wolves Are Back, 15, **42**
    See also arctic environments; ocean
        environments; rain forests; wetlands;
        woodland environment
Europe. *See* France; Great Britain; Italy; London
    (England); Poland; Russia
    *The Champion of Children: The Story of Janusz
        Korczak,* **144**
    Django, **109–110**
    The Fabulous Feud of Gilbert and Sullivan, **115**
    Fartiste, **113–114**
    *The Grand Mosque of Paris: A Story of How
        Muslims Saved Jews during the Holocaust,* **143**
    I Am Marc Chagall: Text Loosely Inspired by My
        Life *by Marc Chagall,* **106**

    Pompeii: Lost and Found, **137–138**
    Through Time: London, **138**
examples, appropriate, 16
explorers
    *Down the Colorado: John Wesley Powell, the One-
        Armed Explorer,* **151**
    The Fantastic Undersea Life of Jacques Cousteau,
        41
    *Into the Deep: The Life of Naturalist and Explorer
        William Beebe,* **40–41**
extinct animals, 73–76
    Sabertooth, **74–75**
    Supercroc: Paul Sereno's Dinosaur Eater, **75–76**
    See also dinosaurs

F

Fala (Dog)
    First Dog Fala, **29**
families, 23–24
    Families, **24**
    Grandma Comes to Stay, **24–25**
    Ikenna Goes to Nigeria, **161–162**
    My Brother Charlie: A Sister's Story of Autism, **25**
    My Little Round House, 5, **156**
    One World, One Day, **159–160**
    Our Grandparents: A Global Album, **23–24**
    *Sisters and Brothers: Sibling Relationships in the
        Animal World,* **50**
farming
    *Cycle of Rice, Cycle of Life: A Story of Sustainable
        Farming,* **89**
    Farm, **86–87**
    Farmer George Plants a Nation, **153**
    Maple Syrup Season, **88–89**
Farnsworth, Philo Taylor, 1906–1971
    *The Boy Who Invented TV: The Story of Philo
        Farnsworth,* **94**
fathers and children
    Hip-Pocket Papa, **57–58**
    See also families
Fibonacci, Leonardo, ca. 1170–ca. 1240
    Blockhead: The Life of Fibonacci, **81**
Fibonacci numbers
    Blockhead: The Life of Fibonacci, **81**
    Growing Patterns: Fibonacci Numbers in Nature,
        80–81
fire engines
    Fire Trucks and Rescue Vehicles, **90–91**

fishes, 54–55
    Fabulous Fishes, **55**
    Sea Horse: The Shyest Fish in the Sea, **54**
    Sharks, **55**
flamenco
    ¡Olé Flamenco!, **112**
flatulence
    Fartiste, **113–114**
fluorescence
    The Day-Glo Brothers, **93–94**
folklorists
    *Home on the Range: John A. Lomax and His
        Cowboy Songs,* **110**
foods and cooking, 85–90
    All in Just One Cookie, **87–88**
    Bug-a-licious, **87**
    *Cycle of Rice, Cycle of Life: A Story of Sustainable
        Farming,* **89**
    Hiromi's Hands, **86**
    Just One Bite, **51**
    Maple Syrup Season, **88–89**
    *Sopa de frijoles: Un poema para cocinar / Bean
        Soup: A Cooking Poem,* **85–86**
    Yum! ¡Mmmm! ¡Qué rico! Americas' Sproutings, 9,
        88
    See also farming
Foucault, Léon, 1819–1868
    *Come See the Earth Turn: The Story of Léon
        Foucault,* **95–96**
France
    Django, **109–110**
    Fartiste, **113–114**
    *The Grand Mosque of Paris: A Story of How
        Muslims Saved Jews during the Holocaust,* **143**
friendship
    *Abe Lincoln Crosses a Creek: A Tall, Thin Tale
        (Introducing His Forgotten Frontier Friend),*
        5, **147**
    Boys of Steel: The Creators of Superman, **103**
frogs
    The Frog Scientist, 7
    Hip-Pocket Papa, **57–58**
    Slippery, Slimy Baby Frogs, **58**

G

Gág, Wanda, 1893–1946
    Wanda Gág: The Girl Who Lived to Draw,
        106–107

García Márquez, Gabriel, 1928–
    *My Name Is Gabito: The Life of Gabriel García
        Márquez,* **101–102**
gardening
    Compost Stew: An A to Z Recipe for the Earth,
        89–90
genetics
    Gregor Mendel: The Friar Who Grew Peas, **38–39**
Ghana
    Grandma Comes to Stay, **24–25**
    *One Hen: How One Small Loan Made a Big
        Difference,* **161**
Gibson, Althea, 1927–2003
    Nothing but Trouble: The Story of Althea Gibson,
        120–121
Gilbert, W. S., 1836–1911
    The Fabulous Feud of Gilbert and Sullivan, **115**
global warming
    The Magic School Bus and the Climate Challenge,
        5, **78**
Golden Kite Award, 172
Graham, Martha
    Ballet for Martha: Making Appalachian Spring,
        113
grandparents
    Grandma Comes to Stay, **24–25**
    Our Grandparents: A Global Album, **23–24**
    See also families
Great Britain
    The Fabulous Feud of Gilbert and Sullivan, **115**
    Through Time: London, **138**

H

hands
    The Handiest Things in the World, **30**
Hanukkah
    Hanukkah at Valley Forge, **131**
    I Have a Little Dreidel, **126**
health
    *I Feel Better with a Frog in My Throat: History's
        Strangest Cures,* **32**
    I'm Getting a Checkup, **33**
    Pierre the Penguin: A True Story, **60**
    Sneeze!, **34**
    *Winter's Tail: How One Little Dolphin Learned to
        Swim Again,* **64–65**
    Your Body Battles a Skinned Knee, **33**
heavy equipment. *See* construction

Hildegard, Saint, 1098–1179
  The Secret World of Hildegard, **132–133**
Hindu religious festivals
  Celebrate Diwali, 6, **129**
Hispanic Americans
  N Is for Navidad, 127
  ¡Olé Flamenco!, 112
  *Sonia Sotomayor: A Judge Grows in the Bronx /
    La juez que creció en el Bronx,* **166–167**
Hispanic authors
  *My Name Is Gabito: The Life of Gabriel García
    Márquez,* **101–102**
holidays, 125–133
  *Book Fiesta! Celebrate Children's Day/Book Day
    / Celebremos El día de los niños/El día de los
    libros, x,* **131–132**
Holocaust, Jewish (1939–1945)
  *The Champion of Children: The Story of Janusz
    Korczak,* 144
  *The Grand Mosque of Paris: A Story of How
    Muslims Saved Jews during the Holocaust,* 143
horses
  Horses, **67–68**
  Seabiscuit: The Wonder Horse, 119
  Stable, 118
Hudson River (N.Y. and N.J.)
  River of Dreams: The Story of the Hudson River,
    139
human body
  Fartiste, **113–114**
  The Handiest Things in the World, 30
  Human Body, 22, **29–30**
  My Bones and Muscles / Huesos y músculos, 31
  Shades of People, 32
  We All Move, 31
  What's inside Your Tummy, Mommy?, 30
  Your Body Battles a Skinned Knee, 33
hurricanes
  Hurricane Hunters! Riders on the Storm, 98
Hypatia, d. 415
  Of Numbers and Stars: The Story of Hypatia, 149

I

Id al-Fitr
  Celebrate Ramadan and Eid al-Fitr, 130
illustrations, 16–17
  attractions of, 2
  in picture books, 7–8

immune system
  Your Body Battles a Skinned Knee, **33**
index in informational books, 18
India
  Celebrate Diwali, 6, **129**
Indonesia
  *Cycle of Rice, Cycle of Life: A Story of Sustainable
    Farming,* 89
informational books
  definition, 3–4
  with fictional elements, 5, 9
  importance of, 2
  as stories, 4–6
insects and spiders, 68–72
  Bug Zoo, **68**
  Bug-a-licious, 87
  The Buzz on Bees: Why Are They Disappearing?,
    70–71
  In the Trees, Honey Bees, 70
  Insect Detective, 71
  Monarch and Milkweed, **69–70**
  Spiders, 6, 36, **69**
  Tarantula Scientist, 7
  Up, Up, and Away, **71–72**
International Reading Association (IRA)
  CBC/IRA Children's Choices, 171
  Children's Book Award, 172
  Global Notable Books, 172
  Teachers' Choices, 173
invented dialogue, 5, 7, 16
inventors and inventions, 93–96
  *The Boy Who Invented TV: The Story of Philo
    Farnsworth,* 94
  *Come See the Earth Turn: The Story of Léon
    Foucault,* 95–96
  The Day-Glo Brothers, 93–94
  Inventions, 96
  *Marvelous Mattie: How Margaret E. Knight
    Became an Inventor,* 95
  Neo Leo: The Ageless Ideas of Leonardo da Vinci,
    93
  Pop! The Accidental Invention of Bubble Gum,
    94–95
invertebrates, 72–73
  I'm a Pill Bug, **72–73**
  Wolfsnail: A Backyard Predator, 72
Iraq
  Silent Music, 5, **162**

Islam
   Celebrate Ramadan and Eid al-Fitr, **130**
   *The Grand Mosque of Paris: A Story of How
      Muslims Saved Jews during the Holocaust,* **143**
islands
   An Island Grows, **78–79**
Italy
   Pompeii: Lost and Found, **137–138**

J

Jane Addams Peace Award and Honor Books, 173
Japanese Americans
   Hiromi's Hands, **86**
jazz musicians
   *Before John Was a Jazz Giant: A Song of John
      Coltrane,* 15–16, **111–112**
   Django, **109–110**
   Jazz, **110–111**
   Piano Starts Here: The Young Art Tatum, **111**
Jewish artists
   I Am Marc Chagall: Text Loosely Inspired by My
      Life *by Marc Chagall,* **106**
Jewish baseball players
   You Never Heard of Sandy Koufax? !, **121–122**
Jewish holidays
   Celebrate Rosh Hashanah and Yom Kippur,
      128–129
   Hanukkah at Valley Forge, **131**
   I Have a Little Dreidel, **126**
Jews
   *The Champion of Children: The Story of Janusz
      Korczak,* **144**
   Emma's Poem: The Voice of the Statue of Liberty, **146**
   See also Holocaust, Jewish (1939-1945)
John Burroughs List, 173
judges
   *Sonia Sotomayor: A Judge Grows in the Bronx /
      La juez que creció en el Bronx,* **166–167**
Jumper, Betty Mae, 1923–
   *She Sang Promise: The Story of Betty Mae Jumper,
      Seminole Tribal Leader,* **163**

K

Kahanamoku, Duke, 1890–1968
   *Surfer of the Century: The Life of Duke
      Kahanamoku,* **117–118**
Kalenjin (African people)
   For You Are a Kenyan Child, **157–158**

Kearton, Cherry, 1871–1940
   *In the Belly of an Ox: The Unexpected
      Photographic Adventures of Richard and
      Cherry Kearton,* **39**
Kearton, Richard, 1862–1928
   *In the Belly of an Ox: The Unexpected
      Photographic Adventures of Richard and
      Cherry Kearton,* **39**
Kellerman, Annette, 1888–1975
   *Mermaid Queen: The Spectacular True Story of
      Annette Kellerman, Who Swam Her Way
      to Fame, Fortune, and Swimsuit History!,*
      112–113
Kennedy, Edward M., 1932–2009
   *My Senator and Me: A Dog's-Eye View of
      Washington, D.C.,* **28**
Kenya
   14 Cows for America, **158**
   For You Are a Kenyan Child, **157–158**
   *Mama Miti: Wangari Maathai and the Trees of
      Kenya,* 20, **164–165**
   *Planting the Trees of Kenya: The Story of Wangari
      Maathai,* 20, *154,* **165**
King, Martin Luther, Jr., 1929–1968
   *March On! The Day My Brother Martin Changed
      the World,* **140–141**
Kirkpatrick, John Simpson, 1892–1915
   *The Donkey of Gallipoli: A True Story of Courage
      in World War I,* **146–147**
Knight, Margaret E., 1838–1914
   *Marvelous Mattie: How Margaret E. Knight
      Became an Inventor,* **95**
Korczak, Janusz, 1878–1942
   *The Champion of Children: The Story of Janusz
      Korczak,* **144**
Koufax, Sandy, 1935–
   You Never Heard of Sandy Koufax? !, **121–122**

L

language, appropriate, 15–16
Latin America. *See* Argentina; Brazil; Colombia;
      Mexico; Panama; Paraguay
   Animal Poems of the Iguazú, **155–156**
   Biblioburro: A True Story from Colombia, 12, **166**
   *Book Fiesta! Celebrate Children's Day/Book Day
      / Celebremos El día de los niños/El día de los
      libros,* x, **131–132**
   Capoeira: Game! Dance! Martial Art!, **116**

Latin America. *See* Argentina; Brazil; Colombia;
    Mexico; Panama; Paraguay (cont.)
    Diego: Bigger than Life, **104**
    Hands of the Rainforest: The Emberá people of
        Panama, **157**
    My Name Is Gabito: The Life of Gabriel García
        Márquez, **101–102**
    Pelé, King of Soccer / Pelé, El rey del fútbol, **117**
Latin American foods
    Sopa de frijoles: Un poema para cocinar / Bean
        Soup: A Cooking Poem, **85–86**
Lazarus, Emma, 1849–1887
    Emma's Poem: The Voice of the Statue of Liberty, **146**
Lee Bennett Hopkins Award for Poetry, 173
Leonardo da Vinci, 1452–1519
    Neo Leo: The Ageless Ideas of Leonardo da Vinci, **93**
    Who Stole Mona Lisa?, **105–106**
libraries
    Biblioburro: A True Story from Colombia, 12, **166**
lightships
    Lightship, **91**
Lincoln, Abraham, 1809–1865
    Abe Lincoln Crosses a Creek: A Tall, Thin Tale
        (Introducing His Forgotten Frontier Friend),
        5, **147**
    Abe's Honest Words: The Life of Abraham Lincoln,
        150
lizards
    Lizards, 6, **56**
Lomax, John A., 1867–1948
    Home on the Range: John A. Lomax and His
        Cowboy Songs, **110**
London (England)
    Through Time: London, **138**
Longworth, Alice Roosevelt, 1884–1980
    What to Do About Alice? How Alice Roosevelt
        Broke the Rules, Charmed the World, and
        Drove Her Father Teddy Crazy!, 6, 15, **148**

M
Maasai (African people)
    14 Cows for America, **158**
Maathai, Wangari
    Mama Miti: Wangari Maathai and the Trees of
        Kenya, 20, **164–165**
    Planting the Trees of Kenya: The Story of Wangari
        Maathai, 20, *154,* **165**
machinery equipment. *See* construction

mammals, 62–68
    Ape, **65**
    The Chiru of High Tibet: A True Story, **66–67**
    Elephants of Africa, **63–64**
    Hello, Bumblebee Bat, **65–66**
    Horses, **67–68**
    How Many Baby Pandas?, **66**
    Ice Bears, **64**
    A Platypus' World, **62**
    Skunks, **67**
    Slow Down for Manatees, 5, **62–63**
    Tracks of a Panda, **63**
    Winter's Tail: How One Little Dolphin Learned to
        Swim Again, **64–65**
manatees
    Slow Down for Manatees, 5, **62–63**
Mandela, Nelson, 1918–
    Long Walk to Freedom, **165–166**
maple syrup
    Maple Syrup Season, **88–89**
maps in informational books, 18
martial arts
    Capoeira: Game! Dance! Martial Art!, **116**
mathematics and mathematicians
    Blockhead: The Life of Fibonacci, **81**
    For Good Measure: The Ways We Say How Much,
        How Far, How Heavy, How Big, How Old, **82**
    Growing Patterns: Fibonacci Numbers in Nature,
        80–81
    Of Numbers and Stars: The Story of Hypatia, **149**
    Zero Is the Leaves on the Tree, **81–82**
measurement
    For Good Measure: The Ways We Say How Much,
        How Far, How Heavy, How Big, How Old, **82**
medical care
    The Donkey of Gallipoli: A True Story of Courage
        in World War I, **146–147**
    I Feel Better with a Frog in My Throat: History's
        Strangest Cures, **32**
    I'm Getting a Checkup, **33**
medium of illustrations, 17
Mendel, Gregor, 1822–1884
    Gregor Mendel: The Friar Who Grew Peas, **38–39**
Mexico
    Book Fiesta! Celebrate Children's Day/Book Day
        / Celebremos El día de los niños/El día de los
        libros, x, **131–132**
    Diego: Bigger than Life, **104**

microfinancing
  *One Hen: How One Small Loan Made a Big
    Difference,* **161**
military. *See* armed services
Mona Lisa (painting)
  Who Stole Mona Lisa?, **105–106**
Mongolia
  Horse Song: The Naadam of Mongolia, **160**
  My Little Round House, 5, **156**
Montezuma, Carlos, 1866–1923
  *A Boy Named Beckoning: The True Story of Dr.
    Carlos Montezuma, Native American Hero,*
    144–145
Moses (Biblical leader)
  Moses, **130–131**
Mount Vernon (estate)
  Farmer George Plants a Nation, **153**
Muir, John, 1838–1914
  John Muir: America's First Environmentalist,
    39–40
muscles
  My Bones and Muscles / Huesos y músculos, **31**
music and musicians, 109–112
  The Fabulous Feud of Gilbert and Sullivan, **115**
  *Home on the Range: John A. Lomax and His
    Cowboy Songs,* **110**
  Odetta: The Queen of Folk, **109**
  See also jazz musicians

N

Naiyomah, Wilson Kimeli
  14 Cows for America, **158**
narrative nonfiction, 5–6
narrative style, 14–15
National Council of Teachers of English (NCTE)
  Notable Books in the Language Arts, 173
  Orbis Pictus Award, Honor, and
    Recommended Book List, 173
Native Americans
  *A Boy Named Beckoning: The True Story of Dr.
    Carlos Montezuma, Native American Hero,*
    144–145
  *Louis Sockalexis: Native American Baseball
    Pioneer,* **122**
  The Navajo Year, Walk through Many Seasons,
    158–159
  *Saltypie: A Choctaw Journey from Darkness into
    Light,* **162–163**

  *She Sang Promise: The Story of Betty Mae Jumper,
    Seminole Tribal Leader,* **163**
naturalists and conservationists
  Bug Zoo, **68**
  The Chiru of High Tibet: A True Story, **66–67**
  Crocodile Safari, **56**
  *Darwin: With Glimpses into His Private Journal
    and Letters,* **40**
  The Fantastic Undersea Life of Jacques Cousteau,
    41
  *In the Belly of an Ox: The Unexpected
    Photographic Adventures of Richard and
    Cherry Kearton,* **39**
  *Into the Deep: The Life of Naturalist and Explorer
    William Beebe,* **40–41**
  John Muir: America's First Environmentalist,
    39–40
  *Mama Miti: Wangari Maathai and the Trees of
    Kenya,* 20, **164–165**
  *Planting the Trees of Kenya: The Story of Wangari
    Maathai,* 20, *154,* **165**
nature, 41–46
  Animal Poems of the Iguazú, **155–156**
  Dark Emperor and Other Poems of the Night,
    45
  *Ubiquitous: Poetry and Science about Nature's
    Survivors,* 9, **52–53**
  Wild Tracks! A Guide to Nature's Footprints, **38**
Navajo Indians
  The Navajo Year, Walk through Many Seasons,
    158–159
New York (N.Y.)
  Lady Liberty: A Biography, **138–139**
  Old Penn Station, **137**
  Pale Male: Citizen Hawk of New York City, 20,
    61
  *Sky Boys: How They Built the Empire State
    Building,* **91–92**
New York Times Best Illustrated List, 173
Nigeria
  Ikenna Goes to Nigeria, **161–162**
night
  Dark Emperor and Other Poems of the Night,
    45
Noguchi, Isamu
  Ballet for Martha: Making Appalachian Spring,
    113
nonfiction. *See* informational books

O

Obama, Barack
 Barack Obama: Son of Promise, Child of Hope,
  163–164
ocean environments
 Down, Down, Down: A Journey to the Bottom of
  the Sea, **43**
 The Fantastic Undersea Life of Jacques Cousteau,
  41
 Into the Deep: The Life of Naturalist and Explorer
  William Beebe, **40–41**
 Looking Closely along the Shore, **44–45**
 See also environments and ecosystems
Odetta, 1930–2008
 Odetta: The Queen of Folk, **109**
O'Keeffe, Georgia, 1887–1986
 Through Georgia's Eyes, **107**
organization of informational books, 15

P

Pakistan
 Listen to the Wind: The Story of Dr. Greg and
  Three Cups of Tea, 15, **164**
paleontologists
 Barnum Brown: Dinosaur Hunter, **76**
 Supercroc: Paul Sereno's Dinosaur Eater, **75–76**
Panama
 Hands of the Rainforest: The Emberá people of
  Panama, **157**
pandas
 How Many Baby Pandas?, **66**
 Tracks of a Panda, **63**
Paraguay
 Animal Poems of the Iguazú, **155–156**
parental behavior in animals
 Ice Bears, **64**
 Sisters and Brothers: Sibling Relationships in the
  Animal World, **50**
 Tracks of a Panda, **63**
Parents' Choice Award, 174
Parkhurst, Charley, 1812–1879
 Rough, Tough Charley, **147**
Pelé, 1940–
 Pelé, King of Soccer / Pelé, El rey del fútbol, **117**
penguins
 Pierre the Penguin: A True Story, **60**
Pennsylvania Station (New York, N.Y.)
 Old Penn Station, **137**

persons with disabilities
 Ballerina Dreams: A True Story, **114–115**
 Django, **109–110**
 My Brother Charlie: A Sister's Story of Autism, **25**
 Piano Starts Here: The Young Art Tatum, **111**
 We All Move, **31**
pets. *See* cats; dogs
photo essays in picture books, 6, 7
photosynthesis
 Living Sunlight: How Plants Bring the Earth to
  Life, 5, **77**
 Why Do Elephants Need the Sun?, **79**
picture books
 definition, 7–8
 as starting point for reading, 2
pioneers
 Bad News for Outlaws: The Remarkable Life of
  Bass Reeves, Deputy U.S. Marshall, **149**
 Rough, Tough Charley, **147**
plants, 46–48
 A Seed Is Sleepy, **46**
 See also trees
platypus
 A Platypus' World, **62**
poetry, 9
 as informational, 4
 Animal Poems of the Iguazú, **155–156**
 Dark Emperor and Other Poems of the Night, **45**
 Diego: Bigger than Life, **104**
 Dinothesaurus: Prehistoric Poems and Paintings,
  73
 Lady Liberty: A Biography, **138–139**
 The Navajo Year, Walk through Many Seasons,
  158–159
 Poetrees, **47**
 Roadwork, 84, **92–93**
 Sopa de frijoles: Un poema para cocinar / Bean
  Soup: A Cooking Poem, **85–86**
 Ubiquitous: Poetry and Science about Nature's
  Survivors, 9, **52–53**
 What Is Science?, **37–38**
 Where in the Wild? Camouflaged Creatures
  Concealed—and Revealed: Ear-Tickling
  Poems, **51–52**
 Yum! ¡Mmmm! ¡Qué rico! Americas' Sproutings,
  9, **88**
 See also stories in rhyme
poets. *See* authors and poets

Poland
  *The Champion of Children: The Story of Janusz
    Korczak,* **144**
polar bears
  Ice Bears, **64**
Pompeii (extinct city)
  Pompeii: Lost and Found, **137–138**
pop-up books, 17
  Moon Landing, **99**
Powell, John Wesley, 1834–1902
  *Down the Colorado: John Wesley Powell, the One-
    Armed Explorer,* **151**
predatory animals
  Flying Eagle, **156**
  Predators, **52**
  Sharks, **55**
  Wolfsnail: A Backyard Predator, **72**
pregnancy
  What's inside Your Tummy, Mommy?, **30**
presidents, South Africa
  Long Walk to Freedom, **165–166**
presidents, United States
  *Abe Lincoln Crosses a Creek: A Tall, Thin Tale
    (Introducing His Forgotten Frontier Friend),*
    5, **147**
  Abe's Honest Words: The Life of Abraham Lincoln,
    150
  Barack Obama: Son of Promise, Child of Hope,
    163–164
  *Big George: How a Shy Boy Became President
    Washington,* **152**
  Farmer George Plants a Nation, **153**
  First Dog Fala, **29**
  Hanukkah at Valley Forge, **131**
  *What to Do About Alice? How Alice Roosevelt
    Broke the Rules, Charmed the World, and
    Drove Her Father Teddy Crazy!,* 6, 15, **148**
Project Apollo (U.S.) Apollo 11
  Moon Landing, **99**
  Moonshot: The Flight of Apollo 11, **98**
  One Giant Leap, **97**
Pujol, Joseph, 1857–1945
  Fartiste, **113–114**

R

radio broadcasts
  *Aliens Are Coming! The True Account of the 1938
    War of the Worlds Radio Broadcast,* **114**

rain forests
  Animal Poems of the Iguazú, **155–156**
  *Hands of the Rainforest: The Emberá people of
    Panama,* **157**
Ramadan
  Celebrate Ramadan and Eid al-Fitr, **130**
read-aloud books
  14 Cows for America, **158**
  *Abe Lincoln Crosses a Creek: A Tall, Thin Tale
    (Introducing His Forgotten Frontier Friend),*
    5, **147**
  Babies in the Bayou, **41–42**
  Biblioburro: A True Story from Colombia, 12, **166**
  Big Belching Bog, **44**
  Celebrate Thanksgiving, **129–130**
  Compost Stew: An A to Z Recipe for the Earth,
    89–90
  Dark Emperor and Other Poems of the Night, **45**
  Dogs and Cats, **28**
  Fabulous Fishes, **55**
  Fartiste, **113–114**
  For You Are a Kenyan Child, **157–158**
  Guess What Is Growing inside This Egg, **50–51**
  Hip-Pocket Papa, **57–58**
  *In the Belly of an Ox: The Unexpected
    Photographic Adventures of Richard and
    Cherry Kearton,* **39**
  Insect Detective, **71**
  Life in the Boreal Forest, **42–43**
  Lizards, 6, **56**
  *Louis Sockalexis: Native American Baseball
    Pioneer,* **122**
  Monarch and Milkweed, **69–70**
  Moonshot: The Flight of Apollo 11, **98**
  Nothing but Trouble: The Story of Althea Gibson,
    120–121
  A Platypus' World, **62**
  Roadwork, 84, **92–93**
  Seabiscuit: The Wonder Horse, **119**
  Sit-In, **142–143**
  Sojourner Truth's Step-Stomp Stride, **150**
  The Story of Snow: The Science of Winter's Wonder,
    77
  Sweet Land of Liberty, 17, 20, **141**
  Turtle, Turtle, Watch Out!, **58–59**
  Under the Snow, **45–46**
  Up, Up, and Away, **71–72**
  Vulture View, **60–61**

read-aloud books (cont.)
  What Is Science?, 37–38
  *Where in the Wild? Camouflaged Creatures
    Concealed—and Revealed: Ear-Tickling
    Poems,* 51–52
  Why Do Elephants Need the Sun?, 79
  Winter Trees, 47–48
  The Wolves Are Back, 15, 42
  You Never Heard of Sandy Koufax?! , 121–
    122
reality as expressed in images, 3
Reeves, Bass
  *Bad News for Outlaws: The Remarkable Life of
    Bass Reeves, Deputy U.S. Marshall,* 149
Reinhardt, Django, 1910–1953
  Django, 109–110
religions, 125–133
  Faith, 124, 125–126
  *Many Ways: How Families Practice Their Beliefs
    and Religions,* 132
  See also specific religions, e.g., Islam
reptiles. *See* amphibians and reptiles
rice
  *Cycle of Rice, Cycle of Life: A Story of Sustainable
    Farming,* 89
Ripken, Cal, 1960–
  *The Longest Season: The Story of the Orioles' 1988
    Losing Streak,* 120
Rivera, Diego, 1886–1957
  Diego: Bigger than Life, 104
roads
  Roadwork, 84, 92–93
Roosevelt, Eleanor, 1884–1962
  *Eleanor, Quiet No More: The Life of Eleanor
    Roosevelt,* 151
Roosevelt, Franklin D., 1882–1945
  First Dog Fala, 29
Roosevelt, Theodore, 1858–1919
  *What to Do About Alice? How Alice Roosevelt
    Broke the Rules, Charmed the World, and
    Drove Her Father Teddy Crazy!,* 6, 15,
    148
Rosh ha-Shanah
  Celebrate Rosh Hashanah and Yom Kippur,
    128–129
Russia
  I Am Marc Chagall: Text Loosely Inspired by My
    Life *by Marc Chagall,* 106

S

saber-toothed tigers
  Sabertooth, 74–75
Schaller, George B.
  The Chiru of High Tibet: A True Story, 66–67
schools
  *Kindergarten Day USA and China /
    Kindergarten Day China and USA,* 25–26
  *Nasreen's Secret School: A True Story from
    Afghanistan,* 26
science
  What Is Science?, 37–38
sea horses
  Sea Horse: The Shyest Fish in the Sea, 54
Seabiscuit (Race horse)
  Seabiscuit: The Wonder Horse, 119
seashore biology
  Looking Closely along the Shore, 44–45
seeds
  A Seed Is Sleepy, 46
Seminole Indians
  *She Sang Promise: The Story of Betty Mae Jumper,
    Seminole Tribal Leader,* 163
September 11 Terrorist Attacks, 2001
  14 Cows for America, 158
series books, 19–20
sharks
  Sharks, 55
ships
  *All Stations! Distress! April 15, 1912: The Day the
    Titanic Sank,* 15, 140
  Pharaoh's Boat, 134, 139–140
Shuster, Joe, 1914–1992
  Boys of Steel: The Creators of Superman, 103
Siegel, Jerry, 1914–1996
  Boys of Steel: The Creators of Superman, 103
skeleton
  Bones: Skeletons and How They Work, 49
  My Bones and Muscles / Huesos y músculos, 31
skin
  Your Body Battles a Skinned Knee, 33
skin color
  Shades of People, 32
skunks
  Skunks, 67
skyscrapers
  *Sky Boys: How They Built the Empire State
    Building,* 91–92

slavery
    Dave the Potter, **105**
    Henry's Freedom Box, **148**
    Moses: When Harriet Tubman Led Her People to
        Freedom, 9, **153**
    Sojourner Truth's Step-Stomp Stride, **150**
Smith, Elinor
    Soar, Elinor!, **97**
snails
    Wolfsnail: A Backyard Predator, **72**
sneezing
    Sneeze!, **34**
snow
    The Story of Snow: The Science of Winter's Wonder, **77**
    Under the Snow, **45–46**
soccer players
    Pelé, King of Soccer / Pelé, El rey del fútbol, **117**
social behavior in animals
    How to Clean a Hippopotamus: A Look at
        Unusual Animal Partnerships, 18, **49–50**
social reformers
    Eleanor, Quiet No More: The Life of Eleanor
        Roosevelt, **151**
    Elizabeth Leads the Way: Elizabeth Cady Stanton
        and the Right to Vote, **152**
    Emma's Poem: The Voice of the Statue of Liberty, **146**
    Sojourner Truth's Step-Stomp Stride, **150**
    Yours for Justice, Ida B. Wells: The Daring Life of a
        Crusading Journalist, **145–146**
Sockalexis, Louis, 1871–1913
    Louis Sockalexis: Native American Baseball
        Pioneer, **122**
solar system
    Boy, Were We Wrong about the Solar System!, **80**
Soriano, Luis
    Biblioburro: A True Story from Colombia, 12,
        166
Sotomayor, Sonia, 1954–
    Sonia Sotomayor: A Judge Grows in the Bronx /
        La juez que creció en el Bronx, **166–167**
soup
    Sopa de frijoles: Un poema para cocinar / Bean
        Soup: A Cooking Poem, **85–86**
sources for informational books, 18
South Africa
    Long Walk to Freedom, **165–166**
space flight to the moon
    Moon Landing, **99**

    Moonshot: The Flight of Apollo 11, **98**
    One Giant Leap, **97**
sphinxes (Mythology)
    How the Sphinx Got to the Museum, **136–137**
spiders. *See* insects and spiders
spies
    Patience Wright: America's First Sculptor and
        Revolutionary Spy, **107–108**
Splash (Dog)
    My Senator and Me: A Dog's-Eye View of
        Washington, D.C., **28**
sports. *See* athletes
Stanton, Elizabeth Cady, 1815–1902
    Elizabeth Leads the Way: Elizabeth Cady Stanton
        and the Right to Vote, **152**
stars and the universe, 79–80
Statue of Liberty (New York, N.Y.)
    Emma's Poem: The Voice of the Statue of Liberty, **146**
    Lady Liberty: A Biography, **138–139**
stories in rhyme
    Compost Stew: An A to Z Recipe for the Earth,
        89–90
    Fabulous Fishes, **55**
    Fartiste, **113–114**
    Flying Eagle, **156**
    Guess What Is Growing inside This Egg, **50–51**
    The Handiest Things in the World, **30**
    In the Trees, Honey Bees, **70**
    An Island Grows, **78–79**
    Jazz, **110–111**
    N Is for Navidad, **127**
    Pierre the Penguin: A True Story, **60**
    Rough, Tough Charley, **147**
    Winter Trees, **47–48**
    See also poetry
subjects of informational books, 13, 14, 20
Sullivan, Arthur, 1842–1900
    The Fabulous Feud of Gilbert and Sullivan, **115**
sun
    Living Sunlight: How Plants Bring the Earth to
        Life, 5, **77**
    Why Do Elephants Need the Sun?, **79**
Superman
    Boys of Steel: The Creators of Superman, **103**
sushi
    Hiromi's Hands, **86**
Suzuki, Hiromi
    Hiromi's Hands, **86**

swimmers
  *Mermaid Queen: The Spectacular True Story of
    Annette Kellerman, Who Swam Her Way to
    Fame, Fortune, and Swimsuit History!*, **112–113**
  *Surfer of the Century: The Life of Duke
    Kahanamoku*, **117–118**

T

taigas
  Life in the Boreal Forest, **42–43**
Tanzania
  Flying Eagle, **156**
Tatum, Art, 1909–1956
  Piano Starts Here: The Young Art Tatum, **111**
television
  *The Boy Who Invented TV: The Story of Philo
    Farnsworth*, **94**
tennis players
  Nothing but Trouble: The Story of Althea Gibson,
    120–121
Thanksgiving Day
  Celebrate Thanksgiving, **129–130**
theater and performers, 112–116
Tibet
  The Chiru of High Tibet: A True Story, **66–67**
time
  *For Good Measure: The Ways We Say How Much,
    How Far, How Heavy, How Big, How Old*,
    82
Tingle, Tim
  *Saltypie: A Choctaw Journey from Darkness into
    Light*, **162–163**
Titanic (Steamship)
  *All Stations! Distress! April 15, 1912: The Day the
    Titanic Sank*, 15, **140**
trees
  *Mama Miti: Wangari Maathai and the Trees of
    Kenya*, 20, **164–165**
  *Planting the Trees of Kenya: The Story of Wangari
    Maathai*, 20, *154*, **165**
  Poetrees, **47**
  Redwoods, 6, **46–47**
  Winter Trees, **47–48**
trucks
  Fire Trucks and Rescue Vehicles, **90–91**
  Heavy Equipment Up Close, **90**
  Roadwork, *84*, **92–93**
Truth, Sojourner, d. 1883
  Sojourner Truth's Step-Stomp Stride, **150**

Tubman, Harriet, 1820?–1913
  *Moses: When Harriet Tubman Led Her People to
    Freedom*, 9, **153**
turkey vulture
  Vulture View, **60–61**
turtles
  Turtle, Turtle, Watch Out!, **58–59**
  Turtle Crossing, **57**
Tutankhamen, King of Egypt
  Tutankhamun, **145**
Twain, Mark, 1835–1910
  *The Extraordinary Mark Twain (according to
    Susy)*, **102–103**

U

Underground Railroad
  Henry's Freedom Box, **148**
  *Moses: When Harriet Tubman Led Her People to
    Freedom*, 9
United States
  Big Alaska, **160–161**
  *Kindergarten Day USA and China /
    Kindergarten Day China and USA*, **25–26**
United States Board on Books for Young People
  (USBBY) Outstanding International Book
  List, 174
United States. Congress
  *My Senator and Me: A Dog's-Eye View of
    Washington, D.C.*, **28**
United States history
  *Abe Lincoln Crosses a Creek: A Tall, Thin Tale
    (Introducing His Forgotten Frontier Friend)*, 5,
    147
  Abe's Honest Words: The Life of Abraham Lincoln,
    150
  *Bad News for Outlaws: The Remarkable Life of
    Bass Reeves, Deputy U.S. Marshall*, **149**
  *Big George: How a Shy Boy Became President
    Washington*, **152**
  *Eleanor, Quiet No More: The Life of Eleanor
    Roosevelt*, **151**
  Farmer George Plants a Nation, **153**
  Hanukkah at Valley Forge, **131**
  Henry's Freedom Box, **148**
  *March On! The Day My Brother Martin Changed
    the World*, **140–141**
  *Moses: When Harriet Tubman Led Her People to
    Freedom*, 9, **153**
  Rough, Tough Charley, **147**

Sit-In, **142–143**
Sojourner Truth's Step-Stomp Stride, **150**
Sweet Land of Liberty, 17, 20, **141**
*Unite or Die: How Thirteen States Became A
  Nation*, 9, **142**
Whale Port: A History of Tuckanucket, 9, **136**
*What to Do About Alice? How Alice Roosevelt
  Broke the Rules, Charmed the World, and
  Drove Her Father Teddy Crazy!*, 6, 15,
  148
United States. Supreme Court
  *Sonia Sotomayor: A Judge Grows in the Bronx /
  La juez que creció en el Bronx*, **166–167**

V

visual literacy
  as starting point for reading, 2

W

War of the Worlds (Radio program)
  *Aliens Are Coming! The True Account of the 1938
  War of the Worlds Radio Broadcast*, **114**
Washington, George, 1732–1799
  *Big George: How a Shy Boy Became President
  Washington*, **152**
  Farmer George Plants a Nation, **153**
  Hanukkah at Valley Forge, **131**
water
  *Our World of Water: Children and Water around
  the World*, **159**
  Why Do Elephants Need the Sun?, **79**
weather
  Hurricane Hunters! Riders on the Storm, **98**
weights and measures
  *For Good Measure: The Ways We Say How Much,
  How Far, How Heavy, How Big, How Old*, **82**
Wells-Barnett, Ida B., 1862–1931
  *Yours for Justice, Ida B. Wells: The Daring Life of a
  Crusading Journalist*, **145–146**
wetlands
  Babies in the Bayou, **41–42**
  Big Belching Bog, **44**
  Crocodile Safari, **56**
whaling
  Whale Port: A History of Tuckanucket, 9, **136**
wildlife photography
  *In the Belly of an Ox: The Unexpected
  Photographic Adventures of Richard and
  Cherry Kearton*, **39**

wildlife reintroduction
  *When the Wolves Returned: Restoring Nature's
  Balance in Yellowstone*, **43–44**
  The Wolves Are Back, 15, **42**
wildlife rescue
  Slow Down for Manatees, 5, **62–63**
  *Winter's Tail: How One Little Dolphin Learned to
  Swim Again*, **64–65**
Williams, Ted, 1918–2002
  *No Easy Way: The Story of Ted Williams and the
  Last .400 Season*, 14, **116–117**
Williams, William Carlos, 1883–1963
  *A River of Words: The Story of William Carlos
  Williams*, 100, **102**
wings (anatomy)
  Wings, **48**
winter
  The Story of Snow: The Science of Winter's Wonder,
  77
  Under the Snow, **45–46**
  Winter Trees, **47–48**
wolves
  *When the Wolves Returned: Restoring Nature's
  Balance in Yellowstone*, **43–44**
  The Wolves Are Back, 15, **42**
women abolitionists
  *Moses: When Harriet Tubman Led Her People to
  Freedom*, 9, **153**
  Sojourner Truth's Step-Stomp Stride, **150**
women air pilots
  Soar, Elinor!, **97**
women artists
  *Patience Wright: America's First Sculptor and
  Revolutionary Spy*, **107–108**
  Through Georgia's Eyes, **107**
  Wanda Gág: The Girl Who Lived to Draw,
  106–107
women athletes
  *Mermaid Queen: The Spectacular True Story of
  Annette Kellerman, Who Swam Her Way
  to Fame, Fortune, and Swimsuit History!*,
  112–113
  Nothing but Trouble: The Story of Althea Gibson,
  120–121
women conservationists
  *Mama Miti: Wangari Maathai and the Trees of
  Kenya*, 20, **164–165**
  *Planting the Trees of Kenya: The Story of Wangari
  Maathai*, 20, *154*, **165**

women cooks
Hiromi's Hands, **86**
women inventors
Marvelous Mattie: How Margaret E. Knight
Became an Inventor, **95**
women journalists
Yours for Justice, Ida B. Wells: The Daring Life of a
Crusading Journalist, **145–146**
women judges
Sonia Sotomayor: A Judge Grows in the Bronx /
La juez que creció en el Bronx, **166–167**
women leaders
Eleanor, Quiet No More: The Life of Eleanor
Roosevelt, **151**
Elizabeth Leads the Way: Elizabeth Cady Stanton
and the Right to Vote, **152**
Emma's Poem: The Voice of the Statue of Liberty,
146
She Sang Promise: The Story of Betty Mae Jumper,
Seminole Tribal Leader, **163**
women mathematicians
Of Numbers and Stars: The Story of Hypatia,
149
women musicians
Odetta: The Queen of Folk, **109**
women mystics
The Secret World of Hildegard, **132–133**
women pioneers
Rough, Tough Charley, **147**
Wong, Anna May, 1905–1961
Shining Star: The Anna May Wong Story,
115–116
wood lice
I'm a Pill Bug, **72–73**

woodland environment
Dark Emperor and Other Poems of the Night, **45**
World War, 1914–1918
The Donkey of Gallipoli: A True Story of Courage
in World War I, **146–147**
World War, 1939–1945
The Grand Mosque of Paris: A Story of How
Muslims Saved Jews during the Holocaust,
143
One Thousand Tracings: Healing the Wounds of
World War II, **141–142**
wounds and injuries
Your Body Battles a Skinned Knee, **33**
Wright, Patience Lovell, 1725–1786
Patience Wright: America's First Sculptor and
Revolutionary Spy, **107–108**
writers. See authors

Y

Yavapai Indians
A Boy Named Beckoning: The True Story of Dr.
Carlos Montezuma, Native American Hero,
144–145
Yellowstone National Park
When the Wolves Returned: Restoring Nature's
Balance in Yellowstone, **43–44**
The Wolves Are Back, 15, **42**
Yom Kippur
Celebrate Rosh Hashanah and Yom Kippur,
128–129

Z

zero (the number)
Zero Is the Leaves on the Tree, **81–82**

CPSIA information can be obtained at www.ICGtesting.com
Printed in the USA
LVOW100823280113

317500LV00003B/280/P

9 780838 911266